THE LAW OF MORTGAGE IN INDIA

THE LAW OF MORTGAGE IN INDIA

RASHBEHARY GHOSE

GYAN

Published by

Gyan Publishing House
5, Ansari Road
Daryaganj, New Delhi-110002
Phone: 011-47034999, 9811692060
E-mail: books@gyanbooks.com

Distribution Network
gyanbooks.com
India, USA, Canada, UK, Australia

ISBN: 978-93-7133-231-6 (PB)

First Published, 1877

2nd Impression 2025

Printed at: Gyan Press, Delhi.

THE LAW OF MORTGAGE IN INDIA
Author: RASHBEHARY GHOSE

Tagore Law Lectures—1875-6.

THE

LAW OF MORTGAGE IN INDIA.

BY

RASHBEHARY GHOSE, M.A.,

TAGORE LAW PROFESSOR.

CALCUTTA:

THACKER, SPINK AND CO.,

Publishers to the Calcutta University.

BOMBAY: THACKER, VINING & Co. MADRAS: HIGGINBOTHAM & Co.

LONDON: W. THACKER & Co.

1877.

TABLE OF CONTENTS.

Page.

LECTURE III.

LECTURE IV.

SIMPLE MORTGAGES.

LECTURE V.

Page.

LECTURE VI.

LECTURE VII.

LECTURE VIII.

Page.

LECTURE IX.

LECTURE X.

LECTURE XI.

Page.

LECTURE XII.

LECTURE I.

Early notions of security—Real security, a development of mature jurisprudence—Short historical sketch of Roman law of pledge—Similar notions traceable in early Hindu and Mahomedan law—Classification of securities by Roman lawyers—Rights of pledgor and pledgee in Roman Law, and in systems founded upon Roman law—Mortgages of land in England—Rights of mortgagor and mortgagee—Influence of oi vil law.

THE history of archaic institutions shows how very slowly the most familiar juridical conceptions of the present day have been matured. Few persons, I venture to affirm, would think of questioning the truth of this assertion at the present day; and yet even a slight acquaintance with juridical literature will show that it is only recently that wild speculation and rash assertion have given place to sober reasoning and careful observation. Comparative jurisprudence in a few short years has accomplished many striking results; but not the least important of these, is the dissipation of the delusions which once clustered round the early history of law. Experience, however, tells us that speculative errors possess remarkable vitality; and it would be rash to suppose that delusions once so common have wholly died out in our time. The tendency to confound the earlier stages of law with its maturity

LECTURE I.

is by no means uncommon even at the present day; and the warning cannot be given too soon, nor repeated too often, that it is only by a careful study of the gradual development of legal conceptions, that we can guard ourselves against mistakes into which we should otherwise be almost sure to be betrayed. In common with the class to which they belong, the delusions of which I speak point to modes of thought from which we cannot emancipate ourselves without a conscious effort of the mind. We find it difficult to realize the intellectual condition of society in its infancy, and are frequently betrayed into transferring to archaic law conceptions which find a place in some of the latest improvements in jurisprudence. The history of the Hindu Will furnishes us with a case in point. I do not mean to deny that testamentary succession was known to the Hindu law; but there can, I think, be no reasonable doubt, that we owe the recognition of the institution by English lawyers to the supposed analogy between a gift and a bequest. The analogy may be very close or merely fanciful. That is a question which I do not propose to discuss. My object in calling your attention to the topic is merely to point out that an examination of archaic institutions shows, beyond the shadow of a doubt, that testamentary succession belongs to a range of ideas very much in advance of that which permits the owner to make a gift of his property during his life; and that in no system whatever has the law regulating wills grown out of, although it may have sometimes shaped itself on the model of, the rules touching gifts during life.

I trust I have said enough to make it unnecessary for me to insist on the interest which attaches to the early history of those legal conceptions which we see only in their maturity. We may not in every case be able to trace the outlines distinctly; but the assertion may be hazarded without rashness that there is not a single juridical conception which may not be historically examined with advantage. A few words therefore on the origin and growth of the law of securities, the immediate subject of the present lectures, will not, I trust, be thrown away.

A learned writer on the law of mortgages has said that pledges must have come into use as soon as the rights of property were recognized. This assertion, however, must be received with considerable reserve. It is true that pledges were known to early law, but the conception when it first shows itself is marked by the crudity peculiar to the infancy of jurisprudence.

Let me pause here for a moment to explain that, according to modern notions, the very essence of a security is the right of the creditor to obtain satisfaction, wholly irrespective of the ability or willingness of the debtor. If the debtor make default, the creditor may either sell the property

LECTURE I. and repay himself out of the purchase money, or the pledge is forfeited to him in satisfaction of his demand. The debtor may be obstinate or unable to pay, but the creditor can always obtain satisfaction out of the property pledged to him, and is therefore wholly independent of the debtor. It is, however, only in the maturity of jurisprudence that the pledgee acquires this right;—a right wihich is justly regarded as the very perfection of a security. In the infancy of law, a pledge was only regarded as a means of compelling satisfaction. The creditor, by detaining the pledge, might compel the debtor to fulfil his engagement; but beyond the pressure which the pledgee was thus in a position to put on the pledgor, the creditor could not turn his security to account. In other words, a pledge only operated on the will of the debtor. The creditor had no authority to sell the pledge, nor was it ever forfeited to him in discharge of his demand.

Modern law furnishes us with an instance of a right closely resembling the right of the pledgee in ancient law. English lawyers have frequently pointed out the unsatisfactory character of what is called a "possessory lien" in English law, a bare right of detention unaccompanied by any power of sale or foreclosure. It is no doubt an anomalous right; and the true explanation of the anomaly lies in the fact that it is a mere "survival." We have here an instance, by on means exceptional, in which a conception, distinctly archaic, is found to linger in a system which has shown no mean capacity for expansion with the multiplying wants of an active commercial age.

I have said that in ancient law a pledge was regarded simply as a means of extorting satisfaction, and that the powers of sale and foreclosure with which we are so familiar at the present day are improvements which are only found in mature jurisprudence. I shall now ask you to test the soundness of the conclusion by an examination of a system of law which, while it has powerfully affected in its maturity the institutions of the greater part of the civilized world, is perhaps also the only system which possesses a continuous history of this branch of jurisprudence. I allude to Roman law. The evidence furnished by the Hindu and Mahomedan law is less authentic, and has to be approached with very great caution. I hope however to be able to show in the next lecture, that there are passages as well in our own law as in the Mahomedan law, which fortify, in a remarkable manner, the conclusions suggested by an historical examination of the Roman system;—passages which can only be explained on the hypothesis that a real security, a security which makes the creditor wholly independent of the debtor, finds its place in every system among the latest improvements in jurisprudence.

LECTURE I. For the present I shall confine myself to the Roman law.

I have not paused to explain with sufficient clearness the meaning of the words "real security," an expression which I have already used more than once. A real security is a security in which the creditor possesses the right to satisfy his demand out of the property pledged to him, and must be carefully distinguished from a real right, which, as I shall have occasion to explain more fully hereafter, is simply a right availing against the world at large, and not merely against a determinate person or persons. A creditor may have a real right in property belonging to his debtor, and yet he may not possess a real security. Thus, if any body should take out of my possession property on which I have a bare lien, I have a right to have the property brought back into my possession, but my right, the security not being real, does not extend, to selling the property in satisfaction of my demand. The distinction is a very important one, and must be carefully borne in mind in the discussions in which we shall presently be engaged.

Let us now turn to the Roman law for the purpose of ascertaining the successive steps by which the law of securities gradually matured itself. The subject has already been investigated by a living German jurist, and the results of his labours have been made accessible to English readers by Mr.

Justice Markby in his Elements of Law. (See the Chapter on Securities in the Appendix to the Elements of Law.)

The earliest form of security known to the Romans appears to have been the Fiducia. This was a proceeding by which the debtor transferred to the creditor the ownership of the property which was intended to be given as a security; the creditor on his part agreeing to restore it to the debtor as soon as the obligation was fulfilled. If the debtor however made default, his right to the property was not extinguished. To use the language of modern law, the debtor possessed an equity of redemption, of which the creditor could not deprive him, either by sale or foreclosure. I shall pass over, for the present, the successive steps by which the Fiducia ultimately ripened into a real security, and proceed to discuss another mode of giving security; which, although a later invention, was ultimately destined to replace the Fiducia in the jurisprudence of Rome.

This was the "pignus" which, in its earliest form, was a proceeding by which the debtor transferred, not the ownership, as in the Fiducia, but the bare possession, to the creditor. The pledgee only possessed the right of detention. Even this right, however, was at first extremely precarious. It was not protected by a real action, as the law refused to recognise a real right in the creditor. So long

LECTURE I. as this was the case, land was rarely given in pledge, as the creditor had no remedy if the debtor made a fraudulent alienation. This was, no doubt, a very unsatisfactory state of things. The law, however, was insensibly developed by the Prætorian jurisdiction to which Roman jurisprudence is indebted for so many reforms. Under the semblance of moulding the procedure of the courts over which they were called upon to preside, the Roman Prætors, by promising to grant a particular action or plea, remodelled almost every branch of the law, and owing to circumstances to which I shall presently refer, the law of security seems to have claimed their attention at an early period. The first improvement was effected by a Prætor named Salvius, who allowed the validity of a pledge, although not followed by a transfer of possession in the case of a tenant pledging his farming stock as security for the rent payable by him. This improvement was followed by the "actio serviana," which allowed the landlord to enforce his claim by a real action, unfettered by the somewhat inconvenient limitations by which the Prætor Salvius had sought to fence in the right of the landlord to follow the pledge into the hands of third persons. Originally confined to the security of the landlord on the farming stock of the tenant, the right was extended in course of time to all classes of pledges, whatever might be the nature of the property, and whether the pledge was accompanied by possession or not. The last improvement was accomplished by the "quasi Servian action," which marks an important epoch in the history of the Roman law of securities. The jealousy with which archaic law guards the creation of a real right has now been relaxed. A real right may now be created without delivery of possession, and the "substantial pledge has been refined into the invisible rights of a hypotheca."

I have said that there were influences at work from without, which, while they hastened the development of this branch of the Roman law, also determined, in a great measure, the direction of that development.

"The most important improvements in the Roman law of security," says Mr. Justice Markby, "were not introduced until, by the extension of the Roman dominion beyond the confines of Italy, very large estates first became common. From this time large numbers of slaves, and even of free persons, began to be employed in cultivating these properties. Small estates also were sometimes let out to farm. Hence the necessity, that the landlord should have some security for his rent, became apparent at Rome, as it has in all places where the land of one person is cultivated by another.

"Under the old law it was not easy for the landlord to obtain this security from the cultivator. Generally the only property which the cultivator

LECTURE I. had was his farming stock (*invecta et illata*); and it was obvious that this could neither be assigned to the landlord by a *fiducia*, nor given into his custody by a *pignus*. It was, therefore, necessary to devise some other means of effecting security; and the mode adopted was, to allow the tenant by a simple agreement, without any formalities, to pledge his farming stock to his landlord as a security for the rent." (Elements of Law, §§ 506, 507.)

I shall now proceed to state the successive steps by which the creditor gained a real *security*, which, as I have already explained, is very different from a real *right*. This was originally accomplished by the introduction of a clause expressly authorizing a sale upon default, a clause which appears to have been suggested by a right possessed by the State of selling land pledged to it. At a somewhat later period, this right was presumed to exist in every pledge. The creditor thus acquired the right to realize his money by the sale of the pledge; in other words, the creditor acquired a real security. The power of sale now came to be regarded as a right inherent in the pledgee; or as a Roman lawyer would perhaps have said, one of the natural incidents of a pledge, and it was probably under the influence of this idea that the law at a later period permitted a sale even when the creditor had expressly agreed not to exercise the power.

We have now reached the stage in which the law

stood in the maturity of Roman jurisprudence. The bare right of detention originally possessed by the creditor has now been succeeded by a right of sale, which, as we have seen, could not be controlled even by the express agreement of the parties; while the somewhat cumbrous formalities which were originally necessary to the validity of the "pignus" (including the transfer of possession) have been replaced by a simple agreement of the parties.

In giving an account of the Roman law of security, I did not notice, at the proper place, the improvements which took place in the Fiducia. The gradual progress of the Fiducia, from a bare right to compel the debtor to make satisfaction, to its latest improvements, when it ripened into something like the mortgage of the English law, or our own conditional sale, is not less interesting than the development of the kind of securities which I have been hitherto considering.

The first improvement was the introduction of a clause, by which it was agreed that the creditor should become, on default, the absolute owner of the property pledged to him. Such a covenant, however, if literally enforced, was likely to operate in many cases with considerable hardship upon the debtor; and the stringency of the condition was relaxed by subsequent legislation. The default of the debtor was not immediately followed by forfeiture, and he was permitted to redeem, if he fulfilled his obligation, within a reasonable time. The position of the creditor now became analogous to that of the English mortgagee, and the conflicting rights of the pledgor and pledgee were, to a certain extent, reconciled with justice and equity. Roman lawyers, however, could not bring themselves to accept such an imperfect reconciliation. It offended their sense of "elegance." A pledge, whatever might be the language used by the parties, was only a security for the debt, and the creditor was not in fairness entitled to anything more. In later Roman law, therefore, the creditor was not suffered to foreclose, but could realize his dues only by the sale of the property pledged to him. You will presently see that the English law is also slowly drifting to the same point. The power of directing a sale instead of a foreclosure, which used to be exercised so very sparingly by the English Courts of Equity, has been extended by a recent statute, while other indications are also not wanting that the total abolition of foreclosure is only a question of time.

From what I have said, I think it is clear that a real security is the most perfect security. The history of the Roman law shows that it was only very slowly that the right of detainer, the only security recognised in early times, ripened into a real security. An examination of Hindu and Mahomedan law also suggests the conclusion that a security in the infancy of law only operated upon the will of the debtor. I shall, however, as I have already said, discuss this point in the next lecture when I propose to give a general outline of the law of security as it is found in Hindu and Mahomedan books.

I shall conclude this part of my lecture with a few general observations on the Roman law of security, and I propose, in the first place, to call your attention to the three-fold division of securities by Roman lawyers, a division which although possibly open to criticism on logical grounds, is eminently convenient.

Roman law divides securities or mortgages into three classes,—conventional, legal, and judicial. A conventional mortgage is one created by the agreement, express or implied, of the parties, and calls for no remark. A legal mortgage is one which is created by the operation of the law. A legal mortgage, however, must not be confounded with implied conventional mortgages, which are really based upon the voluntary consent of the parties, the distinction between the two being precisely the same as that between implied contracts and quasi contracts. The judicial lien of the civil law is a lien created by an order of a Court of Justice for the purpose of compelling obedience to its orders, and corresponds to the process of attachment under the procedure of our own Courts. I do not wish to

LECTURE I. discuss the various rules which governed each of these classes of securities; such a discussion would be beyond the range of the present lectures. Much of our own law of mortgages is, however, still in a floating condition, and I shall, therefore, be obliged to refer occasionally to the Roman law on topics on which our own law cannot be said to be settled. A few general observations will, therefore, I trust, assist you in following me through some of the discussions in which I shall be engaged in the course of these lectures.

The pledgee possessed in later Roman law, as we have already seen, a right to sell the pledge,—a right which might be exercised by him even if he had engaged with the debtor not to sell the pledge in satisfaction of his demand. The creditor, however, was not at liberty to sell until his claim was fully due and payable; and even then he was bound to give the debtor notice of his intention to sell. If, however, the creditor had expressly engaged not to exercise the right of sale, he was bound to issue three successive notices, instead of the one which was ordinarily required by the law. The pledgee was not bound to invoke the process of the Court for the sale of the pledge; but the sale, in the absence of any express agreement to the contrary, must have been effected publicly, and the debtor summoned to be present. The creditor, however, was not entitled to anything in excess of the amount of his debt with interest, if any, and costs. If there was any overplus, the debtor was entitled to it, who, on the other hand, was not released from liability if the proceeds fell short of the demand of the creditor. The creditor, however, could not be compelled to sell, unless the debtor gave security for the payment of the debt in full; but a fraudulent sale rendered the creditor personally liable to the debtor, and if recourse against the creditor was impossible, the purchaser might be compelled to make restitution. If no bidder offered a reasonable price, the creditor might himself obtain an assignment of the pledge for a fair price; such an assignment, however, did not extinguish the debtor's right of redemption.

The debtor, before the exercise of the right of sale by the creditor, was not restrained from dealing with the property in any way he thought proper, provided that the security of the creditor was not thereby impaired. The pledgee could not be affected by any disposition which the pledgor might make of the property pledged by him. The right of the pledgee was a real right, and could not be prejudiced by any alienation made by the debtor. A sale by the creditor therefore passed the property to the purchaser free of all incumbrances subsequently created by the debtor.

It would appear, although the point is not quite free from doubt, that the right of sale could be exercised only by the first pledgee, and not by the second or any subsequent encumbrancer. It was, however, always open to the puisne pledgee to redeem the prior mortgagee, and thus acquire the rights of the latter. This right of redemption was not confined to the second mortgagee, but any mortgage creditor might place himself in the situation of the first mortgagee by the payment or deposit of the amount of his demand. The principle of the English law, however, by which a preference may, in certain cases, be gained over an intermediate incumbrance, was not recognised by Roman lawyers, although the mortgagor was not permitted to redeem without paying to the mortgagee all the debts, whether secured or unsecured, which might be due to him from the mortgagor.

Except in the case of privileged liens, the respective priorities of incumbrances were determined according to the order of time. A privileged lien or pledge was one to which the law allowed priority upon equitable considerations over pledges older in date. For instance, the pledgee who, with an express stipulation for priority, lent money for the purchase of an estate, or who advanced money for the repair of a building, was entitled to priority over encumbrancers whose claims were older in date. There were some other privileged liens recognised by the law, but they do not possess much general interest, and I need not, therefore, refer to them in detail.

Every thing which might be sold, could be lawfully mortgaged. Property which could not be the subject of alienation, could not be the subject of mortgage. A mortgage might be either general, —that is, it might include the whole of the property which the debtor possessed at the time of the mortgage, or which he might subsequently acquire; or it might be special, that is, confined to some specific property. A security might be given not only for the repayment of a debt, but also for other considerations. It might, for instance, be granted by the vendor of a property to the purchaser to indemnify him in case he should be evicted. The creditor might be put in possession of the property pledged to him in order that he might satisfy himself out of the rents and profits. Such an agreement, however, was not permitted to be made the means of obtaining usurious interest.

The above is also very nearly the law followed at the present day in countries whose jurisprudence is founded on the Civil law. There is, however, one important deviation. The creditor is not permitted by most continental systems to exercise the power of sale except through judicial process. Another departure from the civil law may also be noticed. The hypothecation of moveables, although sanctioned by Roman lawyers, is not permitted in any of the modern systems, which are professedly founded on the Civil law.

LECTURE I. There is one other system of law which has a very close interest for the Indian student; and a few words on the English law of mortgages will not, I trust, be thrown away. An English mortgage resembles in its features, as I have already had occasion to remark, the Fiducia of the later Roman law. In form it is a conveyance of land by the debtor to his creditor, with a proviso that, on repayment of the debt on a certain day, the conveyance shall be void, or, as is more usually the case, that the creditor shall reconvey the estate to the debtor. If the money is not repaid on the appointed day, the mortgagee becomes at law the absolute owner of the property, but the Court of Chancery, which has almost exclusive jurisdiction over mortgages, regards the transaction only as a security for the repayment of the debt, and allows the mortgagor to redeem on payment of the principal, interest, and costs within a reasonable time, which is now fixed by statute at twenty years from the date of the entry of the mortgagee, or of an acknowledgment by him of the title of the mortgagor. This right to redeem is known as the "equity of redemption," and as I shall have occasion to explain hereafter, is guarded with peculiar jealousy by the Court. The equity of redemption is not, as the name perhaps would suggest, a mere right. It is an "estate" in the land, and may be devised, granted, or otherwise alienated by the mortgagor, subject however to the right of the mortgagee to foreclose, when, under the decree of foreclosure, the estate passes to the mortgagee free of all incumbrances created since the mortgage.

At any time after the estate has been forfeited at law, the mortgagee, however, has the right to call upon the mortgagor either to redeem, or, in default, to be for ever foreclosed from redeeming the property. This is accomplished by a bill of foreclosure, by which the mortgagee prays that an account may be taken of what is due to him on his security ; and that the mortgagor may be decreed, either to pay the amount, by a short day to be appointed by the Court, or to be foreclosed his equity of redemption. An account is taken, and a day for payment is appointed ; the mortgagor being allowed for that purpose six months from the date of the Master's certificate. If the mortgagor make default, the mortgagee obtains an absolute order for foreclosing, and the estate passes from the mortgagor to the mortgagee. A decree of dismissal of a bill for redemption by reason of non-payment of money at the time appointed by the Court also operates as a foreclosure.

The Court, however, sometimes instead of making a decree for foreclosure, directs a sale of the mortgaged property, when the purchase money is applied in satisfaction of the mortgage, the surplus, if any, being paid to the mortgagor. In case of a deficiency,

LECTURE I. the mortgagee may recover the difference from the mortgagor. A recent statute has considerably extended the power of the Court to make a decree for sale instead of a foreclosure, but the rule of the later Roman law, by which a foreclosure was never permitted, has not yet been adopted in England.

A mortgagee has not only the right to foreclose, but he may proceed to enforce at the same moment all the remedies to which, according to the nature of his security, he may be entitled. He may sue at the same time on his bond or covenant, bring his ejectment, and file his bill of foreclosure. If, however, the mortgagee should enter upon possession before foreclosure, he will be bound to account to the mortgagor for the rents and profits, while an action on the covenant will have the effect of opening the decree for foreclosure, that is of letting in the mortgagor to redeem on the usual terms. I have already explained that after the mortgage has been forfeited by non-payment of principal or interest, the mortgagee is regarded as the absolute owner of the estate at law. He may, therefore, enter upon possession, but Equity will compel him to account for every farthing of the rents and profits realized by him out of the estate.

The best course for the mortgagee, when there is reason to suspect that the security is insufficient, is to obtain an order for sale, or, if that cannot be done, to sue on his bond or covenant first, and then to foreclose for the remainder. LECTURE I.

A decree for sale would seem to be in ordinary cases fair as well to the mortgagor as to the mortgagee.

"The natural course, and certainly the most convenient and beneficial course," says Mr. Justice Story, "for the mortgagor, would seem to be for the Court to follow out the civil law rules on this subject,—that is to say, primarily and ordinarily, to direct a sale of the mortgaged property, giving the debtor any surplus after discharging the mortgage debt; and secondarily, to apply the remedy of foreclosure only to special cases, where the former remedy would not apply, or might be inadequate or injurious to the interests of the parties. This course has, accordingly, been adopted in many of the American Courts of Equity; and it is also the prevailing practice in Ireland. It is done without any distinction, whether there is a power to sell contained in the mortgage or not." "And in most, if not all cases," adds the learned author, "it would be equally beneficial to the mortgagee, as it would prevent the delays incident to the common decree of foreclosure, which is liable to be reopened; and would also prevent any difficulty in obtaining the residue of the debt, when the mortgaged property is not sufficient to discharge it." (Story's Equity Jurisprudence, § 1025.)

LECTURE I. I pass over for the present many topics connected with the English law of mortgage, and shall conclude only with a few observations touching the power of sale, which is generally to be found in English mortgages. Doubts were, at one time, entertained of the validity of an exercise of these powers of sale without the intervention of a Court of Equity, or the concurrence of the mortgagor. These doubts, however, have now been set at rest; and a recent statute enacts that the power may be exercised by every mortgagee unless it is negatived by an express declaration in the security. (23 & 24 Vict., c. 145.) The mortgagee acting upon the power may sell the property mortgaged to him of his own authority, and without the intervention of a Court of Equity. If, however, the power of sale is not expressly given by the deed of mortgage, the mortgagee is bound to give at least six months' notice in writing to the person or one of the persons entitled to the property subject to the charge. When the power of sale is conferred expressly by the instrument of mortgage, there is generally a provision to the effect that the power is not to be exercised until the expiration of a previous notice to the mortgagor.

The mortgagee is regarded as a fiduciary vendor and is bound to adopt every precaution which would be taken by a prudent owner to get the best price for the estate. The exercise of the power, therefore, by the mortgagee for the purpose of oppression, or to accomplish the objects of himself or others, will be prevented in Equity either by restraining or setting aside the sale. The mortgagee cannot proceed to exercise his power of sale upon tender to him of the principal, interest and costs, and the tender may be made even in the auction room.

Notwithstanding the recent statutory extension of the power of sale, the English law does not permit a sale if the creditor expressly engage with the debtor not to exercise the power. A different rule, as we saw, prevailed in the Roman law.

From the short sketch I have been able to give you, you will observe that although the English law of mortgage is in some respects "inelegant," the principles administered by the Court of Chancery have, in a great measure, shaped themselves on the model of those of the Roman law. The jurisprudence of England has been improved on many points by the Civil law; but nowhere is the beneficial influence of that law so perceptible as in the view taken by Equity of the real character of a mortgage transaction. It would be far beyond the scope of the present lectures to trace the gradual growth of this branch of the equitable jurisdiction of the Court of Chancery. But there are few things, I venture to affirm, more remarkable in the history of law than the successive steps by which the law of England touching securities was placed on its present footing.

LECTURE II.

Hindu and Mahomedan law of mortgages—Hindu law—Early notions of pledge—Tradition originally essential to validity of pledge (Shib Chunder Ghose *vs.* Russick Chunder Neogy)—Pledgee had in early times only a right of detention—Foreclosure, and power of sale, innovations—Classification of securities by Hindu lawyers—Rule requiring tradition gradually fell into disuse—Possession still important when any questions touching priority arise—Text of Brihasputty—"Equity of redemption"—Sale by judicious process—Beneficial pledge, and pledge for custody—Important distinction between the two—Right of pledgee to sue when pledge is destroyed without his default—Analogous rule in Code Civil—Rule of Hindu law, interest not to exceed principal—Influence of rule on Hindu law of pledges.

I NOW come to the Hindu law of securities,—a branch of our law which I venture to think may be placed by the side of the most advanced systems of jurisprudence.

An accomplished lawyer, whose memory will be always dear to Sanskrit learning, in speaking of our law of bailments, has said: "It is pleasing to remark the similarity, or rather the identity, of those conclusions, which pure unbiased reason in all ages and nations seldom fails to draw, in such judicial inquiries as are not fettered and manacled by *positive* institution; and although the rules of the *Pundits* concerning *succession* to *property*, *the punishment* of *offences*, and the *ceremonies* of *religion* are widely different from ours, yet, in the great system of *contracts*, and the common intercourse between man and man, the Pootee of the Indians and the Digest of the Romans are by no means dissimilar." The law, however, which moved the admiration of Sir William Jones has ceased, in one sense, to be living law, and it is to be sought at the present day not in our books of reports, but in the texts of our sages and in the writings of the successive jurisconsults by whom Hindu law was gradually moulded into system. It is to that law, the truly indigenous system of the country, that I propose to call your attention in the present lecture. LECTURE II.

I must, however, warn you at the outset that it is by no means easy to thread one's way through the labyrinth of conflicting texts in which the law is sometimes involved. I intend to confine myself only to some of the broader features of this branch of Hindu jurisprudence. But even with this limitation, I cannot but feel a certain degree of distrust in the soundness of my conclusions,—a distrust, I may venture to say, without presumption, perhaps inseparable from the nature of the inquiry upon which we are now engaged.

I have already said that the authorities upon which our conclusions must mainly rest are not unfrequently conflicting. The key to this conflict

LECTURE II. is to be sought in the fact that we have to trust to texts which, although sometimes placed side by side, are of various antiquity,—a fact which must be carefully borne in mind by the student of Hindu law. Whatever truth there may be in the reproach that the Hindus are an unprogressive race, even the most careless student of our law must admit that the charge must be received with considerable reservation. Hindu law is, no doubt, archaic, but there are portions of it which furnish unmistakeable evidence of maturity. A not very friendly critic has said: "There is in truth but little doubt that, until education began to cause the natives of India to absorb Western ideas for themselves, the influence of the English rather retarded than hastened the mental development of the race. There are several departments of thought in which a slow modification of primitive notions and consequent alteration of practice may be seen to have been proceeding before we entered the country; but the signs of such change are exceptionally clear in jurisprudence, so far, that is to say, as Hindu jurisprudence has been codified. Hindu law is, theoretically, contained in Manu, but it is practically collected from the writings of the jurists who have commented on him, and on one another." (Maine's Village Communities, page 46.)

In examining Hindu law, we must, I repeat, carefully distinguish the rudimentary stages of legal thought from its maturity; and it is because this has not always been done, that Hindu law has attracted to itself a cloud of undeserved prejudice. It may be said that it is not always possible to obtain direct evidence of the relative antiquity of the texts of Hindu law; but in this, as in other instances, a knowledge of comparative jurisprudence will, I am sure, greatly assist us in "unravelling the tangled skein" of legal history. Comparative jurisprudence is to the lawyer what comparative grammar is to the philologist; and if the results yielded by the latter are more certain, it is only because its inductions are founded upon a wider basis. The conjecture, however, may be hazarded without rashness or presumption, that Hindu law will, at no distant date, render the same service to jurisprudence that Sanskrit has already done to the sister science of philology.

I will illustrate my position by reference to a question connected with the Hindu law of securities which has provoked no little conflict of opinion.

We saw that in Roman law a pledge was originally required to be accompanied by possession, and that it was only very gradually that hypothecation found a place in the jurisprudence of Rome. In the case of *Shib Chunder Ghose* v. *Russick Chunder Neogy* (Fulton's Reports, p. 36), the question arose, whether a pledge unaccompanied by possession was valid according to Hindu law.

LECTURE II. Conflicting texts were cited in the argument. The plaintiff relied upon the text of Brihasputty,—"Of him who does not enjoy a pledge, nor possess it, nor claim it *on evidence*, the written contract for a pledge is nugatory, like a bond when the debtor and witnesses are dead." The defendant relied upon the text of Naroda: "By the acceptance or actual possession of a pledge the validity of the contract is maintained." "Pledges are declared to be of two sorts, immoveable and moveable, and both are valid when there is actual enjoyment, and *not otherwise.*" The Judges were divided in opinion; but the majority of the Court held that whatever might have been the case in early times, the later Hindu law clearly sanctioned the validity of a pledge although unaccompanied by possession; and they relied as well upon some of the written texts of Hindu law as upon the general usage of the country. Mr. Justice Grant, however, was of a different opinion, and I shall presently call your attention to the reasons given by the learned Judge as a striking illustration of the delusions which had at one time crystallized round the so-called "law of nature;" but before I do so I must enter upon a discussion, which may perhaps at first sight seem to be somewhat outside the range of the present lectures; but which a closer examination will, I trust, show to be relevant. I allude to the important part played by tradition in early law.

It seems that in the rudimentary stages of legal thought there was no distinction between a contract and a conveyance. Sir Henry Maine has shown that, in the Roman law, contracts, as well as transfers, were originally known by the same name, and were accompanied by the same formalities. In course of time, however, the notion of a contract disengages itself from the notion of a conveyance, and then we have the well-known distinction between "real" and "personal" rights. (Ancient Law, Chap. IX.) A "real right," or *jus in rem*, is, as you are aware, a right availing against the world at large; while a "personal right" (*jus ad rem*) is a right availing only against some determinate person or persons. Take the case of an executory contract of sale. If, for instance, A agree to sell a parcel of land to B, B acquires a personal right against A to compel him to fulfil his contract; or if that is impossible, B can compel A to compensate him for the breach. B, however, has no right whatever against third persons who may withhold the land from him. The right is a personal right, arising out of an agreement. But if A, in pursuance of the contract, convey the land to B, B is said to acquire a real right, which he can assert against third persons. Now in archaic law there could be no valid conveyance unless accompanied by tradition. Possession was, therefore, an essential element in the acquisition of a real right. Various explanations have been suggested of the origin of

LECTURE II. this rule. But whatever might be the origin of the rule, there can be very little doubt that it was retained in almost every system of law, because it served a useful purpose. As a conveyance transferred a real right it was very desirable that it should take place openly, and change of possession was, perhaps, best calculated to accomplish that object. The inconvenience of the proceeding, however, must have suggested the gradual relaxation of the rule; and in the maturity of jurisprudence tradition loses its original importance, and is almost everywhere, in time, replaced by a system of registration of titles. It has been thrown out by a learned writer that the first relaxation probably took place in the case of mortgages, and an examination of the Roman law certainly shows that, in the Western world at any rate, this was the case. The Roman prætors, in recognising the validity of a hypothecation, broke in upon what I may call the rule of the common law,—a rule which was retained in Roman jurisprudence to the last, by which no real right could pass without tradition. It is not possible to say whether precisely the same course of development was followed by the Hindu law. There can, however, be little doubt that in mature Hindu law the rule requiring tradition had fallen into disuse, and that a real right, whether by mortgage or sale, could be conferred by a mere expression of the intention of the parties. A close examination of the subject would be beyond the scope of the present lectures; and I shall content myself only with citing a passage from the Mitacshara which shows the state of the Hindu law on the point. "The acceptance of gold, cloths, &c., being completed by the ceremony of bestowing water, and falling, therefore, under either of the means, may be designated as a three-fold acceptance; but in the case of land, as there can be no corporeal acceptance without enjoyment of the produce, it must be accompanied by some little possession, otherwise the gift, sale, or other transfer is not complete. A title, therefore, without corporeal acceptance, consisting of the enjoyment of the produce, is weaker than a title accompanied by it, or with such corporeal acceptance. But such is the case only when of these two the priority is undistinguishable; but *when it is ascertained which is first in point of date, and which posterior, then the simple prior title affords the stronger evidence.*" (Macnaghten's Hindu Law, Vol I, pp. 218-219.)

I have dwelt at some length upon the subject, because Hindu law cannot be properly understood without some general knowledge of comparative jurisprudence, which alone can furnish us with a key to the apparent conflict in our written law. In the digest of Juggannath, side by side with texts which belong to the infancy of law, we find others which belong to a much more advanced stage of legal thought. Our knowledge of the gradual

LECTURE II. progress of law in the Western world will, however, enable us to determine with tolerable certainty the historical order of the different authorities upon which our conclusions must rest. The inductions of comparative jurisprudence are as yet, no doubt, founded upon a limited basis, but I may safely venture to affirm that the written texts of Hindu law, which require the delivery of possession by the mortgagor to the mortgagee, are older than those which do not insist upon tradition. It seems to me, with very great deference, that this simple fact is not sufficiently attended to by Mr. Justice Grant in his elaborate judgment in the case of *Shib Chunder Ghose* v. *Russick Chunder Neogy*, in which this question was fully discussed. In that case Mr. Justice Grant is reported to have said: "In questions, therefore, which concern the laws of countries into which the feudal law has not been introduced, it is of importance to begin by ascertaining what the Roman law was upon those questions, because it is the best digest of the rules which affect the rights and obligations of mankind according to the natural principles common to all nations. If we find the law laid down in any treatise upon the subject which is in question, conformable to the principles of the *Jus gentium* stated in the Roman law, we are entitled to believe that it is correctly laid down. If we find it declared to be otherwise, we are driven to search for some reason in the circumstances of the people which shall account for their institutions in that matter differing from those of the rest of mankind. If we find authorities in their law differing and equally balanced, we must believe those to be correct which agree with the general principles of natural law—still more if we find the majority agreeing with those principles and expressing themselves clearly, and the minority apparently differing from them and expressing themselves more obscurely and less decidedly." LECTURE II.

Mr. Justice Grant then proceeds to examine what he calls the general principles of natural law as they are to be found in the Roman law. After stating that there could be no valid pledge without possession, the learned Judge, referring to the hypothecation of the later Roman law, says: "The *Jus hypothecæ* was limited to certain securities, chiefly, if not solely, over moveable property, and to certain cases, and under certain regulations, afforded by the equity of the prætor. It was *pactum prætorium* not arising out of general principles of law, or forming part of their common law, or *jus non scriptum*, but a municipal institution introduced by that magistrate. Puffendorff confines this security of pledge expressly to the giving the creditor some certain thing in pawn till the debt be paid, and considers the hypotheck of the Romans to have been confined to immoveable property. "The

LECTURE II. distinction," says Sir William Jones, "between pledging where possession is transferred to the creditor, and hypothecation where it remains with the debtor, was originally derived from the Attick law." In what circumstance the Athenians admitted the hypothecation, we do not know. But that with them, as with the Romans, delivery of possession was necessary to constitute pledge by what we may call their common law, there seems no doubt. This, therefore, was the law of the whole ancient world of civilized Europe, extending as well to immoveable as to moveable property *secundum jus gentium*. And it is also the law of the whole of modern Europe in regard to moveables." (Fulton's Reports, page 36.) The learned Judge, therefore, comes to the conclusion that tradition is necessary to the validity of a pledge in Hindu law, a conclusion which we are told is in conformity with "the general principles of natural law." If it were not for the peculiar views about the law of nature so widely prevalent at one time, Mr. Justice Grant could hardly have failed to perceive that the Hindu law might have been developed in course of time in the same manner as the Roman law was developed by the introduction of the hypothecation. We have here an instance of juridical improvements in the West repeating themselves in India.

We have seen how in one respect the Hindu law slowly matured itself. I will now proceed to discuss another question which has also given rise to considerable conflict of opinion,—a conflict which has added not a little to the evil reputation for uncertainty which the Hindu law has acquired.

We saw in the last lecture that in the Western world a security was originally regarded only as a means of compelling the debtor to fulfil his engagement, and that it was only very slowly that Roman jurisprudence emancipated itself from this conception. The questions naturally suggest themselves, was there any analogous movement in Hindu law? Are there any traces in Hindu law of the primitive notions of a security? Now an examination of our law shows, as I have already said, that a real security was comparatively a late development of Hindu jurisprudence. The earliest record of Hindu law which we possess discloses that stage of legal thought in which a security is limited to a bare right of detention. Manu says, "Whatever the length of time, a pledge may neither be sold nor assigned by the pledgee." Here we find the very same restrictions upon the rights of the creditor as we found in early Roman law. In course of time, however, these restrictions were withdrawn, and the security of the pledgee in Hindu law became a true real security. The change was accomplished by the successive jurisconsults, by whom, in the absence of direct legislation, the improvement of our law was carried on. The authority of Manu

LECTURE II. is never openly disowned, and yet we find in the mature Hindu jurisprudence the rule laid down in the code reduced to very narrow limits; the dictum of Manu being confined to the single case of a pledge in which the creditor is permitted to receive the profits in lieu of interest, and the right to redeem the pledge is by the express agreement of the parties unlimited as to time. In order to explain myself I ought to state that, in the later Hindu law, a pledge might either be limited as to time or for an indefinite time. It might also either be a pledge for use, or for mere custody. In the pledge for a limited time, the property, by the express terms of the agreement, passed to the creditor on default. In the pledge for use no interest was permitted to be taken by the creditor in addition to the usufruct. It is not necessary to discuss any of the rules peculiar to each of these classes. All that I wish to observe is, that the division of securities into pledges for a limited period, and pledges for an indefinite time, marks an advanced stage of juridical thought. No trace of any such classification is to be found in Manu, although the distinction between beneficial pledges and pledges for custody is pointed out in the code. In the maturity of Hindu jurisprudence the creditor possessed a real security in every case in which the pledge was for a limited period, and in some cases also where the pledge was for an indefinite time. In the case of a pledge for an indefinite time, if the pledge was one for custody only, the property passed to the creditor when the debt had doubled itself, the rule of Hindu law prohibiting the accumulation of interest exceeding the principal. The law, however, went a step further when it allowed the creditor to sell the pledge and repay himself out of the proceeds even when a forfeiture was guarded against by the express stipulations of the parties. The pledgee was entitled to exercise this right if the pledge happened to be of the class known as a pledge for custody and the debtor failed to redeem after the interest had become equal to the principal. It would seem that in the last case the creditor only possessed the right to *sell* the pledge. In every other case a sale was entirely in the option of the mortgagor.

The foregoing sketch shows how a pledge in Hindu law limited by Manu to a bare right of detention ripened in course of time into a true real security. This was accomplished by a series of limitations imposed upon the very broad proposition which we find in the code. It is not always possible to trace the successive stages of the progress of the Hindu law; but in the present case, I think, the task can be accomplished with tolerable certainty. The first improvement appears to have been the introduction of a clause by which the debtor agreed to the property in the pledge passing to the creditor upon default. The division of

LECTURE II. pledges which we find in the later Hindu law into pledges for a limited and pledges for an unlimited period, is nowhere alluded to by Manu, and there can I think be but little doubt that the classification denotes a very great advance in legal thought. Partly by calling in this distinction, and partly by help of the distinction between pledges for use and those for mere security, the successive commentators cut down the rights of the pledgor to what I will venture to call the most reasonable limits. The commentators, who, as I have already said, always professed the very greatest veneration for the text of the code, explained the dictum of Manu as having reference only to cases in which there was no express agreement that the pledge should be forfeited on default. This was the first of the series of limitations by which the application of the text of Manu was gradually narrowed. Chandeswara, Bachespati, Bhavudeva, all concur in the opinion that the text applies only to a pledge in which there is no special agreement by which the right of the debtor is liable to forfeiture. It was not long before the law was further developed. The process by which this was accomplished was by presuming the existence of a clause of forfeiture when the debt doubled itself in the case of a pledge for custody. The text of Manu was now narrowed down by an ingenious construction only to the single case of a beneficial pledge in which no time was limited for redemption. I have, however, passed over an intermediate stage in the development of the law in which the pledgee for custody was entitled to use the pledge after the accumulation of interest to the extent permitted by the law. The latest improvement, as I have already said, consisted in the right which the law gave to the creditor to sell the pledge even when there was an express stipulation that the property should not be forfeited although the debt was doubled. I shall now call your attention to a discussion in the Mitacshara, which, while it confirms the truth of the proposition that a real security was a late product of Hindu jurisprudence, offers an apt illustration of the method of interpretation followed by Hindu commentators. Referring to the text of Brihasputty,—"Gold having doubled, and the stipulated period having expired, the creditor becomes owner of the pledge after the lapse of fourteen days. If the debtor repays the amount within the time, he shall get back the pledge,"—the author of the Mitacshara says—"A question arises that the pledge is forfeited is not consistent, because there is neither a gift nor sale, &c., by which the right of the debtor can cease; neither is there an acceptance, nor purchase, &c., by which the right of the creditor can accrue; and that it is also contrary to the text of Manu." "However long the time may be" means for whatever length of time the pledge has been in the

LECTURE II. custody of the pledgee. "Assigned," pledged to a third person by the pledgee. Hence, by the prohibition of assignment and sale, it is evident that the right of the pledgee does not accrue. Answered. It is a well known popular notion that a transfer by pledge is a qualified cause of the loss of right; and acceptance of the pledge, a qualified cause of the creation of right. Consequently, after the debt has doubled, and the stipulated time has arrived, the right to satisfy the debt ceases, and by virtue of this text the debtor's right is lost for ever, and that of the creditor accrues. Nor is it contrary to the text of Manu—"after no length of time neither an assignment nor a sale of the pledge can be made." For this is said by the sage (Manu) on the subject of a pledge for use, as he commences by saying,—"if he take a beneficial pledge, he must have no other interest on the loan."

You will remember that the passage in Manu was expounded by the earlier commentators as applying only to pledges whether for use or custody, where there was no express agreement that the property should be forfeited on default. Hindu law, however, had advanced since that time; and accordingly we find the author of the Mitacshara placing a still more restricted interpretation on the text of Manu. This was the way in which Hindu law was gradually improved under conditions which were certainly not very favourable to progress.

Referring to the development of law by successive comments by jurisconsult upon jurisconsult, Sir Henry Maine says:—"Even so obstinate a subject-matter as Hindu law, was visibly changed by it for the better. No doubt the dominant object of each successive Hindu commentator is so to construe each rule of Civil law as to make it appear that there is some sacerdotal reason for it; but subject to this controlling aim, each of them leaves in the law, after he has explained it, a stronger dose of common sense and a larger element of equity and reasonableness than he found in it as it came from the hands of his predecessors." (Village Communities, p. 45.)

We have now arrived at the state in which the Hindu law stood in its maturity. We find that if the debtor committed default, the property in the pledge passed to the creditor, who might, however, in the exercise of his discretion, sell the pledge; when, if there was a surplus, the debtor became entitled to it. In the case, however, of a pledge, for custody, where there was an express stipulation against forfeiture, the creditor could not foreclose, but could only exercise the right of sale. The only case in which there could be neither a sale nor a foreclosure, was when the pledge was of the description known as a "beneficial pledge," and the right of redemption was by the express agreement of the parties not limited to any particular period.

LECTURE II. — The creditor was in no danger of losing his interest, and the law, therefore, left him to the terms of his contract with the debtor.

It would seem that, under the Hindu law, the mortgagee could not sell the pledge except through judicial process. Brihasputty says: "When the pawner is missing let the creditor produce his pledge before the king; it may then be sold with his permission: this is a settled rule. Receiving the principal with interest, he must deposit the surplus with the king." This text, therefore, shows that the creditor was not entitled to sell the pledge of his own authority.

We have already seen that, in later Hindu law, it was not necessary that a pledge should be accompanied by possession.

It must not, however, be supposed that a mortgagee who had omitted to take possession was exactly in the situation of one who had taken the precaution of publishing the mortgage, if I may use the expression, by taking possession of the property pledged to him. Whenever any question of priority arose, the mortgagee in possession, though his mortgage might be later in date, was always preferred to the mortgagee who had neglected to enter upon possession. "If two men, to whom the same property has been pledged, enter into a contest, to him who has possessed the land it shall belong, if no force were used." (Smriti, cited in the Ratnacara; Colebrooke's Digest, Vol. I, p. 217.) LECTURE II.

It would seem from the use of the expression "without force," that the possession must be acquired in good faith, and the text seems to limit the preferable right of the puisne incumbrancer in possession only when the money has been advanced without notice of the prior mortgage.

While upon this subject a few words on a kind of mortgage very common in the Southern and Western Presidencies may not be thrown away. This is the Dristi Bandhak, or a mortgage of visible things. In this kind of mortgage, the mortgagor remains in possession till default is made by him, when the mortgagee becomes entitled to enter upon possession as absolute owner of the property. It is with reference to this class of mortgages that Sir William Strange says :—"It may be doubted whether this mode of pledging be not originally Hindu instead of Attic as has been supposed." The existence of this class of mortgages shows very clearly that Hindu law had long outgrown that stage of juridical thought in which tradition is regarded as essential to the constitution of a mortgage.

I have already shown how, in certain cases, the priority of mortgages was determined by possession. I shall now state some other rules governing priority in Hindu law. A mortgage in writing was

LECTURE II. preferred to a parol mortgage. "If a pledge, a sale, or a gift of the same thing be alleged to be made before witnesses to one man, and by a written instrument to another, the writing shall prevail over the oral testimony, because one contract only is maintained. (Smriti, Colebrooke's Digest, Vol. I, pages 220-21.) Another rule is to be found by which a writing in which the property mortgaged is clearly defined, is preferred to one in which there is no such specification of the property intended to be pledged. (1.) "But, if a man first mortgage land without noticing all circumstances, and afterwards mortgage it with express description by name and the like, that writing which contains an express distinction shall prevail." "If a field or a house be described in a written instrument by its limits, and if villages and the like be so described, the contract is valid." When a distinction is expressed in a writing to one man, and no distinction to another, the express distinction, says Cátyáyána, shall preponderate. (Smriti, Colebrooke's Digest, Vol. I, p. 222.) A general hypothecation does not seem to have been recognised by the Hindu law. A text cited in the Digest says—"If a man pledge his property unexhibited and undescribed as to its nature, and consequently imperceptible like the subtile element, that shall not be considered as a definite pledge." (Colebrooke's Digest, Vol. I, p. 225.) There are one or two more points in connection with Hindu law which deserve notice. "Mortgaged land," says Yágnyawalcya, "being carried away by a rapid stream, or being seized by the king, another pledge of land must be delivered, or the sum lent must be restored to the lender." (Colebrooke's Digest, Vol. I, p. 168.) Similarly, Cátyáyána says, "Whatever pledge has been lost by the act of God or the king, the debt for which it was given shall be paid by the debtor to the creditor with interest." (Colebrooke's Digest, Vol. I, pp. 169 & 170.) Brihasputty also says, "If a pledge be destroyed by the act of God or of the king, the creditor shall either obtain another pledge, or receive the sum lent together with interest." Narada says, "When a pledge, though carefully preserved, is spoiled in course of time, another pledge must be delivered, or the amount of principal and interest must be paid to the creditor. (Colebrooke's Digest, Vol. I, pp. 165 & 166.) An analogous rule is to be found in the French Code, Article 2131, which says: "In like manner, in case the present immoveable or immoveables, subjected to mortgage, have perished, or sustained deterioration, in such manner that they have become insufficient for the security of the creditor, the latter shall be permitted either to sue immediately for repayment or to obtain an additional mortgage."

The Hindu law did not permit the redemption of a usufructuary mortgage for a limited period

LECTURE II. before the expiration of the term. The rights of the mortgagor are, no doubt, guarded with scrupulous care, but the sentimental tenderness for the debtor, which sometimes overlooks the just rights of the creditor, finds no place in our ancient law. "When a house or field, mortgaged for use," says Brihasputty, "has not been held to the close of its term, neither can the debtor obtain his property, nor the creditor obtain the debt." The lawgiver, however, adds,—"After the period is completed, the right of both to their respective property is ordained; but, even while it is unexpired, they may restore their property to each other by mutual consent." (Colebrooke's Digest, Vol. I, p. 199.)

I shall conclude with a few observations on the general rights of the mortgagor. The mortgagor, notwithstanding the mortgage, could deal with the property as owner subject to the limitation that he was not permitted to do anything which might impair the security of the mortgagee. He could make a gift or sale of the property, and the transferee would, in either case, have the right to redeem the mortgage. Raghunandana, in his Dáyatatwa, says,—"Thus also if the pledge be not redeemed by reason of death or the like of the seller or donor, it may be redeemed by the buyer or donee, because a right equal to that of the former owner has been generated by the sale or gift. In such a case if a dispute arise as to the source of the right, then the buyer or the donee (who is admitted as such) is required to prove his possession, and not the commencement of his title." (Dáyatatwa, Translated by Golap Chunder Sirkar Sastri, sec. 16, p. 32.) The passage is also interesting as showing that hypothecation was a common mode of mortgaging property, at least in Bengal, in the sixteenth century. Lecture II.

A text of Vishnu is sometimes cited to show that a second mortgage was not permitted by the Hindu law. "He who has mortgaged," says Vishnu, "even a bull's hide of land to one creditor, and without having redeemed it, mortgages it to another, shall be corporally punished *by whipping or imprisonment;* if the quantity be less, he shall pay a fine of sixteen *suvernas*" (Colebrooke's Digest, Vol. I, p. 216.) The text would seem to point to a fraudulent second mortgage executed by the debtor without disclosing the prior mortgage,—a fraud which the Hindu law, in common with other systems, is careful to guard against. The reasoning of the Bengal lawyer would seem to show that no exception could be taken to a second mortgage honestly created by the debtor; while the extremely severe penalty attached to a violation of the duty which the text imposes on the mortgagor, also points to the same conclusion.

I have now brought down the history of Hindu law to its maturity. I regret that the limits I am obliged to propose to myself will not permit a

LECTURE II. fuller account. The Hindu law of security however deserves very careful study, and I trust I shall not be accused of an idle pride in my own national system if I venture to affirm that although not quite so perfect as the Roman law, it is still on the whole a model of good sense and logical consistency.

LECTURE II.—*(Continued.)*

Mahomedan Law of Mortgage—Difference between Mahomedan Law and Hindu and English Law—*Rahn*, literally detention—Pledge invalid unless followed by transfer of possession—Things capable of being pledged—Those of which possession could be delivered—Things which could be sold, but of which possession could not be given, could not be pledged—Opinion of Shafei—Pledge for contingent debt—Liability of pledgee for loss or destruction of pledge—Interest unlawful—Influence of rule in retarding development of law of pledge—Qualified power of sale—Must be given by contract itself—Bye-bil-waffa, a comparatively modern innovation—Conflicting opinions of Mahomedan lawyers as to its legality—Opinion of Mahomedan law officer in Bussunt Ally's case.—Recognition of validity of Bye-bil-waffas in India—Gradual recognition of hypothecation—Probable influence of Hindu Law—No distinction between pledges of land and pledges of moveables—Moveables, originally the subject of pledge—Gradual extension of pledge of land—Hypothecation.

I WILL now proceed to give a short outline of the Mahomedan law of securities. The Mahomedan law, however, to which I propose to call your attention in this lecture, is not the law which is administered at the present day by our Courts of Justice, but that which is to be found in the authoritative treatises of Mahomedan doctors. Mahomedan law has, no doubt, made great progress since; but in the process it has lost all its distinctive features, and there could, I apprehend, be no better proof of this than the fact that, according to the law as administered in Bengal and the North-Western Provinces, at any rate, the respective rights of mortgagor and mortgagee are the same, whether the parties are Hindus or Mahomedans. The process which Mahomedan law underwent in India may be described as one of gradual assimilation to the Hindu law.

There is one feature of Mahomedan law which distinguishes it as well from the Hindu as from the English law. We saw that in both the latter systems, the ownership of the property mortgaged is liable to pass to the creditor on the failure of the debtor to repay the loan by the appointed time. The transfer is the result of the agreement of the parties, by which the debtor renounces his right to the pledge upon default. In the Roman law, however, we found that another kind of security was invented at a very early period, by which the possession only was transferred to the creditor. This kind of security, as I told you, had a very great fortune in Roman law. It displaced the older form of security, and the respective rights and duties of the pledgor and pledgee were moulded on principles altogether different from those which have obtained in systems in which a conditional transfer of ownership is the recognised mode of giving security. In the later Roman law, the ownership never passed to the creditor upon default. He was only authorised to sell the pledge and satisfy his debt out of the proceeds. Now the pledge of the strict Mahomedan law resembles very closely the pignus of the Civil law. The creditor is not permitted to become the owner of the pledge. His right is confined with certain limitations to be presently noticed to the sale of the pledge, when, if there is a surplus, the debtor becomes entitled to it. It is true that the ingenuity of Mahomedan lawyers soon invented another kind of security analogous to the fiducia of the Roman and the mortgage of the English law. But there cannot be the shadow of a doubt that the early Mahomedan law did not recognise any other kind of security than the *Rahn*, to which I now propose to address myself.

A pledge in Mahomedan law, as signified by its name (Rahn), is defined in the Hedaya as "the detention of a thing on account of a claim which may be answered by means of that thing, as in the case of debts." (Hedaya, Vol. IV, p. 189.) There is a good deal of discussion in the Mahomedan books as to the necessity of possession to the validity of a pledge, but the better opinion seems to be that a pledge is not valid unless accompanied by possession. It is said in the Hedaya that "until the seizin actually take place, the pawner is at full liberty either to adhere to, or recede from, the agreement, as the validity of it rests entirely upon the seizin, without which the end and intention of a pledge cannot be answered." (Hedaya, Vol. IV, p. 190.) In these words you cannot fail to perceive the very same primitive notions which are traceable in early Hindu and Roman jurisprudence. It is also clear that the Mahomedan law had not ceased to be under the dominion of archaic notions when the Hedaya was compiled. The conflicting dicta, however, which are collected by the author, show that the process of emancipation had already commenced, and, it may be presumed, was accelerated by the Hindu law, with which it came into contact in India.

Possession being thus essential to the validity of a pledge, it followed as a corollary that things of which there could be no delivery of possession according to Mahomedan notions, could not be given in pledge. Thus, an undivided share in any property, whether moveable or immoveable, could not be lawfully pledged. One eminent Mahomedan lawyer, indeed, who seems to have entertained sounder notions on the subject, maintains a contrary opinion; but the weight of authority is opposed to his view. The discussion on this point in the Hedaya shows a conflict between archaic notions and modern ideas, which is extremely interesting.

"It is unlawful," says the author of the Hedaya, "to pawn an indefinite part of anything. Shafei maintains that it is lawful. On behalf of our doctors two reasons are urged. *First*, this disagreement arises from the difference of opinion regarding the object of pledges; for, according to us, pledges are taken *to be detained, with a view to obtain payment of a debt*, which cannot be effected in case the pledge be an undefined part of property; because a seizin of things of that nature cannot be made, a real seizin being only practicable with respect to things which are defined and distinguished—whereas, according to Shafei, the *object of pledges is that the pawnee may sell them to effect a discharge of his debt;* and with this object pledges of the nature above mentioned are not in any shape inconsistent. *Secondly*, it is an essential part of the contract of pawn, that the pledge be constantly detained in the hands of the pawnee until the redemption of it by the pawner—a condition which cannot be fulfilled with respect to pledges of the above nature; for, in such cases, it would be necessary that the pawner and the pawnee have possession of the article alternately, whence it would be the same as if the pawner were to say to the pawnee, "I pawn it to you every other day;"—as, therefore, a constant detention is in such case impossible, it follows that the pledge of an undefined part of anything, whether capable of division or incapable, is illegal." (Hedaya, Vol. IV, p. 192.)

I shall now proceed to consider the rights of the pledgee in Mahomedan law. I propose to place before you only some of the broader principles, as

LECTURE II. the details do not possess much interest. The pledgee had the right to sell the pledge on default, but only when the right was given by the contract itself. He was then regarded as the agent of the debtor, but the authority upon principles recognised in every system of law was not revocable. It was not necessary that the authority should be given to the creditor himself. It might be given to a third person, who might be compelled by the Court to exercise the power. A sale, however, through judicial intervention seems to have been unknown, and the Kazee could only compel a person who had been invested with the power of sale to exercise it for the benefit of the creditor. If the power of sale was not given by the original contract, the pledgee had only a bare lien, without the right of getting material satisfaction out of the pledge.

In the Mahomedan law, the debtor was not authorised to deal in any way with the property pledged by him; and a sale without the consent of the creditor was invalid. If, notwithstanding, the debtor sold the property to two persons in succession, the person who was recognised as the purchaser by the pledgee, acquired a preferable right to the property, although the sale to him might be posterior in point of time.

The rule of the Mahomedan law regarding the liability of the pledgee for the destruction of the pledge, even when the destruction is accidental, is somewhat peculiar. It is thus stated by Macnaghten: "Where such property, being equivalent to the debt, may have been destroyed otherwise than by the act of the pawnee or mortgagee, the debt is extinguished; where it exceeds the debt, the pawnee or mortgagee is not responsible for the excess; but where it falls short of the debt, the deficiency must be made up by the pawnor or mortgagor: but if the property were wilfully destroyed by the act of the pawnee or mortgagee, he will be responsible for any excess of its value beyond the amount of the debt." (Macnaghten's Mahomedan Law, page 82, para. 19.)

There are one or two more points which deserve notice. The pledgee was not permitted to enjoy the usufruct of the property pledged to him, but he was not chargeable with the expense of providing for the support of the pledge, although he was bound to provide for its custody. "It is to be observed," says the author of the Hedaya, "that the wants of a pledge are of two kinds: (1) such as are requisite towards the support of the pledge and the continuance of its existence; (2) such as may be necessary towards its preservation of safety, whether wholly or partly. Now, as the absolute property of the pledge appertains to the pawner, the expenses of the first class must, therefore, be defrayed by him; and as he has, moreover, a property in the usufruct of the pledge, its support and the continuance of its existence for this reason also rest upon him, being an expense attendant upon his property,—in the same manner as holds in the case of a trust. Of this class are the maintenance of a pledge in meat and drink, including wages to shepherds, and so forth; and the clothing of a slave, the wages of a nurse for the child of a pledge, the watering of a garden, the grafting of fig trees, the collecting of fruits, &c. The expenses of the second class, on the contrary, are incumbent on the pawnee; because it is his part to detain the pledge; and, as the preservation of it therefore rests upon him, he is consequently to defray the expense of such preservation. Of the second class is the hire of the keeper of the pledge; and so likewise the rent of the house, wherein the pledge is deposited, whether the debt exceed or fall short of the value of the pledge." (Hedaya, Vol. IV.)

A pledge cannot be given as a security against contingencies. Thus, a pledge deposited with a person as a security for anything which may be due in future, is invalid; "although," adds the Hedaya, "it is otherwise in the case of a promised debt, as where a person gives a pledge to another on the strength of his promising to lend him one thousand *dirms*, and the other takes the pledge and promises to lend the money, and the pledge perishes in his hands; for in this case he is responsible in proportion to the sum promised, in the same manner as if it had been actually paid, the promise of debt being considered as an actual existence of it, for this reason that it was made at the earnest desire of the borrower." (Hedaya, Vol. IX, pages 208, 209.) In a case, in which a Mahomedan vendor had deposited with the vendee the title-deeds of a certain estate as a security for his delivering up to the vendee the title-deeds of the property which had been sold to him, and which were not at the time in the possession of the vendor, Lord Kingsdown observed:—"By the Mahomedan law such a contract as the one under consideration for a security in respect of a contingent loss would be one not of pawn but of trust." (*Varden Seth Sam* v. *Lukputty Royjee Lalla*, 9 Moore, p. 320.)

We have seen that the pledgee had not, in the Mahomedan law, an unqualified power of sale, and the reason why no improvement took place in this respect is not far to seek. The Mahomedan law did not authorise the taking of interest, and this rule must have retarded the development of the law of pledge. We saw how common fairness suggested in Hindu law the rule by which the debtor was bound to redeem before the interest became equal to the principal. But no such liability was imposed upon the Mahomedan debtor, because the pledge was thought to be a sufficient security so far as the creditor was concerned, and as the debt

LECTURE II. could not receive any accession, the creditor did not run much risk. The prohibition, however, relating to interest, led to the invention of the bye-bil-waffa—a kind of security analogous to the English mortgage, and possessing a very interesting history.

The Mahomedan creditor being prohibited by law from taking interest, hit upon the expedient of doing so under color of a sale with a clause for repurchase. Such a condition was perhaps strictly legal; but the Mahomedan lawyers were slow to recognise a transaction which had only the semblance of a sale, but which in reality was a loan repayable with interest. You will find the conflicting opinions of some of the most eminent Mahomedan lawyers on the point collected in Baillie's book on Sales. (See Baillie on the Mahomedan Law of Sale, pages 301—302.)

The question seems to have been raised in a very early case in the Sudder Dewany Adawlut, when the Mahomedan Law Officers, who were consulted, gave the following opinion:—"In the deed, there is first stipulated an absolute sale: afterwards, at the end of it, it is additionally stipulated, that, if the seller shall repay the purchase-money within a year, the sale shall become void. The author of the Buhr-i-rayik says such a condition is illegal, except it be for three days only, according to Huneefa and Aboo Yusof; but according to Moohummud it is legal, without restriction, as a *sherti-khiar*, or optional condition." (Select Reports, Vol. I, page 76.) In a note to the case in which the above opinion was given, Mr. Macnaghten adds, "In the cause '*Busunt Ali* against *Ram Coomar*,' decided by the Sudder Dewany Adawlut, on the 4th of January 1799, there was a question put to the law officers respecting the legality of bye-bil-waffa sales, though the cause, as it happened, went off on a question as to the competency of the agent who made the bye-bil-waffa sale in that instance on the part of another. It was stated in the *futwa* then given, that a sale, with optional condition for three days, is good; but for more than three days is not good, according to Huneefa and Yusof: but according to Moohummud, for four days, or even a longer period, is good: that the sort of sale being prevalent in the country, Moohummud's opinion should be followed. The intention of the parties, as collected from the tenor of the deed, shews whether the bye-bil-waffa be a sale with the reserve of an option of retractation within a limited time, or a mortgage for the security of money lent. A stipulation for a short period must be considered to mark that a sale was in the contemplation of the parties; a long term denotes a mortgage, or security for a loan: and such mortgages in the form of conditional sales are very common, and rightly held valid under the opinion here cited." (Select Reports, Vol. I, page 77.)

The bye-bil-waffa is, however, regarded only in the light of a security, when any question arises as to its real character, and the debtor is regarded as the owner, notwithstanding the sale with a condition. Mr. Baillie refers to a case mentioned in the Futwa of Abul Fuzzul, in which a person was allowed to assert a right of pre-emption, notwithstading the ownership of the property, upon the foundation of which the right was claimed, had been transferred to another by a bye-bil-waffa. (Baillie's Mahomedan Law of Sale, p. 103.) This is no doubt a sensible view of the question, although it is extremely open to doubt whether bye-bil-waffas would have obtained any recognition in the Mahomedan law, if the transaction had not originally masked itself as a sale with a clause of repurchase.

I have brought down the history of bye-bil-waffas down to a comparatively recent period. As I have already said, the law relating to Rahn was also considerably modified in time, and hypothecation seems to have been common enough among the Mahomedans in this country when the earlier Regulations on mortgages were enacted. It would seem that by that time, the Hindu and Mahomedan law had been welded together, and the result was a mixed system, which has since been brought to the shape in which we find it by the infusion of some of the doctrines of the English Court of Chancery.

In concluding this account of what I may call

the early and mediæval Hindu and Mahomedan law of pledge, I wish to call your attention to the fact, that neither of the two systems recognises any distinction between a pledge of moveables and a pledge of immoveables. LECTURE II.

A glance at some of the rules which we find will show that moveables alone were originally the subjects of pledge. Indeed, in the political and economic condition of ancient society, it could hardly have been otherwise. Land was of comparatively little value, while its alienation was guarded against with a jealousy common to all systems of archaic law. The necessity of transferring the possession of the pledge to the creditor must also have proved a serious obstacle to land being given as a security. I speak with reserve, but the conjecture is plausible that as land gradually increased in value, the rigor of the ancient rule was insensibly relaxed. The relaxation was probably at first confined only to immoveable property till in course of time it was extended to moveables. It is thus that in the Eastern, as well as in the Western world, the "substantial pledge" becomes ultimately "refined into the invisible rights of the hypotheca."

LECTURE III.

Conventional mortgages—Different kinds of—Simple mortgage—Conditional sale—Usufructuary—*Otti* of Madras—*Gahun lahen* of Bombay—Mortgage how created—Writing not essential—Effect of Registration laws—Parol defeasances inadmissible—Mortgage by deposit of title-deeds—Equitable mortgage in English law—Memorandum—True nature of—Registration—Proper subjects of mortgage—General hypothecation invalid—Capacity to mortgage—Right of mortgagee to accessions—Rights of mortgagor and mortgagee when pledge assumes a different form—Byjnath Lall *v.* Ramdin Chowdhry—Power of sale in Mofussil mortgages—Bhowani Churn Mitter's case.

In the present course of lectures I shall adhere to the classification of securities which we found in the Roman law. Following that classification, I propose in this lecture to make a few general observations upon the various kinds of conventional mortgages in use in India at the present day. From what I have already said, you must have seen that a creditor possessing a security may have either a right to sell the property mortgaged to him, or he may become the absolute owner of the property, on default of the mortgagor to repay the money lent to him. In the first case, the creditor is not entitled to anything in excess of the debt and costs. In the second case, the creditor becomes entitled to the property, whatever may be its value.

In either case, however, the creditor is wholly independent of the debtor. There is, however, another way in which property may be given as a security, and that is by letting the creditor into possession, and permitting him to repay himself out of the rents and profits. Thus, we have three different kinds of securities all of which are to be found in India. The first is called a simple mortgage; the second, a conditional sale; and the third, a usufructuary mortgage. It is true they may be sometimes found in combination, which gives rise to a greater variety; but the three I have mentioned are what I may call the primary divisions of Indian mortgages. There are in some parts of India particular descriptions of mortgages peculiar to those provinces, as the *Otti* of Madras and the *Gahun lahen* of Bombay; but they do not possess much general interest, and one of them, the *Gahun lahen,* in its incidents, closely resembles the conditional sale of Bengal and the North-Western Provinces. I shall discuss the various rights and liabilities created by each of these kinds of mortgages in succeeding lectures. In the present lecture I I shall state the different ways in which conventional mortgages may be created, and the formalities which it is necessary to observe, ending with a few general observations on this class of securities. Neither the Hindu nor the Mahomedan law requires writing for the validity of any transaction, however solemn.

LECTURE III. "Contracts of every description, involving both corporal and spiritual consequences, may be made orally." (Per Holloway, J., 2 Mad., 37.) It is true that writing is often enjoined, particularly by Hindu lawyers, and preference, as we have seen, is sometimes given to a transaction evidenced by writing over a parol contract or transfer. But the fact remains that in no instance is writing absolutely necessary by law. Among Englishmen, however, who can only convey by deed, a parol mortgage is invalid at law. We shall, however, presently see that the strict rule of law has been broken in upon by the introduction of a class of securities, known as equitable mortgages, so called because they are only recognised by the Court of Chancery. Among Hindus and Mahomedans, however, a parol mortgage is as good as a mortgage reduced to writing. This rule of Hindu and Mahomedan law has been left untouched by the Legislature, notwithstanding the introduction of a very stringent system of registration. In practice, however, mortgages are almost invariably reduced to writing; and the language of the earlier Regulations shows that the practice is by no means a recent growth. In conditional sales, however, parol defeasances are not uncommon, although in recent years, they have become much less frequent than before. It must not, however, be understood that a verbal mortgage stands precisely in the same situation as a written mortgage which has been registered. The Indian Registration Acts, although they do not insist upon the necessity of a written instrument, when the laws of the country do not require that the transaction should be evidenced by writing, give as a rule preference to registered instruments over parol agreements or declarations. Section 48 of Act VIII of 1871, the present Registration Act, says,—"All documents, not testamentary, duly registered under this Act, and relating to any property whether moveable or immoveable, shall take effect against any oral agreement or declaration relating to such property, unless where the agreement or declaration has been accompanied or followed by delivery of possession." LECTURE III.

The section is not very happily worded, and the meaning of the words "agreement" and "declaration" has given rise to some discussion. There can be no doubt, however, as explained by Mr. Justice Markby in *Salim Sheik* against *Bydanath Ghuttuk*, that the word "agreement" in the Act is not intended to be used in the sense of what English lawyers call an executory agreement. It evidently embraces conveyances as well as contracts. It seems to me, however, that the language is not very happily chosen, and plausible arguments may be urged in support of a different view. (12 W. R., p. 217.)

While upon this subject a few words upon the real nature of a conventional mortgage may perhaps

LECTURE III. not be thrown away. A mortgage may be viewed in two different aspects. It is a contract creating a personal right so far as the promise of the debtor to repay the loan is concerned. But it is also a conveyance in so far as it passes to the creditor a real right in the property, which is charged with the repayment of the money. Now a real right, as I have already explained to you, is never conferred by a contract; but a mortgage is looked upon so much as a contract that it is precisely one of those transactions in which we are most likely to confound a contract with a conveyance. I shall show hereafter the importance of this distinction which seems to have been overlooked in some of the cases in the books.

Before dismissing the subject of registration, I wish to make one observation. You find that a parol mortgage is protected, only when it has been followed or accompanied by possession; and the reason is because the actual delivery of possession gives publicity to the transaction, and thus lessens the chances of fraud. It is upon this ground that the Court has refused to extend the protection to a case in which a merely constructive possession is delivered to a person already in actual possession either as tenant or under some other title. (*Kirtee Chunder Haldar* v. *Raj Chunder Haldar*, 22 W. R., p. 273.)

I have already alluded to the practice which obtains in this country for the borrower, in the case of a mortgage by conditional sale, to convey the estate absolutely to the lender; the latter agreeing by a contemporaneous agreement, which is sometimes verbal, that he will reconvey the estate to the borrower on repayment of the loan. The question whether such parol agreement could be received in evidence to control the terms of a document which was on its face a deed of absolute sale, was raised in the Calcutta High Court in the case of *Kassinath Chatterjee* v. *Chundy Churn Banerjee* (5 W. R., p. 68), and was referred to a Full Bench, when a majority of the Judges returned an answer in the negative.

It is perhaps necessary to observe that the law laid down by the Court in *Kassinath Chatterjee* against *Chundy Churn Banerjee* does not in any way trench upon any rule of Hindu or Mahomedan law, neither of which, as I have already said, refuses to give effect to parol agreements.

"Admitting that the law allows sale of land or other contracts relating to land to be made verbally, it does not follow that, if the parties choose to reduce their contract into writing, they can bring forward mere verbal evidence to contradict the writing, and to show that they intended something different from that which the writing expresses and was intended to express." "If a man writes that he sells absolutely, intending the writing which he executes to express and convey the meaning that he intends to sell absolutely, he cannot, by mere verbal evidence, show, that at the time of the agreement, both parties intended that their contract should not be such as their written words express, but that which they expressed by their words to be an absolute sale should be a mortgage." (Per Peacock, C.J., in *Kassinath Chatterjee* against *Chundy Churn Banerjee*, 5 W. R., 68.)

The exclusion of parol evidence for the purpose of qualifying the terms of a written instrument rests upon the presumption that when parties choose to reduce the terms of a contract to writing, they intend to insert the whole of the terms. Any other rule would open the widest door to fraud and perjury.

A distinction, however, is taken by the Court between parol evidence of an agreement and evidence of the "acts" of the parties, the Chief Justice being of opinion that parol evidence is admissible to explain the acts of the parties, as for instance, that the document purporting to be a conveyance was not accompanied or followed by possession.

It is perhaps not quite easy to discover the ground upon which the distinction is made,—a distinction which, as pointed out by a learned Judge, is hardly reconcileable with the principle upon which the exclusion of parol evidence is founded. In the case of *Madhub Chunder Roy* against *Gungadhur Shamuntho*, Mr. Justice Markby is reported to have said:— LECTURE III.

"It seems to me to be very difficult to understand the distinction drawn between evidence of a parol agreement contradicting the terms of a written contract being inadmissible, and evidence of the parties contradicting the terms of such a contract being admissible. In all these cases, one starts with the proposition that there was a written instrument which unequivocally and unmistakeably declares the intention of the parties, and I should have thought that it was quite as objectionable, if not more so, to contradict the plain terms of the contract by what are called acts, by the Full Bench, which can only lead to an inference, than to contradict them by an express and unequivocal and unmistakeable parol arrangement between the parties. I should have thought that the principle was this, that when we have once got a clear expression in writing of that which professes to be the intention of the parties, that must conclusively be taken to be the relation which was intended to be created between them, and that to get at their intention, no other evidence, whether of contemporaneous acts or agreements ought to be admitted." (11 W. R., p. 451.)

Since the above observations were made, the Legislature has passed the Indian Evidence Act,

LECTURE III. section 92 of which says,—"When the terms of any such contract, grant or other disposition of property, or any matter required by law to be reduced to the form of a document, have been proved according to the last section, no evidence of any oral agreement or statement shall be admitted as between the parties to any such instrument or their representatives in interest, for the purpose of contradicting, varying, addding to, or subtracting from, its terms."

The language of the Act is not, perhaps, wholly free from ambiguity, but I venture to think that, as the rule is laid down broadly and without any qualification or reservation, parol evidence of the acts or conduct of the parties is no longer admissible for the purpose of varying the terms of a written instrument.

I have said that conventional mortgages may be created either by writing or by parol. They may also be either express or implied. There is one important class of mortgages,—I say class, because in English law they form a class by themselves,—in which the law implies a mortgage from the conduct of the parties. Thus, if money is borrowed on a deposit of title-deeds, the law implies an intention to charge the property covered by the title-deeds with the repayment of the money. This, I need hardly point out, is very different from a true legal mortgage, which is not based upon any express or implied consent of the parties. In English law, a mortgage of the kind is called an equitable mortgage, because following a well-known maxim, equity regards the transaction in the same light as a formal mortgage ; and this sort of mortgage being recognised in equity is called an "equitable mortgage" as opposed to a legal mortgage. The expression is also applied to similar transactions between the natives of this country, although, strictly speaking, it can be properly applied only in a country in which law and equity are administered as two distinct systems.

Equitable mortgages, although very common in the Presidency towns, do not seem to be common in the mofussil. We, indeed, find an instance of it in an early case in the Sudder Dewany Adawlut, but the parties to the transaction seem to have been residents of Calcutta, and the difference of opinion between the learned Judges by whom the appeal was heard, shows that the case was one of the first impression, and that the transaction was by no means common at the time. The report of the case to which I refer is not very full. It would, however, appear that one Ramlochun Paul being heavily indebted to the plaintiff and being pressed for payment, made over to him the title-deeds of certain property belonging to himself. It does not, however, appear that the debtor, when he made over the title-deeds, expressly stated his inten-

LECTURE III. tion to offer them as a security for the debt. The property was afterwards sold under an execution by the Sheriff, and the purchaser bought with notice of the plaintiff's claim. The plaintiff sought to enforce his lien on the property, contending that the purchaser under the execution had purchased the property subject to his lien. The Zillah Judge having given judgment in favor of the plaintiff upon the ground that the deposit by the borrower of the title-deeds was equivalent to a mortgage, the decree was affirmed on appeal to the Sudder Dewany Adawlut, although, as I have already said, one of the Judges was inclined to think that the mere delivery of the title-deeds was not sufficient to clothe the creditor with the rights of a mortgagee. (6 Select Reports, p. 165.) Since the decision in the above case, the Mofussil Courts in Bengal have invariably given effect to a deposit of title-deeds as a valid simple mortgage, although, as I have told you, this is not an usual mode of giving security outside the Presidency towns.

In the case which I have cited from the Select Reports, the Court inferred an intention to create a mortgage from the mere fact of the delivery of the title-deeds to the creditor. The deposit of title-deeds, however, is sometimes accompanied by an agreement, either verbal or written, in which the intention to create a charge is expressly stated. When that is done, the transaction does not substantially differ from an express conventional mortgage; and there is no reason why, as between parties who can pass land without writing and without delivery of possession, such a transaction should not be given effect to. In a case in the Madras Presidency, in which the local Sudder Dewany Adawlut had refused to recognise the validity of such a transaction, Lord Kingsdown, in delivering the judgment of the Lords of the Judicial Committee of the Privy Council in appeal, is reported to have said:—"The decision of the Sudder Dewany Adawlut, so far as it respects the enforcement of the lien against the third and last defendants, appears to have proceeded upon the ground that the principles of the English law applicable to a similar state of circumstances ought not to govern the decision of that suit in those Courts. This was correct if the authoritative obligation of that law on the Company's Courts were insisted on. There is, properly, no prescribed general law to which their decisions must conform. They are directed in the Madras Presidency to proceeed generally according to justice, equity, and good conscience. The question then is, whether the decision appealed against violates that direction or not. The Court of Appeal, reversing the prior decisions, has decided that the contract was not operative as a hypothecation, or pledge, even between the parties to it. Yet the evidence shows that the plaintiff looked not simply to the personal

LECTURE III. credit of the person with whom he contracted, but bargained for a security on land. If any positive law had forbidden effect to be given to the actual agreement of the parties to create that lien, the Court, of course, must have obeyed that law. If the contract of lien were imperfect for want of some necessary condition, effect must have been, in like manner, denied to it as a perfected lien. But nothing of this sort is suggested in the pleadings, or proved. It is not shown that, in fact, the parties contracted with reference to any particular law. They were not of the same race and creed. By the Mahomedan law, such a contract as the one under consideration, for a security in respect of a contingent loss, would be one not of pawn, but of trust. (Hedaya, Vol. IV, p. 208, tit. 'Pawns.') It is not declared that any writing or actual delivery is essential to the creation of such trust by that law; but as the contracting parties are not both Mahomedans, that law would not have governed the question of the validity and force of their contract, even in the Surpeme Court. The plaintiff is a Christian; the contract took place with parties living within the local limits of the Supreme Court of Madras, though it related to land beyond them. It is not shown that any local law, any lex loci rei sitæ, exists, forbidding the creation of a lien by the contract and deposit of deeds which existed in this case; and by the general law of the place where the contract was made, that is, the English law, the deposit of title-deeds as a security would create a lien on lands, though, as between parties who can convey by deed only, or conveyance in writing, such lien would necessarily be equitable. In this case there is an express contract for a security on the lands, to which, no law invalidating it, effect must be given between the parties themselves." (9 Moo. Ind. App., 303.)

I have said that equitable mortgages form a distinct group in the English law of securities. It was, however, very slowly that they found a place in that system, and their ultimate recognition is solely due to the action of the Court of Chancery. The Statute of Frauds provides that all agreements relating to any interest in land must be reduced to writing, and equitable mortgages were supposed to trench upon the statute. They were, however, admitted by the Court of Chancery by a somewhat refined distinction between executed and executory contracts. Equitable mortgages were first introduced by Lord Thurlow, but Lord Eldon and Sir William Grant were both averse to any extension of the doctrine. It was at first attempted to confine the rule only to those cases in which the delivery was made with the object of executing an *immediate* pledge; but the doctrine has since been overruled, and equitable mortgages have maintained their ground in English law, notwithstanding the jealousy with which their

LECTURE III. introduction was at first regarded. We have here an instance, by no means exceptional, in which the law has been compelled to yield to the exigencies of commerce. As observed by Lord Abinger,—"In commercial transactions it may be frequently necessary to raise money on a sudden, before an opportunity can be afforded of investigating the title-deeds, and preparing the mortgage. Expediency, therefore, as well as necessity, has contributed to establish the general doctrine, although it may not altogether be in consistency with the statute." (*Keys* v. *Williams*, 3 Y. & C., 61.)

The objections, however, which apply to equitable mortgages in England, do not apply to them in India. The doctrine, therefore, has been firmly established in this country. A somewhat bold attempt was made to question it in a recent case in the Bombay High Court, but, as might be expected, it was unsuccessful. (7 Bom. High Court Rep., 45, Original Side.)

I have already said that the expression "equitable mortgage" is not properly applicable to a transaction between natives of this country, and if I use it, it is only out of deference to long continued usage. The objection is not a mere verbal one. The case of *Luchmiputty* and *Seth Varden Sam* shows the danger of extending technical English expressions to transactions which have only a partial resemblance to the things denoted by such expressions. In the Madras case, the defendants insisted in their defence upon the doctrine of the English Court of Chancery, that they were protected from the claims of the plaintiff as purchasers for value without notice. Now if you examine the real nature of an equitable mortgage in the English law, and that of a mortgage by delivery of title-deeds in India, you will find a very remarkable distinction. In the English law, an equitable mortgage is only an agreement to mortgage owing to the incapacity of persons subject to the English law to convey otherwise than by deed. In this country, however, there being no such restriction, a delivery of title-deeds of itself operates as a conveyance. Now, as I have already explained to you, a contract does not create any real right, although English Courts of Equity, proceeding upon a very sensible ground, treat the contract as a conveyance as against purchasers with notice of the agreement. In an English Court of Equity, therefore, a purchase for value without notice would be a perfectly good defence to a suit by an equitable mortgagee, but in this country it would not furnish any answer, for the so-called equitable mortgage not being in any sense a *contract* for a mortgage, the Indian equitable mortgagee has a right superior to that of any person claiming under a title subsequently derived from the mortgagor. It seems to me that the defence in the Madras case, to which I have referred, was suggested by the use of the

LECTURE III. unhappy expression "equitable mortgage" to denote the nature of the right of the plaintiff in that case. I think I have said enough to put you on your guard against the misconceptions, which an inaccurate use of technical terms, borrowed from an extremely artificial foreign system, seldom fails to occasion. (See, however, *Bunsheedhur* v. *Heera Lall*, 1 All., 166.)

I have already stated that the deposit of title-deeds is sometimes accompanied by a memorandum in writing, setting forth the nature of the transaction. Even in this case, however, the memorandum is not the contract between the parties; but the contract is implied by the Court from the deposit of the title-deeds and the advance of the money on such deposit. In the case of a mortgage in writing, if the instrument is unregistered, the mortgagee cannot, generally speaking, enforce his security against the land, because the contract is evidenced by the instrument itself, and that being inadmissible in evidence, no other evidence is allowed to be given. In the case, however, of a mortgage by deposit of title-deeds, although there may be a memorandum, the memorandum is not looked upon as the instrument creating the mortgage, but, as observed by the Court in *Kedarnath Dutt and another* v. *Sham Lall Khettry* (20 W. R., p. 150) "the mortgage is created by the agreement which is evidenced by the loan and the deposit of the title-deeds. The mortgagee may, therefore, rely upon the parol agreement, which is implied by the deposit of the title-deeds. It must, however, be remembered that the mortgage would not be a mortgage in writing, but a parol mortgage, and therefore subject to all the incidents of a parol mortgage. The distinction is an important one, and requires to be illustrated by one or two recent cases in which the question has been raised. In the case of *Kedernath Dutt and another* v. *Sham Lall Khettry*, to which I have already alluded, the facts were shortly these. The plaintiff, who asked the Court to declare his rights as an equitable mortgagee on certain premises, had advanced to Woomachurn Banerjee a certain sum of money on the deposit of the title-deeds of certain property, belonging to the borrower. Woomachurn also executed a promissory note, whereby he promised to pay to "Sham Lall Khettry or order the sum of Rs. 1,200, with interest at the rate of 24 per cent. per annum, for value received in cash." There was an endorsement on the promissory note in these words:—"For the repayment of the loan of Rs. 1,200, and the interest due thereon of the within note-of-hand, I hereby deposit with Baboo Sham Lall Khettry, as a collateral security by way of equitable mortgage, title-deeds of my property situate at No. 11 in Fuckeer Chand Mitter's Street at Mirzapore in Calcutta." "Woomachurn Banerjee."

LECTURE III. There was some question as to whether the transaction was completed when the promissory note was given, but the Appeal Court thought that the question whether there was a complete equitable mortgage before the promissory note was given, or whether that was the completion of the transaction, was not material. It seems that after the deposit of the title-deeds the property was sold under an execution against Woomachurn and purchased by the defendants Kedernath Dutt and Madhub Chunder Bose. These defendants resisted the plaintiff's suit on the ground that the mortgage was created by an express agreement which was reduced to writing, and, as the endorsement was not registered, the plaintiff could not enforce any claim against the land which, as I have already said, had intermediately passed to them under an execution against Woomachurn Banerjee. The objection, however, was overruled. Sir Richard Couch in giving the judgment of the Court observed:—"The rule with regard to writings is that oral proof cannot be substituted for the written evidence of any contract which the parties have put into writing. And the reason is that the writing is tacitly considered by the parties themselves as the only repository and the appropriate evidence of their agreement. If this memorandum was of such a nature that it could be treated as the contract for the mortgage, and what the parties considered to be the only repository and appropriate evidence of their agreement, it would be the instrument by which the equitable mortgage was created and would come within section 17 of the Registration Act. But it was not a writing of that character. As I have said, the equitable mortgage was created by the agreement which was evidenced by the loan and the deposit of the title-deeds. The promissory note, whether given either at the same time or some hours afterwards in pursuance of the understanding between the parties, was evidence of the terms upon which the loan was made, *viz.*, that the interest should be at the rate of 24 per cent.

" But as regards the contract between the parties, if there had been no memorandum at all on the promissory note, there would have been a complete equitable mortgage. When we consider what the memorandum is, we find it is not the contract for the mortgage, not the agreement to give a mortgage for the Rs. 1,200, but nothing more than a statement by Woomachurn Banerjee of the fact from which the agreement is inferred. It is an admission by him that he had deposited the deeds upon the advance of the money for which the promissory note was given. It is not by the memorandum that the Court takes the agreement for the mortgage to be proved, but by the deposit of the deeds. This is no more than a piece of evidence showing the fact of the deposit which might be proved by any other

11

LECTURE III. evidence. The memorandum need not have been produced.

"On the ground, therefore, that this was not a writing which the parties had made as the evidence of their contract, but only a writing which was evidence of the fact from which the contract was to be inferred, I think it does not come within the description of documents in the 17th section of the Registration Act." (20 W. R., 150.)

There is another case to be found in the books (7 Bombay, 50) which is somewhat stronger. In that case the plaintiff had agreed to lend a certain sum of money to Devji Keshavji on a deposit of the title-deeds of certain property belonging to the debtor. The title-deeds having been deposited, the plaintiff continued to advance certain sums of money from time to time till the whole sum advanced amounted to that which the plaintiff had originally agreed to advance. On the 13th of June 1865, after the Registration Act of 1864 had come into force, and when the last advance was made, a Guzrati document was executed by the debtor in which, after stating the amount which had been advanced from time to time by the plaintiff, the debtor proceeded to say,—"According to these particulars I have received or borrowed from you at interest Rs. 25,000 in cash and currency notes. On account of the same (there are mortgaged) at your place my piece of land at Naigáni, namely, a garden with a building (or) a bungalow, which (land) is registered under No. 36 in the Collector's books, and the building or dwelling-house built on the said piece of land that is registered under No. 9 in the books of the house-assessment Collector. All the deeds and other 'vouchers' relating to the said land having been left in mortgage at your place, Rs. 25,000, namely, twenty-five thousand, have been received (or borrowed) at interest thereon for an unlimited time." LECTURE III.

This document was not registered, and the question arose whether the writing being inadmissible in evidence, the plaintiff could enforce his rights as mortgagee. The question was answered in the affirmative, and Mr. Justice Bayley in giving judgment is reported to have said:—"I consider that the contract for a security on the land was created when the loan was applied for and agreed to, and the deeds were handed over to Karsandas; and that the receipt then and those subsequently given did not, nor did the Guzrati document of the 13th of June 1865, on which day Rs. 25, the last instalment of the Rs. 25,000, was advanced, create or declare any right or interest within the meaning of the Registration Acts. The rights of the parties, be they legal or be they equitable, had already been created and perfected on the 31st of October 1864, and it required no memorandum or writing to render such rights valid, nor in fact was there evidence that any

LECTURE III. such document, or any deed or writing, was on the 31st of October 1864 contemplated by the parties. Suppose the receipts and the instrument of the 13th of June 1865 had never existed, the lien or charge on the property would still, in my opinion, have been perfect and valid. The fact of such informal native document being subsequently given and executed after the transaction had been completed, cannot, I think, in any way be held to affect the validity of that which Sir Lawrence Peel, in the Calcutta case, calls *a perfected contract of pledge*, or, to borrow the words of Lord Kingsdown, was a '*contract which created between the parties a lien on the land.*'

" In general, no doubt, where a contract has been reduced into writing by the parties, the writing is the best evidence of it, and must be produced. But it is not in every case necessary, where the matter to be proved has been committed to writing, that the writing should be produced. If, for instance, the narrative of an extrinsic fact has been committed to writing, it may yet be proved by parol evidence. Upon this principle a receipt for money given on unstamped paper will not exclude parol evidence of the payment, and the paper on which it is written may be produced not as evidence of itself, but as a material memorandum which a witness who saw it given may refer to, and give parol evidence of the fact of payment. (*Rambert* v. *Cohen;*

1 Taylor on Evidence, p. 412, 5th ed.) So a verbal demand of goods is admissible in trover, though a demand in writing was made at the same time : *Smith* v. *Young*. The fact, too, of birth, baptism, marriage, death, or burial may be proved by parol testimony, though a narrative or memorandum of these events may have been entered in registers which the law requires to be kept, for the existence or contents of these registers form no part of the fact to be proved, and the entry is no more than a collateral or subsequent memorial of that fact, which may furnish a satisfactory and convenient mode of proof, but cannot exclude other evidence, though its non-production may afford grounds for scrutinising such evidence with more than ordinary care." (7 Bombay, 62-63.)

These cases, therefore, show that where the conduct of the parties is such as to raise the inference of a mortgage, such conduct may be relied upon, although there may be a statement of fact in writing from which the same inference may be made. If, for instance, I borrow money on the deposit of title-deeds, I may state the fact of deposit in writing, but the writing is not the only evidence of such deposit, and it may be proved by other means. If, however, a formal document is executed, I apprehend such document must be taken to be the only evidence of the transaction, although there are certain expressions in the judgment of the

LECTURE III. Bombay Court which might perhaps lead to the inference that even in such a case the parties might, so to speak, go behind the writing and rely upon the deposit coupled with the advance. If such was really the meaning of Mr. Justice Bayley, I venture to say, with great deference, that the dictum cannot be supported to that extent. The distinction is clear between a writing containing a statement of fact from which the Court may infer a contract, and a document in which the contract itself is reduced to writing.

From what I have already said it is clear that a memorandum of the description mentioned above is not a document the registration of which is compulsory. This was substantially decided in both the cases I have mentioned. I have gone at some length into the subject because I think the nature of what is called an equitable mortgage cannot be properly understood without a careful study of the distinction between mortgages of this class, and what I have called express conventional mortgages; and this distinction is very clearly brought out in the cases in which questions of the admissibility of the memorandum, which sometimes accompanies the deposit, have been raised.

I have already said that an equitable mortgage, although it may be accompanied by writing, is still only a parol mortgage. It is, therefore, liable to all the disadvantages imposed by the Registration Act on parol transactions. If the mortgage is not followed or accompanied by possession, and equitable mortgages are very seldom followed by delivery of possession, it is liable to be postponed to subsequent incumbrances which may be registered. A somewhat difficult question may perhaps arise if the memorandum is registered, but that is not generally practicable owing to the provisions of the Registration Act; Section 21 of which says,—"No document, not testamentary, relating to immoveable property, shall be accepted for registration unless it contains a description of such property sufficient to identify the same." Even if the memorandum accompanying an equitable mortgage be registered, I should venture to think that the mortgagee would not be in the same position as one who holds a registered express conventional mortgage.

To go back. Every species of property, whether moveable or immoveable, which can be alienated, may be also the subject of mortgage, but it seems that a general hypothecation will not be recognised as valid by our Courts. (N. W. P., Vol. VII, p. 265; S. D. A., 1855, p. 353; compare 2 All., 263). The question, however, is not now of much practical importance, as no document which does not sufficiently specify the property comprised in it, can be registered, and a general hypothecation, therefore, cannot be created by registered instrument.

As regards the power to mortgage, it may be said

that, generally speaking, a mortgage being a qualified alienation, the same rules which regulate the power to sell also regulate the capacity to mortgage. A detailed examination of these rules, which you will find in Mr. Justice Macpherson's treatise on Mortgages, would carry me much beyond the range of the present lectures. A doubt may, however, sometimes arise when trustees are empowered to sell, and no express power to mortgage is given. The law on the subject in England is that a trustee empowered to sell has presumably the right to mortgage, except when there is clear indication in the language of the intrument that no such authority was intended to be given. The question does not seem to have been ever distinctly raised in this country; but there can be no doubt that if it should arise the point will be decided in the same way.

I shall now proceed to discuss the rights of the mortgagee, when the property pledged to him has received any accession, or undergone any alteration. The general law on the subject is that the creditor has not only a right against the property mortgaged to him, but also to any augmentation or increase. Thus, if a flock of sheep be mortgaged, the creditor acquires the same rights to any natural increase, as he has against the animals which composed the flock at the time of the mortgage. On the same principle, accessions to the mortgaged property by alluvion become subject to the mortgage. In some systems of law, the right of the mortgagee to whom land has been pledged extends to any buildings which may be subsequently erected by the debtor on the land. The right has not, however, so far as I am aware, been carried to a similar extent in India. LECTURE III.

The right of the mortgagee will, however, not extend to anything which was never pledged to him, although it may be substituted in the place of the property originally pledged. Thus, to take a familiar instance from the Roman law, if a farm together with the slaves upon it be pledged, and the slaves die and are replaced by others, the right of the creditor shall not extend to the latter, except, as I have already said, where they are the issues of the deceased slaves.

This limitation of the right of the creditor however must not be confounded with cases in which the pledge is not actually destroyed, but to use the language of Sir James Colvile, only "assumes a new form."

A question of considerable nicety on this point arose in the case of *Byjnath Lall* v. *Ramdin Chowdhry*, which was heard in the last resort by the Lords of the Judicial Committee of the Privy Council. In the case before the Privy Council, which was heard on an appeal from a decree of the Calcutta High Court, the facts were somewhat peculiar. It seems that the mortgagor Gopalnarain Dass

LECTURE III. was, when he executed the deed of conditional sale, which was the foundation of the plaintiff's title, the undisputed owner of an eight-anna undivided share in an estate consisting of three Asli mouzas called Gunniporebija, Pemburinda and Tajpore Ruttompore, to each of which certain Dakhila villages were appurtenant. There was no partition or division among the shareholders, and the interest of the mortgagor therefore in the whole estate was an undivided moiety. In this state of things Gopalnarain executed the mortgage, out of which the suit arose, of the whole and entire eight-anna of the whole 16 annas of Mouzas Gunniporebija and Pemburinda, expressly excepting from the deed the eight annas of Tajpore Ruttompore. It should seem that before the execution of the mortgage, application had been made by some of the co-sharers of the mortgagor for a partition of the estate under Regulation XIX of 1814. A partition was made by the Collector, and the result was that, instead of an undivided moiety of the whole estate, the whole of Mouza Pemburinda, the whole of Tajpore Ruttompore, and whole of another mouza, a dependency of the third Mouza, Gunniporebija, were allotted to Gopalnarain, to be held by him in severalty. Shortly after the partition, Gopalnarain's rights and interests in the mouzas, which fell to his share, were sold at execution sales, and purchased by certain persons, who were the substantial defendants, and who resisted the right of the plaintiff, the mortgagee, to take anything under his mortgage deed in excess of the eight-anna share of the mouzas which had been mortgaged to him, the mortgagee insisting upon his right to the whole sixteen annas of the mouzas which had fallen to the share of the mortgagor in lieu of the undivided moiety which was held by the mortgagor at the time of the execution of the mortgage. The Court of first instance gave judgment in favor of the plaintiff, proceeding upon the principle that the mortgagee was entitled to whatever was allotted to the mortgagor on the partition in lieu of his undivided eight-anna share in the Mouzas Gunniporebija and Pemburinda, which was the subject of the mortgage. On appeal, however, to the High Court, the right of the mortgagee was limited to the share which was expressly named in and covered by the mortgage deed, *i.e.*, only to an eight-anna of Mouza Pemburinda and an eight-anna share of Mouza Gunniporebija. The case then went on appeal to the Privy Council, and the Judicial Committee affirmed the decree of the first Court, and declared that the principle laid down by the first Court was correct. In giving the judgment of the Privy Council, Sir James Colvile is reported to have observed:—"Let it be assumed that such a partition has been fairly and conclusively made with the assent of the mortgagee. In that case, can it be

LECTURE III. doubted that the mortgagee of the undivided share of one co-sharer (and for the sake of argument, the mortgage may be assumed to cover the whole of such undivided share), who has no privity of contract with the other co-sharers, would have no recourse against the lands allotted to such co-sharers; but must pursue his remedy against the lands allotted to his mortgagor, and, as against him, would have a charge on the whole of such lands. He would take the subject of the pledge in the new form which it had assumed. In the present case there is not a suggestion of fraud, nor is there any ground to suppose that the partition was other than fair and equal. The mortgagee is content to accept what has been allotted in substitution of the undivided interest as the fair equivalent of it. Their Lordships are of opinion, not only that he has a right to do so, but that this, in the circumstances of the case, was his sole right, and that he could not successfully have sought to charge any other parcel of the estate in the hands of any of the former co-sharers. There is, therefore, no question here of election, or of the time when the election was made." (21 W. R., p. 237; compare N. W. P., Vol. VIII, p. 669; S. D. A., 1857, p. 359.)

I shall now proceed to consider the validity of a power of sale contained in a mofussil mortgage. The question appears to have been for the first time raised in the case of *Bhowani Churn Mitter* v. *Joykishen Mitter*, heard before the late Sudder Dewany Adawlut of Calcutta in the year 1842, when the Judges were unanimously of opinion that a sale by the mortgagee under the power did not pass a valid title to the purchaser. LECTURE III.

The decision has been criticised by Mr. Justice Macpherson in his work on Mortgages (pp. 45—47), and there is no doubt that some of the reasons given by the learned Judges will not bear examination. But the judgment of the Court substantially rests upon the broad ground that it would be inexpedient to allow the mortgagee in this country to exercise the power. It is true that such a power has been found beneficial in England, but English mortgagors as a class are perfectly competent to take care of their own interests. In India, however, we have to deal with a very different order of men. The mass of mortgages in this country consist of mortgages of ancestral fields by ignorant ryots to a class of people not remarkable for their scrupulousness, and any one having experience of Indian litigation, must admit the danger of arming our money-lenders with the right to sell the properties pledged to them without the intervention of a Court of Justice. As observed by the Court in *Bhowani Churn Mitter* v. *Joykissen Mitter*:—"This Court has only to declare such a condition legal, and in the course of a short time

LECTURE III. not a mortgage bond would be without it. The mortgagee would then sell his debtor's property to suit his own time, and in such manner and with such publicity and formalities as he thought proper. Fraud, it is to be feared, would frequently accompany the transfers, and the property fall into the hands of the mortgagee, or some of his connexions (even as in this case it is alleged the purchaser is the son-in-law of the mortgagee) at an inadequate price, leaving the lender at liberty still to pursue the borrower for the balance that may remain after the sale." (7 Select Reports, p. 429.)

With reference to the argument that the exercise of the power of sale was not unfair to the debtor, the learned Judges observe:—"It is urged for the plaintiff that the public sale of the mortgagor's property cannot be a disadvantageous mode of proceeding towards the latter, that his property is sold to the highest bidder, and that if a surplus remains it belongs to himself. We have not to deal with abstract theories or bare possibilities, but with what experience and the principles of the Regulations furnish us, as our guides in the determination of a novel and unprecedented case. In a case of execution of a decree of Court, the proclamation of sale is an invitation to others interested to come and state their claims. If no claim is preferred, the title of the purchaser may generally be considered a pretty fair one. If claims are preferred, they are summarily investigated, and, should they appear fraudulent, are rejected; and in this case, too, the purchaser may generally be considered in a good position, as few are willing to incur the expense of a regular action on grounds already declared by a Court of Justice to be *primâ facie* fraudulent. And yet, with all the formalities and securities of a transfer of real property by sale made by a Court of Justice, how frequent are the complaints that the property has been sold at an inadequate price, how much more frequent would they be, had not this Court held that inadequacy of price, at a regularly conducted sale, forms no ground for its reversal! If such be the case in such sales, the evils to be apprehended from permitting private individuals to sell their debtor's property, in satisfaction of their claims, must be ten-fold. But few purchasers at a fair price will be found, when, in all probability, a law-suit (as the order granting the review expresses it) will be tacked to the purchase. The object of the Regulation is to prevent improvident and injurious transfers of landed property at an inadequate price; the result of such a practice as that which the contract before us involves would be to render them universal." (7 Select Report, pages 440-41.)

It is true that the utmost latitude ought to be given to the parties to contract in any manner they

LECTURE III. please, but freedom of contract wears a very different aspect according as it is allowed to the English landowner or the Hindu ryot, and I am fortified in my view by the recommendation of the Indian Law Commissioners, who propose in their Sixth Report that a sale under a mortgage should in every case be conducted by the Court. (See also the observations of Melvill, J., in *Kesub Rao* v. *Bhowaneejee*, 8 Bom., p. 142.)

We have already seen that in most continental systems a sale without judicial process is absolutely void. Article 2078 of the French Code says,—"The creditor cannot in default of payment dispose of the pledge, saving to him the power of procuring an order of the Court that such pledge shall continue with him in payment, and up to its due amount according to an estimate made by competent persons, or that it shall be sold by auction."

"Every clause which shall authorise the creditor to appropriate the pledge to himself, or to dispose thereof without the abovementioned formalities, is void."

You will remember that the French Code, equally with the other systems of law on the Continent, is largely shaped by the Roman law, and if the power which the Roman pledgee possessed has not been retained in those systems, it may fairly be presumed that the exercise of the power is not suited to every condition of society. But for the peculiar economic conditions under which land is owned in England, it may indeed fairly be doubted whether the system would have worked well even in that country. Be that, however, as it may, there can be no doubt that it would be dangerous to trust the Indian money-lender with a power which is so much liable to abuse. (See Appendix I.)

LECTURE IV.

SIMPLE MORTGAGES.

What constitutes simple mortgage—Conflicting dicta—Nature of security possessed by simple mortgagee—How made available—Decree for sale—What passes under such decree—Rights of puisne encumbrancers—Haran Chunder Ghose *against* Dinobundhu Bose—Law of execution—Practice of Continental Courts—Effect of clause against alienation in mortgage deed—*Lis pendens*—Mortgagee not bound to proceed against pledge—May waive his rights as mortgagee—Sale of property "subject to mortgage"—Sec. 271 of Act VIII of 1859—Sec. 270 how construed—Right of simple mortgagee, a real right—Defence of purchase for value not available—Period within which security must be enforced—Court in which mortgagee must sue—Conflicting decisions on the point.

A SIMPLE mortgage is a mortgage in which the land is pledged as a collateral security, the right of the creditor in default of payment being limited to a sale by judicial process of the land hypothecated to him. In this kind of mortgage the personal liability of the mortgagor is not excluded. It corresponds to the hypothecation of the Civil law and the systems of law which are founded upon it. In a pure simple mortgage the mortgagor is not put into possession of the property pledged to him. He has not, therefore, the right to satisfy the debt out of the rents and profits, nor can he acquire the absolute ownership of the estate by foreclosure.

No particular form of words is necessary to constitute a simple mortgage. Difficulties, however, not unfrequently arise owing to the extremely inartificial language of Indian instruments. In the case of *Gunga Persaud Sing* v. *Lalla Behary Lall*, in which the question arose whether a bare covenant by the debtor not to alienate his property till the debt should be repaid, constituted a simple mortgage so as to confer a real right on the creditor, the Court observed:—"As a general rule we adhere to the principle laid down in the case of *Chunder Kishore Surma* (9th July 1855), that the title of a person who purchases in good faith is not vitiated by any contract into which the vendor may have previously entered with a stranger binding himself not to alienate his property. If a party is desirous of obtaining a valid lien on any particular property, he should adopt the simple means which the various kinds of mortgage in use in this country afford. If he does not choose to do so, the fault is his own, and the innocent purchaser should not be made to pay the penalty of his negligence." (S. D. A., 1857, p. 825.)

It may, no doubt, be said that such a doctrine would very frequently defeat the intentions of the parties; but the rule of construction founded on the presumed intention of the parties, unless carefully fenced in, is calculated to introduce the very greatest confusion. It would carry me much

LECTURE IV. beyond the limits of the present lecture to examine the various aspects of this doctrine, and there are probably many among you who are familiar with the controversies on the point in some famous writings, both ethical and juridical. There is, however, a speciousness about the rule which is betrayed only on a close examination. It is true that if the intention can be collected from the instrument, the form of expression is not material. But the real difficulty lies in collecting the intention when it is not formulated in apt words.

In the Reports of the Agra High Court you will find two cases, in one of which the Court thought that the debtor intended to create a mortgage, while in the other it was held that there was nothing to show an intention to create a charge on any property. The language of the two instruments, so far as can be gathered from the report, was almost precisely the same, the debtors covenanting with their creditors in both the cases not to alienate their properties till the debts were repaid. (*Chuney Lall* v. *Pallowun Sing*, 4 Agra H. C., 217; *Martin* v. *Purrissrum*, 2 Agra H. C., 124. See also 7 W. R., 309; 13 W. R., F. B., 82; compare N. W. P., vol. VII, p. 124; vol. VIII, p. 669.) The caustic observations of Mr. Fearne on *Perrin* v. *Blake* will suggest themselves to every one familiar with the writings of that accomplished lawyer.

I will now proceed to discuss the rights of the

mortgagee under a simple mortgage. We have seen that he has no right to enter upon possession of the property mortgaged to him, or to foreclose the mortgagor's equity of redemption. The only mode in which he can avail himself of his security is by a sale through judicial process of the property pledged to him under a decree of the Court, the mortgagee having a right to be paid out of the purchase money.

According to the usual practice of the mofussil Courts the mortgagee asks by his plaint for the sale of the mortgaged property, and if he succeeds he obtains a decree for the money due to him with a declaration that the mortgaged property should be sold for the realization of the money. I may mention that in the Madras Courts a period of six months is usually allowed to the mortgagor to pay the money found due to the mortgagee on his security. This indulgence, however, which seems to be borrowed from the practice of the English Court of Chancery, is not allowed to the mortgagor elsewhere, and the propriety of extending it to a decree for sale is perhaps open to question; such a decree standing upon very different ground from a decree for foreclosure. Even in England an immediate decree for sale is not unfrequently made by the Court.

The question, however, is not of much practical importance, and I have referred to it only to show

LECTURE IV. how largely even in details our law of mortgage is shaped by the practice of the English Courts of Equity.

It used to be thought at one time that a purchaser under a decree which did not direct a sale, acquired no higher rights than one under an ordinary execution. Those cases, however, are no longer law, and it is now settled that the mortgagee conveys to the purchaser the benefit of his own lien and the equity of redemption of the debtor, as well when the sale is under a decree for sale as when it is under a "money decree." (*Haran Chunder Ghose* v. *Dinobundhoo Bose*, 23 W. R., 186.)

The doctrine that a sale under a money decree passed to the purchaser only the rights and interests of the debtor, was apparently founded on the notion that the mortgagee by accepting a money decree waived the benefit of his lien, for it could not be contended with any show of reason that the mortgagee, notwithstanding the sale, would retain the benefit of his security. But if the doctrine rested on any such notion, it was not reconcileable with the principle recognised in a large number of cases that if the mortgagee was unable to take the land mortgaged to him in execution of a money decree, he might bring a fresh suit for the purpose of making his security available on the land. It is, however, unnecessary to pursue the discussion further, as the cases in which the right of the purchaser was limited to the bare equity of redemption possessed by the mortgagor, if the decree was only for money, are no longer law.

The Full Bench ruling, however, made another important alteration in the law as it was previously understood. It used to be thought that a sale under a mortgage passed the property to the purchaser as it stood at the date of the mortgage, and that a decree for sale made in the presence of the mortgagor, but in the absence of the puisne encumbrancers or other persons possessing only a qualified interest in the equity of redemption, was a good decree and passed a complete title to the purchaser.

As the law, however, now stands, it would not be safe for the mortgagee to sell the property pledged to him under a decree not made in the presence of the subsequent encumbrancers, who cannot be concluded by an order for sale made in their absence.

"If there be persons not parties to the suit claiming an interest in the property, no form of dealing with the property in their absence can prejudice their rights." (Per Couch, C.J., in *Haran Chunder Ghose* v. *Dinobundhoo Bose*, 23 W. R., 190.) The rights, however, of the subsequent encumbrancers are nowhere defined in the judgment. It is only said that the purchaser under a decree made in their absence purchases the property sub-

LECTURE IV. ject to their rights. He buys the lien of the creditor and the equity of redemption of the debtor, the entire interest which they could jointly sell, and if there are no third persons interested in the property, it becomes absolutely vested in the purchaser.

The doctrine, therefore, which is to be found in some of the cases in the books that a sale by a mortgagee conveys the property to the purchaser free of all subsequent encumbrances must now be received with some qualification. A mortgagee is no doubt competent to transfer the property to the purchaser in the state in which it was pledged to him, but this can only be effected by a sale under a decree in which the subsequent encumbrancers are represented. If the sale take place under a decree against the mortgagor alone, no complete title passes to the purchaser.

I have already said that the Court did not, in the case of Haran Chunder Ghose, define the rights of the subsequent encumbrancers as against the purchaser under a decree made in their absence.

The question, however, arose in the subsequent case of *Nobocoomar Ghose* against *Uzir Shikdar*, in which the debtor having mortgaged his property to two persons in succession, the first mortgagee brought a suit and obtained a decree, but only against the debtor. The property was sold under the decree and purchased by the mortgagee himself. The second mortgagee also sued the debtor, and the property was again sold under the decree and purchased by the creditor. The Court held that the purchaser under the first decree was entitled to possession, but that, as the puisne mortgagee was not a party to the decree under which the purchaser acquired his title, the purchaser under the second decree had a right to pay off the amount due under the first mortgage, and that upon such payment he would be the "holder of the first charge" on the property. You will observe that this case recognises the right of a puisne encumbrancer to pay off the debt on account of which the estate may have been sold, and thus to treat the purchaser as the owner of the estate subject to his claim. As to the question of possession the Court held that the right to the possession was in the debtor and passed to the purchaser under the first execution. The question which we are now considering is a somewhat difficult one, and I shall, therefore, try to illustrate the principle laid down by the Court by putting a hypothetical case. Now suppose an estate is worth Rs. 20,000, and that it is mortgaged first to A for Rs. 15,000 and then to B for Rs. 3,000. The interest which remains in the debtor after the execution of the mortgage is, therefore, worth only Rs. 2,000. Now suppose the property is sold by A in execution of a

LECTURE IV. decree against the debtor and in the absence of B. The purchaser purchases only the lien of the creditor and the right of redemption subsisting in the debtor, which together is by the hypothesis worth Rs. 15,000 plus 2,000 = Rs. 17,000. Now B would have a right to pay off the debt due under the first mortgage, and to treat such payment, together with the amount due to him, as a charge on the property, *i.e.*, by paying off to the purchaser the fifteen thousand due under the first mortgage, he would acquire a charge on the property for Rs. 15,000 plus 3,000 = Rs. 18,000. Now, in order to enforce that charge he would have to bring a suit against the purchaser who, as we have seen, has acquired the right of redemption of the debtor. Now if the purchaser pays him off, he acquires an absolute title to the property. But in that case he would have to pay altogether Rs. 17,000 minus 15,000, *i.e.*, Rs. 2,000 plus 18,000 = 20,000, which we have assumed to be the value of the property. But suppose the purchaser does not choose to pay off the consolidated charge on the property, the property must be sold, and assuming that it fetches its proper price, the mortgagee gets Rs. 18,000, and the purchaser gets back the two thousand rupees which he had laid out. If the property is so heavily burdened that the right of redemption is worth nothing, the purchaser would not be safe in paying anything in excess of the debt due under the first mortgage. To that extent he would be secure

against the claims of subsequent encumbrancers. LECTURE IV.
If the purchaser pays less than the amount of the debt secured by the first mortgage, he cannot insist upon the second mortgagee paying to him anything in excess of the purchase money, although I am not to be understood as saying that the case might not be different if the creditor himself became the purchaser.

The principle applicable to subsequent mortgagees has been extended on the authority of *Haran Chunder Ghose* v. *Denobundhoo Bose* to other persons possessing a qualified interest in the equity of redemption—lessees, for instance, holding under beneficial leases created subsequently to the mortgage.

In the case of *Byjnath Singh* v. *Goburdhun Lall* (24 W. R., 210) the purchaser under a sale by the mortgagee sought to set aside a lease created by the debtor subsequently to the mortgage. The lessee was not a party to the suit by the mortgage creditor, and the order directing the sale was made in his absence. It was contended on behalf of the purchaser under the execution that the lessee was not a necessary party to the suit, and that as the lease had been executed subsequently to the mortgage, it was not binding upon the purchaser. The Court, however, held otherwise, being of opinion that the sale did not pass the property absolutely to the purchaser, and that the rights of the lessee who

LECTURE IV.

claimed an interest in the property could not be prejudiced by a sale under a decree made in his absence. It would, however, seem, although the point was not before the Court, that the purchaser, as assignee of the lien of the creditor, would have a right to insist upon the lessee's redeeming him, and on his failure to do so, to sell the property, the purchaser being entitled to a charge on the purchase money to the extent of the lien of the creditor who first put up the property to sale; and this would seem to be the only course open to him if the mortgage security was impaired by the creation of the term by the debtor. Under the law as it stood before the Full Bench ruling in *Haran Chunder Ghose's* case (23 W. R., 187), the sale by the mortgagee would have avoided the lease, and the right of the tenant would have been confined to the surplus proceeds of the sale. (*Brojo Kishoree Dassee* v. *Mahomed Solim*, 10 W. R., 151. See also 7 W. R., 67 ; 10 W. R., 291.)

The security which is possessed by a mortgagee under a simple mortgage is, as I have endeavoured to explain, the right to sell the entire estate of the mortgagor as it existed at the date of the mortgage free of any charges on the property subsequently created by the debtor. The Calcutta High Court has not made any alteration in respect to the nature of the security to which the mortgagee becomes entitled under this form of mortgage, the rule laid down by the Court being a mere rule of procedure. The mortgagee has still the right to sell the entire estate of the mortgagor as it existed at the date of the mortgage, but he must take care to bring the puisne encumbrancers before the Court. Under a decree for sale obtained in their absence, the mortgagee can only transfer to the purchaser the benefit of his own lien and such interest, if any, as may be possessed by the debtor at the time of the institution of the suit. LECTURE IV.

As far as I have been able to discover, the ruling of the Calcutta High Court has not been followed in the other provinces, and a purchaser under a decree for sale obtains a complete title to the property although such decree may have been made in the absence of the puisne encumbrancers.

It is perhaps idle to expect that the case of *Haran Chunder Ghose* v. *Denobundhoo Bose* will be reconsidered. It is, however, doubtful if the Court did not in that case go too far in their anxiety to protect the interests of posterior encumbrancers. It is true that no person ought to be affected by an order made in his absence. But how is the puisne encumbrancer affected by the conversion of the estate into money ? He may have a right to the surplus proceeds, and if that is secured to him, it is difficult to discover how he can be possibly prejudiced by a decree for sale. In every system of law in which the pledgee possesses the right of sale, what he sells is

LECTURE IV. the property pledged to him, and not merely an undefined interest in the pledge, and no claimants upon the property posterior to the first pledgee can interfere with this right. (See the observations of Markby, J., in *Haran Chunder Ghose* v. *Denobundhoo Bose.*) I do not deny that very different considerations would arise if the mortgagee asked not for a decree for sale, but one for foreclosure. A decree for foreclosure stands upon a very different footing from a decree for sale, and any argument founded upon analogy would be sure to mislead.

There is besides another aspect of the question which I have not yet considered. It is very seldom, indeed, that an estate sold under an execution realizes an adequate price, and the encouragement offered to speculative purchasers is one of the principal sources of a good deal of litigation never very healthy, and frequently dishonest. It is not difficult to foresee that the result of the Full Bench ruling will be to aggravate the evil, and that both mortgagee and mortgagor will suffer by the sale of rights which must be to a great extent uncertain. The mischief is carefully guarded against in other systems of law by provisions which, while they secure to the creditor his just rights, prevent a needless sacrifice of the property of the debtor. Indeed, in this respect the interest of the debtor is identical with that of his creditor, as the object of both must be to secure the best possible price for the property.

Under the law as it was understood before the Full Bench ruling to which I have had occasion to refer so frequently, this might be always accomplished by a sale by the first pledgee, who it was thought could pass the property free of all subsequent encumbrances. In the case of a puisne encumbrancer the result was, no doubt, different, as the sale by him was, as it still is, subject to all prior mortgages. It may, however, be suggested that even in this case it might perhaps be more convenient to allow the creditor to sell the estate, the preferential right of the prior mortgagee to the purchase money being secured to him. I am afraid that the suggestion may be regarded as somewhat wild, and I am free to confess that it is one which I should not have ventured to make if I had not found similar provisions in the law of France and other countries, whose jurisprudence is moulded on the Roman law. Broadly speaking (for I do not pretend to give a detailed account) a sale under an execution extinguishes all hypothecary rights or debts affecting the property, the right of the creditor being transferred to the purchase money. For this purpose the proceeds of the sale are deposited in the Court, and the creditors of the mortgagor are cited to appear and assert their claims. A proceeding is then adopted by which the respective priorities of the creditor are ascertained, and the proceeds divided according to the result of the investigation.

LECTURE IV. This proceeding is called the *præferentia* and concurrence of creditors. Its object is to comprise the adjudication and assertion of those claims which are prior or preferred, as well as those which are concurrent. Each claim to be preferred or ranked concurrently is regularly brought to issue and debated, and the Court, by its sentence, declares the order in which the parties are to rank on the proceeds. (Code de Proced. Civile, tit. 14; see also Burge's Foreign and Colonial Law, Vol. II., pp. 592-3; Vol. III, pp. 229-30.) This is a very simple and intelligent rule. It secures to the debtor a fair price for his property, and thus, as I have already explained, effectually protects the interests of the creditor. Trafficking in doubtful claims, one of the least interesting phases of litigation, finds no encouragement in such a system, while the rights of the creditors are guarded with a jealousy not less scrupulous than that which we find in systems with which we are more familiar.

I have ventured to detain you with this slight sketch of the continental system of execution, not because I think there is much likelihood of the introduction of the principle into our own law, but because I think the student ought to have some acquaintance with the leading features of a system of jurisprudence which obtains in a large part of the civilized world. A too exclusive attention to any one system is likely to induce a habit of mind, which I am afraid is to be found in other persons besides the worthy English conveyancer, who thought that an attempt by the legislature to preserve contingent remainders without the intervention of trustees was about as absurd as an attempt to alter the laws of nature. Certain doctrines, true only in a limited sense, come to be regarded as fundamental principles of jurisprudence, and acquire such a firm hold that even the most gifted minds become intolerant of criticism. We have not to go far to seek for illustrations.

To return: As the law at present stands, the right which passes under a sale by a mortgagee is the entire interest which the mortgagor and mortgagee could jointly sell. Where the subsequent encumbrancers are parties, and the order for sale is made in their presence, the purchaser acquires a higher right which may be described as the entire interest which the mortgagee together with the puisne encumbrancers and the mortgagor could jointly convey. This is not distinctly stated in the judgment of the Court in *Haran Chunder Ghose* v. *Denobundhoo Bose* (23 W. R., 186), but there can be very little doubt that this would be so. In the case, however, of the second mortgagee, the interest which the purchaser acquires must be necessarily subject to the prior charge, and the presence of the first mortgagee as a party would not, I apprehend, make any difference. In this respect, as I have

LECTURE IV. already said, the Full Bench has made no change in the law as it was previously understood. It is only in the case of a sale by the first mortgagee that the rule laid down in the earlier cases has been qualified by making the presence of the puisne encumbrancers essential to the passing of the estate absolutely to the purchaser. I have already explained that the doctrine has been extended to the case of a lessee, and there can be no doubt that it will be applied for the protection of all persons having an interest in the property, and not parties to the decree under which the property is sold.

I have said that the Full Bench ruling in *Haran Chunder Ghose* v. *Denobunhoo Bose* has made no change as regards second mortgagees. The proposition, however, must be understood with the necessary qualification that the second mortgagee stands in the same relation to posterior mortgagees that the first mortgagee does to him, and that he is, therefore, under the same obligation towards them as the first mortgagee is towards him. Thus a purchaser under a sale by the second mortgagee, although he must in any event purchase subject to the rights of the first mortgagee, acquires a very different estate accordingly as the posterior mortgagees are parties to the decree or not. If the order for sale is made in their presence, the purchaser acquires the estate absolutely as against them, but if it be otherwise, the purchase is made subject to their right to redeem. I may also point out that although it has been always held that a purchaser of the mortgagor's interest is a necessary party to a suit by the mortgagee to enforce his charge, the rule was never extended to persons possessing a more qualified interest in the estate. The rights of these persons were recognized, so far as I am aware, for the first time, in *Haran Chunder Ghose* v. *Denobundhoo Bose* (23 W. R., 186). LECTURE IV.

I have said that a sale by the mortgagee conveys to the purchaser the entire interest which he and the mortgagor could jointly sell. I may, however, point out that this refers to the interest which they could jointly pass, not at the time when the property is sold, but at the time of the institution of the suit in which the decree under which the property is sold, is made. This is a necessary consequence of the doctrine *lis pendens*, which I shall have occasion to discuss in a subsequent lecture. I may also point out that the language of section 259 of the Civil Procedure Code is perhaps, in strictness, inapplicable to a sale by a mortgagee which takes place under a decree for sale, and not as in an ordinary execution. The right, title, and interest of the judgment-debtor, of which the section speaks, must be understood in a somewhat wider sense than the right possessed by the debtor at the time of the sale. As I shall have occasion to explain presently, the provisions of the Procedure Code with respect to

LECTURE IV. executions are far from being clear on the rights of the mortgagee.

In connection with this subject I may mention that a question may arise, but which, so far as I am aware, has not been decided, as to the effect of a clause against alienation contained in a deed of mortgage. Such clauses are frequently found in Indian mortgages. I have already explained that ordinarily a clause against alienation does not prevent the alienee from acquiring a title to the property. The covenant does not affect the thing itself, although in some cases the covenantor may render himself liable to an action for a breach of his contract. It would, however, seem that in the Civil law a clause against alienation by the mortgagor is allowed to bind the property itself, and a subsequent alienation is therefore void. In consequence of this doctrine the mortgagee is not bound to recognise any alienee of the property mortgaged to him, if there be a clause against alienation in the mortgage. It seems that in some of the earlier cases to be found in the books, the doctrine was carried by the Indian Courts further than equity or good conscience would seem to justify; but it may be a question whether, in the presence of such a stipulation, a decree obtained by the mortgagee, and a sale thereunder, although made in the absence of persons who acquired an interest in the property subsequently to the mortgage, would not pass an absolute title to the purchaser. In the absence of any distinct authority I do not venture to offer any opinion one way or the other. I simply call attention to the point as one which must not be taken to be concluded by the Full Bench ruling in *Haran Chunder Ghose's* case. (23 W. R., 186.)

It was thought at one time that a creditor whose debt was secured by a mortgage, was bound to proceed in the first instance against the property mortgaged to him, and that he could only proceed against other properties for the deficiency, should there be any. (*Brohmomoyee Debea* v. *Bykunt Chunder Gangoolly*, 5 W. R., Mis., 52.) It is, however, now settled that a mortgagee is under no such liability, and that he is at liberty to proceed against any property belonging to his debtor in the same way as an unsecured creditor, and this right is not qualified, although the decree should say that execution should be first had against the property pledged to the creditor, and afterwards against the person. It is always competent to the creditor to say, "I am content to rest upon the decree which I have obtained for the money due upon the bond, and to waive the right which I have as mortgagee." (*Fakeer Buksh* v. *Chutterdharee*, 14 W. R., 209; see also *Purmessaree Dossea* v. *Nobin Chunder Tavan*, 24 W. R., 305.) I need hardly point out that these observations do not apply to cases in which the creditor has lost his right either by the operation of

LECTURE IV. the statute of limitations, or otherwise to proceed upon the covenant contained in the mortgage, and is restricted by the decree to proceedings against the land on which the debt is secured.

I will now call your attention to section 271 of the Civil Procedure Code—a section which I may venture to say is by no means a favorable specimen of legislative workmanship. The section says as follows:—"If, after the claim of the person on whose application the property was attached has been satisfied in full from the proceeds of sale, any surplus remain, such surplus shall be distributed rateably amongst any other persons who, prior to the order for such distribution, may have taken out execution for decrees against the same defendant, and not obtained satisfaction thereof. Provided that, when any property is sold subject to a mortgage, the mortgagee shall not be entitled to share in any surplus arising from such sale."

Now the first observation which I think it necessary to make upon this section is that its language clearly points to a case in which there is a surplus, and there are rival judgment-creditors among whom it has to be distributed. It has no application where the mortgagee is the only creditor who seeks to be paid out of the surplus proceeds as being money payable to his debtor in the hands of the Court. In other words, the judgment-debtor cannot object to the mortgagee's demand to be paid out of the surplus purchase money. (24 W. R. 305.) The only ground upon which he could do that would be that the mortgagee was bound to satisfy his debt, as far as he could, in the first instance, by the sale of the property pledged to him. But as we have already seen, the mortgagee is not under any such liability, and the result of the recent authorities is that a mortgage creditor is not in a less favorable situation than an unsecured creditor in respect of the proceedings allowed by the law for the purpose of enforcing a judgment for money.

The next question which arises upon the section is whether in a contest between unsecured creditors and a mortgagee, where the money in the hands of the Court is not sufficient to pay all the creditors in full, the mortgagee can waive his rights as mortgagee, and insist upon sharing in the surplus as an ordinary creditor. You will see that the considerations which arise here are very different from those which would arise if the contest was solely between the debtor and the creditor. The law seems to be anxious to guard against a wanton sacrifice of the rights of the unsecured creditors, and upon a principle which has its foundation in equity and good conscience—a principle which I shall explain in a subsequent lecture—the mortgagee is not permitted to share in the purchase money which is paid, not for the absolute interest in the estate, but only for the equity of redemption. The mortgagee has

LECTURE IV. in his mortgage ample security for the realization of his dues, and his rights are in no way prejudiced by refusing to permit him to share in the surplus proceeds, while very great injustice might be done if a different course were followed. Thus, for instance, suppose an estate is worth Rs. 50,000, and that it is mortgaged for Rs. 25,000. If the estate is sold subject to the mortgage, it will sell only for Rs. 25,000, being the value of the equity of redemption. The mortgagee is, therefore, sure to get his money out of the estate, but suppose he is permitted to share in the surplus proceeds, the result will be that the purchaser will be benefited, and the debtor and his creditors will suffer to the extent to which the lien is reduced. Thus, suppose the mortgagee gets Rs. 5,000 under an order for distribution. The fund available to the unsecured creditors will be less by that amount, while the purchaser under the execution will get property worth Rs. 50,000 for only Rs. 45,000. It seems to me, therefore, notwithstanding certain expressions in the judgment of the Court in *Fakeer Buksh* v. *Chutterdharee* (14 W. R., 209), which might seem to support a contrary view, that a mortgagee is not entitled to share in the surplus arising out of the sale of property which is sold subject to his mortgage, *i.e.*, as I have already explained, when the contest is one between him and the unsecured creditors of the debtor. If there should be any surplus after satisfying the claims of the unsecured creditors, the mortgagee may have a right to such surplus. LECTURE IV.

I have said that the result of the recent authorities seems to place the mortgagee's right to proceed against any property belonging to his debtor beyond all doubt. It may, however, be doubted whether the doctrine does not require some qualification—a qualification which is based upon the same principle which excludes the mortgagee from the benefit of an order for distribution under section 271 of the Procedure Code. I think there can be no doubt that the mortgagee has ordinarily the right to proceed against any property belonging to the judgment-debtor, but should not this right be restricted when the equity of redemption has passed away from the judgment-debtor to a third person. Thus, to take the illustration given in the last paragraph, the purchaser pays only Rs. 25,000 for the property purchased by him, as it is sold subject to a mortgage for Rs. 25,000. Now if the mortgagee is permitted to proceed against other properties, without in the first instance proceeding against the property pledged to him, the purchaser may acquire an estate worth Rs. 50,000 for one-half the sum. It is probable that the judgment-debtor may not be wholly without a remedy, and he will be perhaps entitled to the benefit of the lien, and the equities between the parties may possibly be worked out in a regular suit between the purchaser

16

LECTURE IV.

and the debtor. But I think this would be a perfect waste of litigation, and the limitation which I have ventured to suggest on the right of the mortgagee to proceed against his debtor ought to be accepted, if for no better reason, at least for the prevention of that circuity of action which the law is generally supposed to abhor. The legislature also would seem to have guarded against this very evil by refusing to permit the mortgagee to share in the surplus proceeds of property sold subject to his mortgage, for I conceive that even if there had been no such provision, the unsecured creditors would have been permitted to stand in the place of the mortgagee to the extent to which the fund to which they were exclusively entitled to look for the satisfaction of their dues, was reduced by the action of the mortgagee; and this upon a doctrine which is by no means peculiar to any particular system of jurisprudence, but which has its foundation in the broadest principles of equity and good conscience. It may be said that it would be beyond the province of the Court to impose limitations and restrictions on the rights of creditors which are not to be found in the Code of Civil Procedure, but the principle to which I refer is in no sense whatever a part of the law of procedure, and its introduction would not, I apprehend, be regarded as in any way trenching upon the province of the legislature. (*Mirza Futteh Ali* v. *Gregory*, 6 W. R., Mis., 13 ; 4 Madras, 49.)

The question as to what is meant by "sold subject to a mortgage" has given rise to considerable discussion. In a recent case, *Fakeer Buksh v. Chutterdharee Chowdhry,* the Court observed: "We think that section 271, Act VIII of 1859, or rather the proviso in that section, is intended to apply to a case where the property is actually sold subject to a mortgage, and where the transaction is such that the purchaser is buying the property subject to the mortgage, where he is, in fact, only buying the equity of redemption which remains in the judgment-debtor ; and it does not apply to a case where there is merely the right by law in the mortgagee to enforce his mortgage against the purchaser. This appears to have been the view taken by this Court in a decision reported in 6 Weekly Reporter, Miscellaneous Rulings, page 13.

"There the Court says:—'It is not equitable that the purchaser who purchased and paid for only the mortgagor's interest in this property, should hold it released from Gregory's lien.' Now, here it does not appear that the sale to the purchaser was in fact subject to the mortgage. By 'in fact' we mean that it was not so subject by the contract of sale, and there was merely a legal right existing which might be capable of being enforced. It seems that a petition which was presented by the present appellant was not taken notice of, and neither in the proclamation of sale, nor in any of

LECTURE IV. the sale proceedings, is mention made of the existence of any mortgage. Nor is there anything to show that only a limited right of the judgment-debtor was to be sold. Therefore, upon that construction of section 271, we should say that the proviso does not apply to the present case." (14 W. R., 209-10).

According to this decision the mortgagee may share in the surplus proceeds, although the purchaser—aware that the property was in law subject to a mortgage—paid only the price of the equity of redemption, and not that of an absolute interest in the property. If the contest had been between parties who had induced an honest purchaser to lay out money in the *bonâ fide* belief that he was purchasing the property free of all encumbrances, such a construction might be supported on the ground that it tended to prevent a circuity of action, for the consequence of refusing the mortgagee to share in the distribution would be to throw him upon the mortgaged property, with the further consequence that the purchaser would have a right to ask the unsecured creditors to refund a portion of the purchase money equal to the amount of the mortgage. But the doctrine of a purchase in good faith for valuable consideration without notice has not been ever applied to a purchaser under an execution, who purchases only the rights and interests of the debtor, while its extension to every case in which no mention is made of the mortgage at the time of the sale, would be wholly without precedent. It seems to me, therefore, with very great deference, that the proposition laid down by the Court in *Fakeer Buksh* v. *Chutterdharee Chowdhry* (14 W. R., 209), cannot be supported to its full extent, as the only foundation upon which it could be placed, the prevention of a multiplicity of suits, fails. I say the only foundation, because I think that it is quite clear from what I have said that the doctrine would be open to the same objection as permitting the mortgagee to share when the property is sold expressly subject to a mortgage.

I have already said that a sale by an unsecured creditor passes only the equity of redemption. There may, however, be cases in which the purchaser acquires a higher right. Thus, for instance, in the case of *Mudhusudun Sing* v. *Mukundloll Sahee* (23 W. R., 373),—where execution was taken out by one of the creditors against an estate which was subject to a mortgage in favor of another creditor, who also had placed an attachment on the property, and the property was subsequently sold at the instance of the first creditor, but without any mention of the mortgage—it was held by the Court that what passed to the purchaser under the sale was not the bare equity of redemption, but the property itself, free of the mortgage held by the other creditor; and the case of *Nadir Hussen*

LECTURE IV. — v. *Baboo Pearoo* (19 W. R., 255) lays down still more broadly that when an estate is sold pending an attachment by the mortgagee, the lien is transferred from the property to the purchase money, and the purchaser acquires the property discharged from the lien. The rule laid down in these cases is likely to prevent, in some measure, the evils which attend all sales in execution in this country; it being by no means an uncommon thing for the same property to be sold successively five or six times, first by an unsecured creditor, and then by the mortgage creditors of the debtor; the third mortgagee probably coming in first, then the second mortgagee, the first mortgagee closing the scene; and this although execution had been taken out and the property attached by all the creditors, when the sale took place at the instance of an unsecured creditor.

I shall now refer to another section of the Procedure Code which also has created no little difficulty. I allude to section 270 of the Code. That section says:—"Whenever property is sold in execution of a decree, the person on whose application such property was attached shall be entitled to be first paid out of the proceeds thereof, notwithstanding a subsequent attachment of the same property by another party in execution of a prior decree." Now this section in terms gives to the creditor by whom the property is first attached, *i.e.*, first made available to the creditors of the debtor, the right to be paid first. But suppose the property is sold by a mortgagee who comes in after the property has been attached, but whose mortgage is prior to the attachment. It cannot be said that his claims should be postponed to that of the unsecured creditor, and yet the language of the section would seem to leave no discretion to the Court of execution in the matter. It is unnecessary to discuss if this is the right view, for, as explained by the Court in a recent case (22 W. R., 98), the enactment was never intended to alter or limit the rights which a person may have acquired by contract independently of the rules embodied in the Code of Civil Procedure. As the law, therefore, at present stands, the Court of execution is frequently obliged to make an order which the Court knows, and which the parties perhaps know equally well, will be set aside in what is called a regular suit. I speak with reserve, but it seems to me that the whole chapter on execution in the Civil Procedure Code relates to sales in *execution* of decrees for money, and not to sales under decrees for that purpose obtained by mortgagees. The provisions relating to attachments and the language of section 259 of the Code leave on my mind a very distinct impression that the legislature had before them only one class of sales, those in execution of decrees for money.

LECTURE IV.

I will end with a few general observations on the security to which the mortgagee becomes entitled under an ordinary simple mortgage. Now it is necessary to bear in mind that a simple mortgage creates a real right, and that the defence of purchase for value without notice is not applicable to a suit by a mortgagee to enforce his security. I have already explained the origin of this doctrine introduced by the English Court of Chancery for the purpose, among others, of guarding against the consequences of treating a contract as a conveyance. It is, therefore, that, as a general rule, the defence is not allowed when the right sought to be enforced is a legal right, and not one which is recognised only by equity. It would be beyond the province of these lectures to explain the doctrine at length, and if I recur to it, it is only because its somewhat indiscriminate application in this country has attracted to it a cloud of prejudice, much of which, when kept within reasonable limits, the doctrine certainly does not deserve. The real truth seems to be that the doctrine is in some measure a 'survival,' and points to times when a conveyance was a transaction which never could take place secretly, while a mere agreement was not attended with any such publicity. In these days, when the title to real property passes by mere writing, a conveyance may be attended with as little publicity as an agreement to transfer at a future time, and it is this feeling apparently which has led to the extension of this doctrine to real rights. In all enlightened systems of jurisprudence, however, the somewhat cumbrous formalities which our forefathers insisted upon as a protection against fraudulent practices, are gradually giving way to a system of Registration of Assurances.

The question whether a security is available against a purchaser from the mortgagor without notice of it, was raised in the Calcutta High Court in the case of *Moharajah Moheshur Bux Singh Bahadoor* v. *Bhikha Chowdhry*, and was answered in the affirmative. Sir Barnes Peacock, in giving the judgment of the Full Bench, observed: "As to the *second* ground which has been raised for our opinion, —namely, that the purchaser under the bill of sale was a *bonâ fide* purchaser without notice, and therefore entitled to priority,—if the bond was really and *bonâ fide* executed before the date of the defendant's purchase, it would *primâ facie* be entitled to priority, and the defendant could not, according to the decision in the case of *Verden Seth Sam* v. *Luckpathy Royjee Lallah* (Marshall's Reports, p. 461), succeed without proof that he was a *bonâ fide* purchaser for value without notice. But even if the defendant were to satisfy the Court upon that point, he would not, in my opinion, be entitled to priority, unless the plaintiff was bound to give notice of his bond. If he was not bound to register

LECTURE IV. it in order to retain priority over subsequent purchasers for value, I do not see what notice he could give, or was bound to give. The mere charge upon an estate does not give a right to the possession of title-deeds; and even if it would, the plaintiff in the present case had a charge, not upon the entire estate, but only on one or two villages, which would not give him a right to the possession of the title-deeds to the whole estate.

"But if the defendant should prove that he was a *bonâ fide* purchaser for value, he would throw the onus on the plaintiff of proving that he actually advanced the money as alleged in the bond creating the charge, and that the bond was executed before the defendant's purchase." (5 W. R., 63. See also 4 Madras, 434; 5 Madras, 457.)

Mr. Justice Campbell, who was of a different opinion, pointed to the "frightful consequences which may result if it be established as law that a lien on real property without either publication or possession will suffice to defeat the most cautious purchaser." "I should fear," adds the learned Judge, "that in this country the result would be an entire insecurity of title; that it would be impossible for any man by any amount of caution to buy real property with any confidence or any security that secret lien-holders may not start up with documents (or possibly even asserting verbal engagements) proved, as proof here goes, and which he cannot disprove, and may defeat or harass him." (5 W. R., 67.) LECTURE IV.

It is impossible to deny that there is a good deal of truth in these observations. In countries where the Roman doctrine of hypothecation obtains, the evil is guarded against by the device of public hypothec books, and the same purpose is served by the new system of registration which has been introduced into this country since the passing of the 16th Act of 1864.

The fact that hypothecation confers a real right seems also to have been overlooked in some of the earlier cases on the Statute of Limitations, in which it was held that a mortgagee was bound to enforce his security within the time limited to suits for breaches of contracts. (*Seetul Singh* v. *Baboo Sooraj Bux*, 6 W. R., 318, since overruled. See *Sarwar Hossein* v. *Shazada Golam Mohamed*, 9 W. R., 170.) In the last case it was held that a suit to enforce a security is a suit to recover an interest in immoveable property within the meaning of clause 12 of the first section of Act XIV of 1859. It must not, however, be understood that the same extended period was allowed to the mortgagee to sue on the covenant which must be enforced within the same period as any other contract. (10 W. R., 379; 10 W. R., 56.) The new Limitation Act has, by Art. 132, Schedule II, expressly provided for suits "for money charged upon immoveable

LECTURE IV. property," and the period of limitation is stated to be twelve years from the time when the money becomes due. It would seem, although the language is not very precise, that, as under the old law, the remedy on the covenant must still be sought within the period limited for contracts.

It follows from what I have said as to the nature of the right created by a simple mortgage, that a suit to enforce the security must, like any other suit for land, be brought in the Court within whose jurisdiction the land is situated, although the remedy against the person may have to be sought in a different forum. There is indeed a case at 9 Bombay, page 12, in which a different view is taken, but I presume it cannot be supported. (See 18 W. R., 269; 18 W. R., 287.) As the law was understood before the Full Bench ruling in *Haran Chunder Ghose's* case (23 W. R., 187), it was of the utmost importance to the plaintiff to bring his suit in the proper Court, as no other Court than that within whose jurisdiction the land was situated, could make a decree expressly directing a sale of the mortgaged property; and this declaration was always sought by the mortgagee, although the mortgagor had not in any way parted with his interest in the property either by a sale or a second mortgage. It is true that, under a recent ruling of the Calcutta High Court, a mere money decree is, as between the parties, as good as a decree for sale, but the mortgagee would certainly act safely in expressly asking for the usual decree for sale, which, as I have already explained, can only be made by the Court within whose local limits the land is situated.

LECTURE V.

Conditional sales—Differences in form between conditional sales and English mortgages—Difference between mortgages by conditional sale and sales with clause for repurchase—Mortgagor does not generally incur any personal liability—Construction of the Sudder Dewany Adalut—True meaning of "construction"—Implied warranty of title by mortgagor—Remedy for breach of warranty—Remedy of mortgagee when pledge is accidentally destroyed—Principle on which damages should be assessed—Right of mortgagee to prevent waste when security is insufficient—Reg. XVII of 1806—Process of foreclosure in Bengal—Meaning of "stipulated period," "legal representatives"—Duty of Court on receiving application—Provisions of Regulation mandatory and not merely directory—Distinction between mandatory and directory enactments—Proceedings under Regulation merely ministerial—Regular suit—Process of foreclosure elsewhere than in Bengal—Moulded on the practice of the English Court of Chancery—Right of mortgagee to possession immediately on default—How far qualified in Bengal by Regulation XVII of 1806—Limitation—Acts XIV of 1859 and IX of 1871.

A MORTGAGE by conditional sale is, as its name denotes, a conditional conveyance of land as a security for the repayment of a loan "with a stipulation that, if the money borrowed be not repaid with or without interest by a certain day, the sale shall become absolute." It resembles very closely in form an English mortgage, both of them belonging to that class of securities in which the property pledged is liable to pass from the debtor to the creditor on default. There is, however, some difference in the form of the instruments. In an English mortgage the ownership is wholly transferred to the creditor, liable, however, to be divested by the repayment of the loan on the appointed day. The English mortgagor says to his creditor, "I sell my property to you, but if I repay the debt by a certain day, the conveyance shall be void or (as is now more usually the case) you shall reconvey the property to me." In the Indian mortgage, on the other hand, the creditor acquires only a qualified ownership, which, however, by the terms of the agreement ripens into absolute proprietorship immediately on default. In the English mortgage, therefore, the mortgagee, by the terms of the agreement, has the right to enter upon possession of the property mortgaged to him immediately upon the execution of the deed, but the mortgagee under a conditional sale can have no such right. The possession of the mortgagor is, therefore, generally protected in an English mortgage by a covenant for quiet possession till default, a covenant which would be wholly superfluous in an Indian mortgage, for the simple reason that with us only a qualified ownership passes to the mortgagee, which before default does not carry with it the right to the possession of the property.

A practice, however, obtains in this country, which also seems to have prevailed in England in former times, by which the debtor executes a deed purport-

LECTURE V. ing on the face of it to be an absolute conveyance, the creditor, on the other hand, engaging to reconvey the property to the debtor on repayment of the loan. In such cases the conditional sale differs but very little in form from an English mortgage. The practice, however, is open to very serious objection, and is gradually dying out.

In the case of *Rajah Heera Singh* (N. W. P., Vol. VIII, p. 564), where there was an absolute sale together with an agreement by the purchaser to reconvey the property, if the purchase money, together with interest, were paid by a certain day, it was contended that the transaction between the parties was not a mortgage, but only "a redeemable sale," and, therefore, not subject to the rules relating to mortgages. The Court, however, held that a redeemable sale was identical with a mortgage, and that the vendor in a redeemable sale had an equity of redemption which must be foreclosed in the same way as in an ordinary mortgage. (See also *Arman Pandey* v. *Norrotun Koonwar*, 3 Sel. Rep. 78.)

There can be no doubt that the case was rightly decided, but the proposition about "redeemable sales" is stated in terms which are somewhat unnecessarily broad. It is true that the rights of the mortgagor may not be defeated under color of a redeemable sale, but care must be taken to distinguish a mortgage from a *bonâ fide* sale with a clause for repurchase. The two things resemble one another closely in form, but differ widely in their incidents. If there is a *bonâ fide* sale with a condition for repurchase, the power must be exercised strictly in compliance with the terms of the condition, while in the case of the mortgagor, a failure to fulfil the strict terms of the agreement is not immediately followed by a forfeiture of the property. The reason of this difference is, that in the case of a *bonâ fide* sale with an option to the vendor to repurchase within a given time, there is no equity whatever to relieve against the sale, the rights of the purchaser being entitled to protection equally with those of the vendor; while in the case of a mortgage the transaction is regarded only as a security, and the mortgagee is sufficiently compensated by receiving interest in default of payment at the appointed time. The distinction is illustrated in several English cases, in which Courts of Equity, notwithstanding the jealousy with which such transactions are viewed, have refused to relieve the vendor from the consequences of his own default, and has been acted upon by our own Courts in more than one reported case. (*Rajah Lakshmi Chelliah Garu* v. *Rajah Sri Krishna*, 7 Mad., 6; *Venkappa Chetti* v. *Akku*, 7 Mad., 219.)

It is not perhaps always very easy to determine the class to which a particular transaction belongs. The question always is, was the transaction a *bonâ*

LECTURE V. *fide* sale with a contract for repurchase, or was it a mortgage under the form of a sale? In this, as in every other case, the intention of the parties must be looked to, and that intention may be shown by the deed itself, by other instruments, or even by oral evidence. (*Alderson* v. *White*, 2 De and J., 97; see also *Nallana Gaundan* vs. *Palani Gaundan*, 2 Mad., 422.) The test sometimes applied by English Judges, *viz.*, the existence or absence of a power to recover the sum named as the price for the repurchase, cannot safely be applied in this country, because, as you will presently see, there is in general no personal liability incurred by the debtor in a mortgage by conditional sale. There are, however, other circumstances which may furnish a key to the real character of the transaction. If, for instance, the conveyance is not followed by possession, or if there is any covenant for the payment of interest, I presume the transaction will be regarded as a mortgage, while, if the purchaser is let into possession as owner with no power to recover interest upon the purchase money paid by him, the instrument will be regarded as an absolute sale with an option to the vendor to repurchase. It is, no doubt, possible to suggest a case in which the creditor might agree to take the rents and profits in lieu of interest, and conceal the real nature of the transaction under the appearance of a sale with a clause for repurchase, but even in this case the adequacy or inadequacy of sum mentioned in the instrument as the purchase money would perhaps throw some light on the transaction. "The intention of the parties, as collected from the tenor of the deed, shows whether the *bye-bil-wafa* be a sale with the reserve of an option of retractation within a limited time, or a mortgage for the security of money lent. A stipulation for a short period must be considered to mark that a sale was in the contemplation of the parties; a long term denotes a mortgage, or security for a loan, and such mortgages, in the form of conditional sales, are very common." (Note I, Select Reports, p. 77; compare 7 Mad., 6, and 7 Mad., 219, with 2 Mad., 422.) I shall close the subject with the remark that in doubtful cases the Court will lean strongly to the construction most favorable to the person claiming the right to redeem. LECTURE V.

There is a kind of mortgage much in use in the provinces of Bombay and Madras to which I have already had occasion to allude. The *Dristibundhuk* is in its nature essentially the same with our own conditional sale, the debtor agreeing with his creditor to put him in possession on default of the property pledged to him as absolute owner. The *Gahen Lahen* of Bombay is also analogous to our conditional sale, and I propose to treat of all of these varieties of mortgages in the present lecture as they belong to the same group of securities in

LECTURE V. which the ownership of the pledge is liable to be transferred from the debtor to his creditor.

I intend, in the first place, to call your attention to the rights acquired by the mortgagee under a conditional sale, although the mutual rights and duties of mortgagor and mortgagee are so interwoven with one another that I cannot discuss the rights of the mortgagee without in some measure touching upon those of the mortgagor.

Now the first observation which I think it necessary to make is, that in a conditional sale the mortgagor does not ordinarily incur any personal liability. The creditor can only look to the land pledged to him for the satisfaction of his debt. If the debtor make default, he may foreclose the equity of redemption and become the absolute owner of the estate. If the property is worth less than the amount due to him, he must suffer the loss, and cannot enforce payment from the debtor. This was laid down in a very early "construction" by the Sudder Dewany Adalut of Calcutta, and this view of the law has not, so far as I am aware, been since questioned. The "construction" says—"If the mortgage be of the nature of a conditional sale and the money be not repaid, the lender, unless good and sufficient cause be shown, can only sue for possession of the property pledged, and has not the election of suing for the money or to be put in possession of the property as he may deem most advantageous to his own interest." (Vide Select Reports, Vol. VII, p. 92.) LECTURE V.

The language is not perhaps very precise, and it would seem that the proposition that the mortgagee must ordinarily look to the land is somewhat broadly laid down. The question, I presume, must depend upon the particular language of the instrument, and all that can be affirmed as a proposition of law is, that personal liability shall not be presumed in the absence of an express covenant. Thus qualified, the proposition would not seem to be open to any reasonable objection. Possibly this was all that was meant to be laid down in the construction, although the language used might have been more precise. I have in my own experience found very distinct covenants for repayment in Bengali mortgages, and it would not, I conceive, be just to say to the mortgagees in such cases, "You must not sue upon the covenant, but must proceed to foreclose the equity of redemption."

I find that Mr. Justice Macpherson in his treatise on Mortgages defines a conditional sale as a mortgage, in which "the borrower, *not making himself personally liable for repayment of the loan*, covenants that, on default of payment of principal and interest on a certain date, the land pledged shall pass to the mortgagee." (Macpherson's Mortgage, p. 11.) This definition, or rather description, of a conditional sale, is taken from the judgment of the

LECTURE V. Court in a very early case in the Sudder Dewany Adalut. But the learned author does not express any opinion of his own.

In making the foregoing observations, I must not be understood as expressing an opinion that the mortgagee will be permitted in this country to pursue all his remedies concurrently, or that he may not be put to his election. The case of *Mohanund Chatterjee* v. *Govind Nath Roy* (7 Sel. Rep., 110) is a direct authority that a mortgagee having elected to foreclose will not be suffered to sue the mortgagor personally for the debt secured by the mortgage.

The question whether or not there is an implied warranty of title in a mortgage by conditional sale, is perhaps not wholly free from doubt. In the case of an out-and-out sale of immoveable property, there are conflicting dicta, if not decisions, and I presume the same uncertainty must extend to the case of a mortgage. The weight of authority, however, so far as mortgages are concerned, seems to be in favor of the existence of an implied warranty. (*Dwarka Dass* against *Rutton Singh*, 2 Agra, 119.) The question, however, is not of much practical importance, as there are few mortgages in which some expressions may not be found sufficient to constitute an express warranty of title.

The question next arises what is the remedy of the mortgagee if the title of the mortgagor is found to be bad. This is pointed out by Mr. Justice

Markby in delivering the judgment of the Court in *Syud Sayet Ali* v. *Syud Mohamed Jowad Ali.* In that case the title of the mortgagor having proved defective, the mortgagee brought a suit, in which, after stating the result of a certain action between the mortgagor and a third person, in which such third person was declared to be the owner of the property which had been mortgaged to the plaintiff, the plaint proceeded to state—"Hence, the right of Sayet Ali ceased to exist, and he held no longer any lien on the property sold. That for this reason your petitioner has become entitled to recover the consideration money with interest accrued thereon." (7 W. R., 197.)

The plaint was filed on the 20th February 1864, before the time fixed for the repayment of the loan had expired. The defendant in his answer insisted that the suit was premature, as it was substantially a suit for the money which had been advanced, and which had not become due when the plaint was filed. Mr. Justice Markby, in overruling the objection, points out the real nature of the suit. The learned Judge observes,—"With regard to the defence that the action is premature, because the time for repayment of the loan has not elapsed, we think that it is not well founded. The defendant has misunderstood the cause of action; it is not brought to enforce repayment of the loan, but it is an action for damages for breach of contract. A warranty of title amounts to a contract by the seller that, in consideration of the buyer purchasing the property and pay the consideration money, he (the seller) will make good to the buyer any loss which the buyer may incur by reason of the seller not having a good title to the property. This is an absolute contract from the moment it has been entered into, and the buyer can sue upon it at once, if he can show that the seller has not a good title in accordance with his undertaking, and that he has sustained loss in consequence." (7 W. R., 196.) Further on the learned Judge observes,—"It is perhaps desirable to point out that though, as above stated, the buyer may at once bring an action on a warranty of title, if he can show a breach of that warranty, it does not follow, as a matter of course, that he is entitled to recover back as damages the whole of the consideration money. Nor do we assent to an argument which has been put forward on the part of the plaintiff, and has received some countenance from the Principal Sudder Ameen, that, on its being ascertained that the seller had no title, the conditional sale was (to use the expression of the judgment below) *nullified*." (7 W. R., 196.) We thus find that the mortgagee has a right to bring an action for damages if the title of the mortgagor is found to be bad. The remedy of the mortgagee is not quite so clear when the pledge is destroyed by what is called an act of God, or suffers deterioration so as to become insufficient for the security of the creditor. I have not been able to find any reported case on the subject, although I find it difficult to persuade myself that the precise point never came before any of the superior Courts in this country. We have already seen that the Hindu law in such cases permitted the creditor either to demand another pledge or to sue the debtor immediately for the debt secured by the pledge. A similar right is given by the French Code Napoleon, and I may, therefore, venture to affirm that the principle will be adopted by our own Courts as founded in justice and equity, and open to no reasonable objection.

While upon the subject I may venture to suggest that a similar rule may perhaps be applied with advantage to cases in which the mortgagor's title is found to be bad. It is perfectly true that the creditor would be sufficiently protected by permitting him to sue for damages for the breach of the warranty, but I think there would be very great difficulty in assessing the damages. As pointed out by the Court in *Sayet Ali* v. *Mohamed Jowad Ali* (7 W. R., 196), it does not follow that the mortgagee is entitled to recover as damages the whole of the "consideration money." For the purpose of this enquiry, I shall assume, as the Court apparently did in the case to which I have referred, that this would be one of those cases in which the mortgagor would be personally liable; for otherwise

LECTURE V. there can be no doubt that the mortgagee would be at least entitled to recover as damages the whole of the money lent by him. The question then arises what, assuming that the mortgagor is liable to be sued upon his covenant, is to be the measure of damages for the breach of the warranty. Now the principle on which the damages ought to be assessed would seem to depend upon the difference to the creditor in the risk incurred by him under the altered circumstances, and this difference ought to be the measure of the damage suffered by the creditor. Now the difference in the risk is, I apprehend, capable of a money valuation in this way. What would be the rate of interest which the creditor would demand if the money were advanced on the personal security of the debtor? and the difference between this hypothetical rate and the rate at which the money was actually lent, would represent the loss to the creditor, not indeed with mathematical certainty, but with that substantial accuracy which is alone attainable in such cases. It is, however, evident that the principle cannot be worked out satisfactorily in practice. It would impose upon the Courts of Justice a duty which it would be next to impossible for them to perform. There can therefore be no serious objection to the extension of the rule that where by reason of an accident the mortgagee loses the benefit of the security, the mortgagor is bound either to repay the debt, or to give another pledge. The debtor surely cannot complain with reason of being obliged to repay, before the appointed time, money which would perhaps have been never lent to him but for his offer of a security which turns out to be worthless; while the creditor will be only too glad to call in his money. In the case of an out-and-out sale the difficulties which I have suggested do not occur, but I think it would be unsafe to apply the same rule to a transaction which is essentially different, and which must, therefore, be governed by other rules.

In the foregoing observations, I have confined myself to the rights acquired by the mortgagee immediately on the execution of the mortgage, and before any default has been committed by the mortgagor. In connection with this subject I may mention that, although the mortgagor is treated as the owner of the land before foreclosure, the mortgagee has the right, where the security is insufficient, to ask the Court to interfere to prevent waste by the mortgagor. I have not indeed been able to find any Indian case directly bearing upon the point, but the rule is founded in good sense, and there can be no possible objection to its application in this country.

I shall now proceed to discuss the rights of the mortgagee after default made by the mortgagor to repay the debt by the appointed time. If we were

LECTURE V. to look only to the terms of the contract between the debtor and his creditor, the ownership passes absolutely to the creditor immediately on default, and this would seem to have been actually the case in this country before the legislature interfered and engrafted on, what I may call, the common law of India, the rule borrowed from the practice of the English Court of Chancery, by which the mortgagee is permitted to redeem within a reasonable time after he has forfeited his right to do so by the terms of his own agreement. The preamble of Regulation XVII of 1806, which was passed for the Presidency of Bengal, points out the necessity of "an equitable provision" for allowing a redemption within a reasonable and limited period, as the only means of guarding against improvident and injurious transfers of landed property by the forfeiture of mortgages accompanied with a condition of sale. In the other provinces the legislature does not seem to have thought it necessary to interfere, but the same result has been accomplished by what is called, not perhaps very felicitously, judicial legislation.

I propose in the first place to call your attention to the provisions of the Bengal Regulation, by which the mortgagee was prevented for the first time from insisting upon a strict enforcement of the terms of his contract with the mortgagor. The mortgagee, in order that he may become the absolute owner of the property pledged to him, must proceed to foreclose the right of redemption, and the procedure which he has to adopt is pointed out by the 8th section of the Regulation, which says:—"Whenever the receiver or holder of a deed of mortgage and conditional sale, such as is described in the preamble and preceding sections of this Regulation, may be desirous of foreclosing the mortgage, and rendering the sale conclusive on the expiration of the *stipulated period*, or at any time subsequent before the sum lent is repaid, he shall (after demanding payment from the borrower or his representative) apply for that purpose by a written petition, to be presented by himself or by one of the authorized *vakils* of the Court to the Judge of the zillah or city in which the mortgaged land or other property may be situated. The Judge, on receiving such written application, shall cause the mortgagor or his legal representative to be furnished, as soon as possible, with a copy of it, and shall at the same time notify to him by a *purwana* under his seal and official signature, that, if he shall not redeem the property mortgaged in the manner provided for by the foregoing section within one year from the date of the notification, the mortgage will be finally foreclosed, and the conditional sale will become conclusive."

The preceding section declares the mortgagor entitled to redeem on payment of the principal

LECTURE V. sum with the interest due thereon. Now the language of this section has given rise to a good deal of discussion, and I cannot do better than call your attention to some of the questions which have arisen upon it from time to time. In the case of *Shoroshee Bala Dabee and others* v. *Nund Lall Sein* (13 W. R., 364; S. C., 5 B. L. R., 389) the question arose as to the meaning of the words "stipulated period" which occur in the eighth section of the Regulation. The facts in that case were shortly these. On the 4th of September 1863, Shoroshee Bala Dabee and her son Hemendro Nath Mookerjee executed a mortgage of certain landed property at Chittagong to one Gobind Chunder Sein. The deed was in the English form, and by it the property was conveyed to Gobind Chunder absolutely, subject to the proviso that in the event of the mortgagors paying Gobind Chunder the principal sum of Rs. 54,437-10-4 on the 4th September 1868, and in the meantime paying interest on that sum at 10 per cent. per annum half-yearly, (*i.e.*, on the 4th March and 4th September), with annual rests in the case of default of such payment, then and in such case Gobind would reconvey.

The mortgagors failed to pay all the interest which became due under the terms of the mortgage, and on the 4th December 1866, Gobind Chunder applied by written petition to the Judge of Chittagong for a foreclosure of the mortgage pursuant to the provisions in that behalf of section 8 of Regulation XVII of 1806. Thereupon, the prescribed notification seems to have been made to the mortgagors by the Judge.

Upon the footing of this petition and notification, Nund Lall Sein, the son of Gobind Chunder, on the 15th April 1868 (his father having meanwhile died), instituted a suit for the establishment and confirmation of absolute purchase and to obtain possession of the mortgaged property accordingly.

It is obvious from this statement of the facts of the case that the application to foreclose, as well the suit based upon it, were instituted before the period fixed for the repayment of the loan secured by the mortgage had elapsed. It was contended for the plaintiff that the suit was not premature, as, according to the terms of the deed, the defendants had lost their right to ask for a reconveyance; and the Regulation was never intended to give a right to the mortgagor other than a right to redeem within a certain time, even after he has lost all right to the property under the strict terms of the contract, and that the stipulated time within the meaning of the Regulation had therefore arrived as soon as there was a breach by the debtor. The contention, however, was overruled, and the Court in giving judgment observed:—"If the Zillah Court was at liberty, and had the machinery to deal with this matter precisely upon the principles which

LECTURE V. govern the English Court of Chancery, the facts of the case are possibly such as would give the plaintiff a right of suit even before the expiration of the time agreed upon for repayment of the principal debt. For, whenever that has occurred by reason of which the mortgagor has lost his right under the deed to call for a reconveyance of the property, and he can only get back the mortgaged premises by virtue of the right of redemption which the Court of Equity still preserves to him, then also that Court allows the mortgagee to come in and insist that the mortgagor shall elect between the exercising of this right of redemption and being foreclosed. But we think that this mortgage transaction, notwithstanding that it wears a completely English aspect, falls within the operation of Regulation XVII of 1806. It is in all respects parallel with the mortgage common in this country, which is effected by means of a bill of absolute sale, together with a contemporaneous ekrar for reconveyance; and mortgages of this sort have always been treated as being subject to the Regulation. The words 'conditional sale' as explained by the preamble, are broad enough to cover them, and there is no doubt that they are especially within the mischief against which the enactment was directed. This being so, the mortgagee can only obtain a foreclosure by following the procedure which is laid down by section 8 of the abovementioned Regulation. And although there is some ambiguity in the words of that section relative to the time when the mortgagee may first prefer his petition for foreclosure, this is cleared up by reference to the previous section. The last clause of the 7th section runs thus :—" The whole of the provisions contained in section 2, Regulation I of 1798, and section 12, Regulation XXXIV of 1803, as applied therein to the *stipulated period* of redemption, are declared to be equally applicable to the *extended period* of one year granted for an equitable right of redemption by this Regulation."

" This makes it evident that the year of grace, commencing as it does with the notification which follows on the mortgagee's application for foreclosure, is intended by the Legislature to be additional to the period which is stipulated for redemption in the mortgage contract; and, therefore, it follows that the application itself cannot be made before the expiration of that 'stipulated period.'

" Now the stipulated period of redemption referred to by the Legislature in this Regulation appears to us to be the whole period prescribed by the mortgage contract for the performance of the conditions, upon the fulfilment of which the mortgagor is to be entitled to a reconveyance. We do not think that it in any case means less than this, or depends upon whether the mortgagor duly performs all those

LECTURE V. conditions or not. We see no reason for supposing that the Legislature by those words spoke, not of the period of redemption originally specified in the contract (as the words themselves certainly imply), but merely of the shorter period during which the mortgagor by performance of the conditions may have preserved his strict right to redeem under the contract.

"From the very object of the Regulation it is obvious that the framers of it had expressly in view the case of a mortgagor who fails to perform the conditions necessary to give him the contract right to redeem, and if they thought of the 'stipulated period' as a period terminating in the first default of the mortgagor, they would surely have used some apter expression than this to convey their meaning.

"According, then, to our view, in the case before us the 'stipulated period' did not expire until the 4th September 1868, and consequently both the presenting of the petition for foreclosure and the filing of this plaint occurred before the mortgagee had any right to take a single step towards foreclosing the mortgagor's equity of redemption. All the proceedings in this matter are, therefore, inoperative: the suit is without legal foundation and must be dismissed." (13 W. R., 364; S. C., 5 B. L. R., 389.)

I shall presently ask you to contrast the case of

Shoroshee Bala with another recent case in which also a question arose as to the meaning of the words "stipulated time." But before I do so I wish to make one observation. The Regulation seems to provide only for that class of mortgages in Bengal in which a forfeiture takes place by reason of the "money advanced not being repaid within a stated period," and although it is perfectly true that a forfeiture for breach of any other condition is equally within the mischief of the Act, the statute does not in terms embrace such cases.

According to the law as administered in the English Court of Chancery, and which is followed in the other provinces, the mortgagee is entitled to sue at any time after default in payment of interest, where his right to do so is not qualified by a covenant not to call in the money during a certain period.

As the law, however, stands at present in this Presidency, the mortgagee cannot call upon the mortgagor to elect between exercising his right of redemption and being foreclosed at any time before the period fixed for the repayment of the loan secured by the mortgage, whatever may be the nature of the covenants contained in the deed.

The case of *Omachurn Chowdhry* against *Behary Lall Mookerjee* (21 W. R., 274), however, shows that the object of the mortgagee may be indirectly accomplished by the fixing of an early date for the repayment of the money, followed by a covenant that the money shall not be called in for a certain term if the interest is paid regularly, and the other covenants observed by the mortgagor. The distinction may seem to be somewhat refined, but it seems to be the only way in which the rights of the parties can be reconciled with the enactments contained in the Bengal Regulation.

In the case of *Omachurn Chowdhry* against *Behary Lall Mookerjee*, the question arose upon a mortgage deed in the English form by which the 3rd of January 1866 was fixed as the date for the repayment of the loan. This was, however, accompanied by a proviso that in the event of the debtor continuing to pay the interest on the principal sum regularly, the money should not be called in by the creditor before the 3rd of July 1871. The debtor having failed to pay the interest regularly, the mortgagee proceeded to foreclose under Regulation XVII of 1806 without waiting till the extended period mentioned in the proviso. It was contended for the mortgagor that the application was premature, as the 3rd of July 1871 was the "stipulated period" for the repayment of the loan within the meaning of the Regulation. The contention, however, was overruled, the Court observing that the last clause in the deed had not the effect of making the 3rd of July 1871 the stipulated period to which the Regulation would apply. Referring to the case of Shoroshee Bala,

Chief Justice Couch, who gave the judgment of the Court, observed,—"That is a different case from the present; and the decision rather supports the view which we take in this case, namely, that we are to look at the time which is stipulated for the payment of the principal sum, and that the intention of the parties is to be collected from the whole of the deed. To my mind, in all these cases, it is a question of intention, what have the parties fixed upon as the time for payment."

You will see that Sir Richard Couch says that the question is one of intention. This is no doubt perfectly true, and yet the language is somewhat misleading. In English mortgages a very early day is generally appointed for the repayment of the loan, but it is seldom "intended" that the principal is to be paid on the day named in the condition. Now, suppose the question arose under the Regulation, whether or not the day named in the deed was that which the parties intended to be the stipulated time for repayment; I suppose the question would be answered in the affirmative, although in a certain sense it might be said that the parties knew very well that the repayment of the loan would not be insisted upon on the very day mentioned in the deed. The fact is, the words "intended" and "intention" are somewhat ambiguous, and, unless clearly explained, apt to be misleading.

To return to the provisions of section 8 of

LECTURE V. Regulation XVII of 1806. We find that the application must be preceded by a demand for payment. It is, however, not necessary that the demand should be for the specific sum which may be ultimately ascertained to be due. (*Forbes* v. *Amerunnissa*, 10 Moo. Ind. App., 340.) Indeed it is very doubtful whether a foreclosure, otherwise regular, can be questioned merely on the ground that it was not preceded by a demand for payment.

The section then points out the Court to which the application should be made, and the only point which it is necessary to notice on this part of the enactment is, that where the properties are situated in two districts, the application may be made to either of the Judges within whose jurisdiction the property or a portion of it is situated. (*Rashmonee Debea* v. *Prankissen Doss*, 4 Moo. Ind. App., 392.)

The statute next defines the duty of the Judge on receiving the application, who is directed to cause the mortgagor or his legal representative to be furnished with a copy. Now the expression "legal representative" has given rise to a good deal of discussion. The earlier authorities were all reviewed in *Gunga Gobind Mondul* v. *Banee Madhub Ghose* (11 W. R., 548; S. C., 3 B. L. R., 172), in which the question was whether the purchaser of a portion of the mortgaged property was entitled to notice. Mr. Justice Markby, in delivering the judgment of the Court, observed:—

"The question turns entirely on the construction to be given to the words 'legal representative' in Regulation XVII of 1806. In the first place, it is contended broadly that those words did not mean the legal representative of the mortgagor in respect of the particular property mortgaged, but *universal* legal representative, such as an heir: and there is no doubt some color for this contention. These words are sometimes used in the latter sense, as for instance, in section 210 of the Code of Civil Procedure, and this is the idea which these words would at first sight rather suggest to my mind. But it appears to me to have been settled by long practice and authority that they were not used in this Regulation in this sense. The late Sudder Court held that the purchaser at a sale in execution of civil process is entitled to notice, and that doctrine has, I believe, ever since been acquiesced in. Now, this completely negatives the construction contended for. An auction-purchaser, as he is called, is not the universal legal representative of the mortgagor; he is only the assignee of a portion of his property.

"It also appears to me to have been decided by a great preponderance of authority in this Court (although I admit that the decisions are not altogether reconcilable), that a purchaser out-and-out of the mortgagor's interest, whether by public or private sale, and whether he be in possession or not,

LECTURE V. must be served with notice, except where any alienation of the mortgagor's interest has been prohibited by contract between the mortgagor and mortgagee. It is not necessary to go through the cases which are all collected in Macpherson on Mortgages, 5th edition, page 179.

"Nor do I think that there is any ground for putting upon these decisions the restrictions which have been now contended for, namely, that they do not apply to cases where the whole of the property comprised in the mortgage has not been sold by the mortgagor, or to cases where the mortgagee has no notice of the subsequent sale, both which peculiarities are said to be found in the case now under consideration. I do not see that a purchaser out and out of a distinct and definite portion of the property is in a different position from a purchaser of the whole. And as to the question of consent, I see no ground whatever for introducing that consideration. If, as is now decided, the words 'legal representative' include an assignee of the mortgaged property, it appears to me that they must include *all such assignees*, and that to make a distinction between assignments to which the mortgagee has or has not consented, would be an unwarrantable addition to the provisions of the Legislature."

We thus find that a purchaser of a part of the mortgaged property is a legal representative equally with an assignee of the whole of the property. In the case of *Mohun Lall Sukul* v. *Brojonath Kundu* (10 Moo. Ind. App., 1), the words were construed in a still more extended sense. In that case the mortgagee, after an unsuccessful attempt to withdraw an attachment which had been taken out against the mortgaged property by a judgment-creditor of the mortgagor, applied to the District Judge for foreclosure under Regulation XVII of 1806. The notice of foreclosure was served only on the widow and heiress of the mortgagor, and not on the creditor by whom the property had been taken in execution. The property was subsequently sold under the attachment which had been unsuccessfully contested by the mortgagee, and the purchaser under the execution, as the assignee of the debtor's equity of redemption, brought a suit for possession against the mortgagee upon the ground that the mortgage debt had been paid off from the rents and profits of the mortgaged property. The mortgagee in his defence relied upon the proceedings taken by him under the Regulation, and contended that the equity of redemption had been foreclosed. The Privy Council, however, were of opinion, that there was no valid foreclosure as no notice had been served upon the attaching creditor; Lord Justice Knight Bruce who delivered the judgment of their Lordships, observing that the mortgagee, when he filed his application for foreclosure, not only had notice that the interest of the mortgagor had been taken

LECTURE V.

LECTURE V. in execution, but was actually disputing the right of the creditor to put up that interest to sale. Under such circumstances his Lordship thought that the notice ought to have been served on the decree-holder, adding, "It was quite clear upon the authorities that if the sale had taken place before the application for foreclosure, such application could not have been effectual unless the purchaser had been served with it."

This reference to the peculiar circumstances of the case would seem at first sight to suggest that it was not decided solely with reference to the meaning of the words "legal representative" in the Regulation, but this decision must be read with another decision of their Lordships (*Pattabhiramier* v. *Vencatarow*, 7 B. L. R., p. 136), in which it was held that in the absence of any express legislative enactment, the interest of the mortgagee becomes absolute according to the terms of the contract by the mere failure of the mortgagor to redeem. We are therefore bound to suppose that in the earlier case of Mohun Lall Sukul, the Privy Council considered that the words "legal representative" were sufficiently wide to embrace an attachment creditor who, as we shall hereafter see, acquires a sort of statutory hypothecation by virtue of the attachment. It follows that a puisne mortgagee, whether by way of simple mortgage or conditional sale, is entitled to notice under the provisions of the Regulation. (*Nuddiar Chand Chuckerbutty* v. *Roop Doss Banerjee*, 22 W. R., p. 475.)

The Regulation is silent as to the person on whom the notice of foreclosure is to be served when the person entitled to redeem is an infant. When a guardian has been appointed by the Civil Court, or the estate has been taken charge of by the Court of Wards, there can be no difficulty whatever, service on the guardian being a perfectly good service. If, however, no guardian has been appointed, it would seem that service on the person who would have a preferable claim to the guardianship of the minor would be deemed a good service. (*Debee Persaud* v. *Manu Khan*, 2 All., 444. See also *Rashmonee Debea* v. *Prunkissen Doss*, 4 Moo. Ind. App., 392.) The safest course, however, for the mortgagee would be to apply to the District Court for the appointment of a guardian, who might be served with the notice of foreclosure.

Where there are more mortgagors or legal representatives of such mortgagors than one, the notice ought to be served on each of them. A more difficult question arises when the mortgage is executed by one of several co-sharers, a practice not uncommon in this country, but under circumstances under which if the transaction had been an out-and-out sale, it would be binding upon all the coparceners. Thus, for instance, A, the managing member of a joint Hindu family, executes a mortgage of an estate belonging to the joint family, the other members assenting to the transaction, either according to

LECTURE V. the usual practice by subscribing their names as attesting witnesses, or otherwise ratifying the transaction. There is little doubt that in such cases if the mortgagee is not aware of the rights of the other members, it would be sufficient if the notice is served on the person by whom the mortgage was executed. The difficulty arises only where the mortgagee is aware of the fact that the mortgagor is not the sole owner. It would seem, although the authorities are not very clear or consistent on the point, that even in such cases there may be a valid foreclosure on the foundation of a notice served only on the person who is the mortgagor on the face of the instrument by which the charge is created. (S. D. A., 1849, p. 36; S.D. A., 1856, p. 923; S.D.A., 1852, p. 423.)

I may mention that persons deriving title subsequently to the application of the mortgagee to foreclose are not entitled to any notice. If it were otherwise, proceedings in a foreclosure suit would be endless, as a fresh alienation might be made every day in the course of the proceedings. (*The Bishop of Winchester* v. *Paine*, 11 Vesey, 194; see also *Bhanoomutty Chowdrain* v. *Prem Chand Neogee*, 15 B. L. R., 28.) The rule, however, as I have already explained, does not apply to a purchaser under an execution, whose purchase, although subsequent in date to the application for foreclosure, was made under an attachment executed before any application to foreclose by the mortgagee. (*Anundmoyee Dassea*

v. *Dhunindro Chunder Mookerjee*, 16 W. R., P. C., 19; S. C., 14 Moo. Ind. App., 111.) In such cases, however, it would seem that notice to the execution creditor would be sufficient. As to the nature of the service, it must, where practicable, be personal, and substituted service will not be good except where the mortgagor is shown to be keeping out of the way. In the case of *Syud Esaf Ali Khan* v. *Mussamut Azumtoonessa* (W. R., 1864, p. 49), Mr. Justice Norman, in delivering the judgment of the Court, said,—"We may observe that, by the section now under consideration, the notification is not merely a preliminary proceeding leading up to a judgment of foreclosure to be subsequently pronounced in Court. It not only fixes the date from which the period during which the mortgagor is to retain the right to redeem is to be computed, but it is of itself the operative act in the foreclosure proceeding. We think, therefore, that the service of the notice must be evinced by the clearest proof, and must in all cases be, if not personal, at least such as to leave no doubt on the mind of the Court, that the notice itself must have reached the hands, or come to the knowledge of, the mortgagor."

You will observe that the Regulation directs that a copy of the application should be furnished to the mortgagor or his legal representative. This provision is mandatory and not merely directory,

LECTURE V. and an omission in this respect will, it seems, vitiate the whole proceedings. In the case of *Santi Ram Jana* v. *Modoo Mytee* (20 W. R., 363), where the mortgagor had not been served with a copy of the application, the Court observed,—"It is urged, first, that the notice contained all the information which would be contained in the written application; and, secondly, that it was not the fault of the mortgagee, but of the Court peon, that the mortgagor was not furnished with a copy of the written application. But these are not considerations upon which we are at liberty to enter. The law prescribes two conditions which are to be fulfilled before a mortgage can be foreclosed, and we cannot say that the mortgagee before us, who has only fulfilled one of them, is in a position to foreclose." (See also *Denonath Gangooly* v. *Nursing Pershad Dass*, 22 W. R., 90.)

The Allahabad Court has carried the principle of a close adherence to the provisions of the Regulation somewhat further, holding that a notice of foreclosure bearing the seal of the Court issuing it, but signed only by the Munsirim, and not by the Judge, is not a sufficient compliance with the law, and cannot be the foundation of a decree for foreclosure. (*Seth Harlall* v. *Manick Pal*, 3 All., 176.) In saying that this is carrying the doctrine further than the Calcutta High Court has done, I do not mean to suggest that the decision is not perfectly good law, although it may possibly work hardship in particular cases. At any rate it is better to adhere closely to the plain directions of a statute than to fritter it away by calling in the distinction between mandatory and directory enactments, a distinction which, unless carefully fenced in, would introduce the greatest uncertainty into the law.

An examination of the general question to which the discussion has conducted us would be beyond the range of these lectures. Those of you who wish to know more on the subject may consult the following English cases. (*Morgan* v. *Parry*, 17 C. B., 334; *Henderson* v. *The Royal British Bank*, 7 E. and B., 356; compare *Bowman* v. *Blyth*, 7 E. and B., 26; and *Friend* v. *Dennett*, 4. C. B., N. S., 576.)

I may here mention that the notification to the mortgagor ought to tell him distinctly that if he do not redeem the mortgage within one year, the mortgage will be finally foreclosed, and the conditional sale will become absolute. In one case, when the notice, after stating that an application had been made for the purpose of foreclosing the mortgage, called upon the mortgagor to appear and state any objection which he might have to the proceeding, the Court held that there was no notification as directed by the law, and refused to make a decree for foreclosure. (*Bheekhun Khan* v. *Bechun Khan*, 3 All., 35.)

To return once more to the Regulation: we find

that if everything is regularly done, the conditional sale becomes absolute unless the mortgagor takes the proper steps for the purpose of protecting his right of redemption within one year from the date of the "notification." I shall consider in the next lecture the steps which the mortgagor must take for that purpose. It is, however, necessary to state that these proceedings are not judicial proceedings, and any question between the parties may be raised in a regular suit. (10 Moo. Ind. App., 340.)

"It has been ruled by the Circular Order of the 22nd of July 1813, No. 37, and has ever since been settled law, that the functions of the Judge under Regulation XVI of 1806, section 8, are purely ministerial, and that a mortgagee after having done all that this Regulation requires to be done in order to foreclose the mortgage and make the conditional sale absolute, must bring a regular suit to recover possession if he is out of possession, or to obtain a declaration of his absolute title, if he is in possession.

"In that suit the mortgagor may contest on any sufficient grounds the validity of the conditional sale, or the regularity of the proceedings taken under the Regulation in order to make it absolute. He may also allege and prove, if he can, that nothing is due, or that the deposit, if any, which he has made, is sufficient to cover what is due; but the issue, in so far as the right of redemption is concerned, will be whether any thing at the end of the year of grace remained due to the mortgagee, and if so, whether the necessary deposit had been then made. If that is found against the mortgagor, the right of redemption is gone." (Per Lord Kingsdown, delivering the judgment of the Judicial Committee in *Forbes* v. *Amerunnessa.*)

Although in one sense it may, therefore, be said that the title of the mortgagee is not complete till he obtains a decree in a regular suit, it must not be understood that the decree creates any title in favor of the mortgagee. It only establishes, beyond all question, that as between the mortgagor and mortgagee, the ownership has passed absolutely from the former to the latter. The title of the mortgagee in reality dates from the end of the year within which the mortgagor is permitted to redeem, and it is for this reason that the mortgagee may maintain an action for mesne profits against the mortgagor for the period between the expiration of the year of grace and the actual recovery of the land. (*Jeora Khun Singh* v. *Hookum Singh*, 5 Agra, 358. See also *Suroop Chunder Roy* v. *Mohender Chunder Roy*, 22 W. R., 539.)

I have been at some pains to explain the real character of the proceedings under Regulation XVII of 1806, and the relation they bear to the regular suit which the Circular Order enjoins, because I find there is some misconception on the point, arising probably from the observation made by

LECTURE V. — the Privy Council in the case of *Forbes* v. *Amerunnessa* that the "title of the mortgagee is not even then (when the mortgagee has failed to redeem within the year of grace) complete." The context shows that all that was meant by these words was that the title of the mortgagee might be impeached by the mortgagor in a regular suit notwithstanding the regularity of the proceedings under the Regulation; in other words, that the mortgagee's title was not so secure as under a decree for foreclosure.

Before quitting the subject of foreclosure, I wish to call your attention to the precise nature of the restrictions imposed by the Regulation upon the strict rights given by the contract to the mortgagee. It has only extended the period of redemption to any time within one year from the date of the notification to the debtor that the creditor is desirous of enforcing the repayment of the debt, but any other covenants which may be contained in the deed are left wholly untouched. If, therefore, there is a covenant that the mortgagee shall enter upon possession on default, he will not be restrained from taking possession, although he should attempt to do so before foreclosing the debtor's equity of redemption. He can, however, only take the rents and profits as mortgagee, liable to account to the mortgagor. The question whether a mortgagee in this country has a right to bring ejectment immediately upon default, was discussed in the case of *Denonath*

Gangooly v. *Nursing Pershad Dass* (22 W. R., 90), which deserves very careful study. It is true that in that case, as well as in the Privy Council cases which are cited in the judgment of Mr. Justice Markby, the right to possession on default was expressly stipulated for, and it may therefore be said that none of these cases is an authority for the proposition that a right of entry would accrue on default where the instrument is wholly silent as to any such right, and only provides for a transfer of the right of ownership. I, however, venture to think that a right of entry may fairly be presumed from the express agreement of the debtor that the ownership shall pass, although the relation of mortgagee and mortgagor is so anomalous that any deduction from general principles must be made with caution. (See the observations of Mr. Justice Markby in *Denonath Gangooly* v. *Nursingh Pershad Dass*, 22 W. R., 90.) Any other construction, however, would lead to absurd consequences, as I shall have occasion to point out to you when I discuss the question of limitation, and it seems to me that the only way out of the difficulty is to presume that in every mortgage there is an implied right of entry given to the mortgagor as necessarily accompanying the right of ownership, the implied right not being controlled by any law, and having the same operation as an express stipulation, and for the same reasons. There is, however, another class of cases in

LECTURE V. which the mortgagor stipulates that on default the mortgagee shall have authority to foreclose and to take possession after foreclosure as absolute owner. In instruments of this class, and they are by no means uncommon, I think there is no room for presuming any right of entry on default, and I am afraid the anomaly to which I have alluded in connection with the statute of limitations cannot be avoided.

I shall now ask you to compare the law of foreclosure in Bengal with that which obtains in the other provinces, and which is based on the practice of the English Court of Chancery. The mortgagee wishing to foreclose brings a suit praying that an account may be taken of the principal and interest due on the security, and that the defendant may be directed to pay the same by a day to be appointed by the Court, or be foreclosed his equity of redemption. An account is then taken, and a decree is made for payment within a certain time, generally six months, the mortgage being foreclosed in the event of default, when the mortgagee may obtain an absolute order for foreclosing.

I have not been able to discover any reported case in which a sale has been ordered instead of a foreclosure. In a recent case the High Court of Madras made a decree for foreclosure, although the District Court had made a decree for sale. We have seen that English Courts of equity have been armed by a recent statute with extensive powers of directing a sale instead of a fore- closure, and it is to be hoped that the Indian Courts will follow the same practice.

I may mention that a decree for foreclosure is not binding upon one not a party to the decree. It is therefore necessary that all persons entitled to redeem should be represented in the suit. Who those persons are I shall discuss more fully in the next lecture. The question whether a mortgagee is entitled to pursue all his remedies concurrently does not seem to have been directly raised. In England, where the mortgagee suspects his security to be deficient, the proper course for him would seem to be to proceed against the mortgagor on the collateral securities in the first instance, and then apply for foreclosure for the deficiency. It is true that the mortgagee is at liberty to foreclose and then to proceed against the mortgagor on his collateral securities, but this has the effect of opening the decree of foreclosure, and is therefore attended with inconvenience. It is difficult to say how the Indian Courts will deal with such cases. In Bengal it would seem that the mortgagee, if he elect to foreclose, will not be suffered to proceed personally against the mortgagor even when there is a covenant for the repayment of the debt. There is no provision in the Regulations for re-opening a decree of foreclosure, and this of itself would be a ground for putting the mortgagee to his election. The

LECTURE V. same difficulty does not occur where the mortgagee applies for foreclosure for the deficiency after having proceeded against the debtor personally.

As in Bengal, the mortgagee is entitled to enter upon possession on default subject to his own right to foreclose and the right of the mortgagor to redeem. There being no distinction between Courts of Equity and Courts of Common Law in this country, the law will not permit ejectment where the mortgagor would have a right to relief in equity. In the case of *Sitaram Dandekar* v. *Ganesh Gokhle* (6 Bom., 121), where the mortgage deed contained a clause to the effect that the mortgagee should be entitled to possession on default by the mortgagor in payment of the interest on the principal money secured by the mortgage, the Court refused to make an absolute decree for ejectment, and directed the mortgagor to pay to the mortgagee the arrears of interest due to him within three months, or that in default the property should be delivered to the mortgagee to be held by him under the terms of the mortgage bond.

I will conclude by discussing the question of the time within which the mortgagee is permitted to assert his rights under the statute of limitations. I shall, in the first place, discuss the question with reference to Act XIV of 1859, and then with reference to Act IX of 1871, the present Statute of Limitations. Now, in order to clear up the matter as much as possible, I shall first take up the case in which the mortgagor himself continues in possession and is the party defending the suit. It would be tedious to go through the various conflicting decisions on the point before the law was finally settled in the case of *Denonath Gangooly* v. *Nursingh Pershad Dass*, in which all the earlier authorities are reviewed, and a clear and consistent doctrine is laid down. (22 W. R., 90.)

Now the provision of Act XIV of 1859, which is applicable to mortgages, is that laid down in clause 12 of the first section of the Act, which says,—"To suits for the recovery of immoveable property, or of any interest in immoveable property, to which no other provision of this Act applies—the period of twelve years from the time the cause of action arose."

The words "cause of action" are nowhere defined in the Act, but as pointed out by Mr. Justice Markby in Denonath Gangooly's case, which is the leading case on the subject, it is clear that two things are necessary to constitute a cause of action; —a right to possession, and an adverse withholding of that right. "If the plaintiff had not a right to immediate possession, or if having a right to possession the defendants were holding with the plaintiff's permission, and acknowledging his right, no suit could be brought in the one case, because the right to possession had not accrued; and in the other, because

LECTURE V. it had not been disturbed or denied." (Per Markby, J., in delivering judgment in *Denonath Gangooly* v. *Nursingh Pershad Dass.*) Now we have already seen that, generally speaking, a right of entry accrues immediately to the mortgagee on default, but still no cause of action would arise if the mortgagor continued in occupation acknowledging the title of the mortgagee, and, as is commonly the case, paying the interest on the principal sum regularly to the mortgagee, who from various causes might be reluctant to assume possession of the pledge. In such a case as this it would be monstrous to contend, that by allowing the mortgagor to retain possession for a period of twelve years, the mortgagee loses his right to the security. "It would be confounding adverse occupations with those which have not the semblance even of such a character, and would establish a bar arising from simple occupation and not from the laches of the demandant or others before him." (Per Lord Kingsdown, 6 Moo. Ind. App., 353.)

A difficulty, however, may arise in those cases in which the mortgagor neither pays any interest nor does anything else to indicate that he acknowledges the right of the mortgagee. In such cases it may, I think, be fairly presumed, in the absence of any evidence to the contrary, that the possession of the mortgagor is only permissive, and cannot, therefore, be urged as a bar to an action by the mortgagee.

If, however, the mortgagor retained possession under such circumstances as would rebut the presumption of a permissive occupation, the mortgagee's suit must fail. "A default may be made by the mortgagors, which may give the mortgagee a right to sue or to enter into possession (if he chooses to assert such right), but which may, notwithstanding, have no effect whatsoever in altering the nature of the mortgage title. So long as the mortgagor in possession, or those who claim under him, assert merely a title to redeem, and advance no other title inconsistent with it, such possession must *primâ facie* at least be treated as perfectly reconcileable with, and not adverse to, the title of the mortgagee, and the continuation of the lien on the property pledged." (*Buldeen* v. *Golab Koonwar*, Agra, Full Bench, 108.) LECTURE V.

It was thought at one time that no cause of action could accrue to the mortgagee before foreclosure, and as there is no limit as to the time within which an application for foreclosure may be made, the curious result followed that a mortgagee might, if he chose to do so, enforce his security at any time, and no safe title could possibly be acquired against a mortgagee in this country. The doctrine rested on the supposition, which I have shown to be erroneous, that no right of entry accrued to the mortgagee till foreclosure. I have, however, already referred you to a class of securities which may possibly admit of different considerations.

LECTURE V. I shall next consider the case in which the rights of the mortgagor have been transferred to a third person. Now if such third person purchased with notice of the mortgage, the same presumption would be made as to the character of his possession as if the mortgagor himself had been in occupation. But if the purchase was made without any such notice, there can be no pretence whatever for treating the possession of the purchaser as permissive, or as that of a person holding in privity of the mortgagor. In the case of *Anund Moye Dassee* v. *Dhunindro Chunder Mookerjee* (14 Moo. Ind. App., 111), the Privy Council observed:—"Their Lordships think that the title of a judgment-creditor, or a purchaser under a judgment decree, cannot be put on the same footing as the title of a mortgagor or of a person claiming under a voluntary alienation from the mortgagor. They are of opinion that the possession of a purchaser under such circumstances is really not the possession of a person holding in privity of the mortgagor, or holding so as to be an acknowledgment of the continuance of the title of the mortgagee. The possession which the purchaser supposed he acquired was a possession as owner. He thought he was acquiring the absolute title to the property, and that he was in possession as absolute owner."

I have not considered the case of a trespasser holding adversely both to mortgagor and mortgagee. If the trespasser enter into possession after default, there can be no difficulty whatever, as that would be a much stronger case than that of a purchaser without notice of the mortgage. The difficulty arises only when the occupation commences before default, and the mortgagor takes no steps for the purpose of vindicating his rights. There does not seem to be any method in this country by which the mortgagee may interrupt the prescription, and it would seem to be a hardship upon him to hold that the time would run against him before he had acquired a right of entry. The authorities are not very clear on the point. In a case reported in the Weekly Reporter for 1864, Mr. Justice Jackson observed:—"The question to be decided is, when did plaintiffs' cause of action arise? They have alleged that the date of expiry of their year of grace is the date from which the cause of action should be calculated. This may be the rule in those cases where the mortgagor remains in peaceable and undisturbed possession of the estate mortgaged. But the rule no longer stands good when the mortgagor is dispossessed, and his title disputed, and another person obtains possession of the estate. The possession of this new holder becomes a possession adverse to both the plaintiff's mortgagor and to the plaintiff, the mortgagee. If the mortgagee submits to this possession for more than twelve years, he loses his right to contest the title of the new holder. His cause of action against the new

LECTURE V. holder arose on the date on which the latter obtained such adverse possession of the mortgaged estate. Circumstances may occur which will defer the mortgagee's cause of action. If the mortgagor, for instance, contests the title of the new holder, and a litigation ensues between them, the mortgagee is not bound to take action upon his mortgage until that litigation is decided. But if the mortgagor's title is rejected, and his possession is disturbed by an adverse one, the mortgagee's cause of action against the new holder commences from the date on which the latter obtains possession on his title adverse to the mortgagor, which has been confirmed by the Courts. This is the law on the subject which has been laid down in the Privy Council." (*Prannath Roy Chowdhry* v. *Rookeea Begum*, W. R., 1864, p. 375.)

I may mention that section 6 of Act XIV of 1859 contained a special enactment with regard to suits on mortgages in Courts established by Royal charter. "In suits in the Courts established by Royal charter by a mortgagee to recover from the mortgagor the possession of the immoveable property mortgaged, the cause of action shall be deemed to have arisen from the latest date at which any portion of principal money or interest was paid on account of such mortgage debt."

It might perhaps be plausibly argued upon the language of this section, that in cases to which it did not apply, the mortgagee's right of action would not be kept alive by the payment of any portion of the principal money or interest. This, however, does not necessarily follow. The object of the legislature was probably to put mortgages in the English form, when sued upon in the Supreme Court, on the same footing as English mortgages. If this be a correct view, it would seem that, under Act XIV of 1859, English mortgages were placed in a less favorable position as regarded limitation than Mofussil mortgages, for, in the latter case, as we have already seen, the cause of action did not necessarily arise with the last payment of any portion of the principal or interest.

The new Act (IX of 1871) contains a distinct provision for suits for possession of immoveable property by mortgagees. The period allowed under the new law is the same as that under the old statute, but it runs not from the accrual of the cause of action, but from the time when the mortgagee first becomes entitled to possession. It may, therefore, be presumed that the old doctrine of adverse and permissive occupation has been abolished, and the mortgagee must sue for possession within twelve years of the date fixed for the repayment of the loan. In a recent case the Court observed:—"The question raised in the earlier cases as to the accruing of the cause of action does not arise here, the legislature having in

LECTURE V. Article 135, Act. IX of 1871, substituted for that occurrence a specific time, *viz.*, the time when the mortgagee was first entitled to possession. This was confessedly the 29th Cheyt 1260.

"In this view of the case, the nature of the defendant's possession, whether adverse or permissive, is immaterial. The mortgagee having his time expressly limited by the Act was bound to guard himself, and if he did not do so, and allowed the time to pass, he loses his remedy." (*Lall Mohun Gungopadhya* v. *Prosonno Chunder Banerjee*, 24 W. R., 433.)

I may, however, venture to suggest that the clause was not perhaps intended to apply to a case in which the mortgagor is permitted to retain possession so long as he pays interest. In such cases, I presume, a new cause of action, or right of entry, would accrue on the determination of the permission. Thus, suppose a landlord makes a lease for a term of years ; according to the provisions of the new Act, the landlord would be bound to bring ejectment within twelve years of the determination of the tenancy. But suppose the tenant holds over with the consent of the landlord, who receives rent from the tenant, it would be absurd to contend that the landlord would be barred if he allowed the tenant to retain possession for a period of twelve years. The answer to such a contention would be, that there was a fresh contract between the parties, and

I conceive that the same answer would be given to a defence by the mortgagor founded on clause 135, the mortgagor having been all the while in possession with the assent of the mortgagee, who continued to receive the interest regularly. The word "first" may possibly create some difficulty, but it was probably introduced for the purpose of indicating clearly that it was not intended that the period should run from the end of the year of grace. (For Courts established by Royal Charter, see art. 149 of the Act.)

LECTURE VI.

Equity of redemption—Origin of expression—Position of mortgagor before foreclosure—Right to redeem—Bengal Regulation XVII of 1806—Recognized by Courts of Justices in other Provinces—Opinion of the Privy Council—*Puttaveramier* v. *Vencatta Row Naiker*—"Once a mortgage always a mortgage"—Meaning of maxim—Persons entitled to redeem—Regulation XVII of 1806—Practice of English Courts of Chancery—Mortgage security indivisible—Effect of mortgagees purchasing portion of mortgaged property—Contribution—Redemption under Bengal Regulations—Deposit or tender—What a good deposit—*Rukea Begum* v. *Prannath Roy Chowdry*—Time within which deposit must be made—Practice in Bombay and Madras—Limitation—Acknowledgment—Effect of acknowledgment by one of several mortgagees—Difference between English Statu te and Indian Act.

I NOW propose to call your attention to the position of the mortgagor before the mortgage is finally foreclosed, and the ownership of the pledge transferred from the debtor to the creditor. I have already pointed out that the mutual rights and obligations of the parties to a mortgage transaction are so closely interwoven with one another, that, in discussing the rights of the one, you necessarily suggest those of the other. There are, however, some points which will be more conveniently dealt with in the present lecture, and it is to these points that I shall confine myself.

The interest which resides in the mortgagor before foreclosure is known in this country by an expression borrowed from the English law — an expression which is open perhaps to more serious objection than others which we have borrowed from the same source. The interest of the mortgagor is known as the equity of redemption, or, as it is sometimes called, the right of redemption. Now, even the expression "right of redemption" is not wholly unexceptionable. It suggests the idea, in common with the kindred expression "equity of redemption," that the interest of the mortgagor is a bare right; something essentially different from what we call ownership, which is supposed to be vested in some other person who must be the mortgagee. It would, however, be more correct to say, that the ownership resides in the mortgagor notwithstanding the mortgage, the mortgagee acquiring by the contract only the right to foreclose. If we, however, examine the history of the English law of mortgage, we shall find that the expression "equity of redemption" first made its appearance at a time when the mortgagor was supposed to have parted with the estate retaining only the right of redemption or repurchase—a right, which being under the peculiar protection of equity, came to be known as the equity of redemption. The expression originally served to distinguish the interest of the mortgagor from the "estate" which was supposed to pass to the mortgagee. In

LECTURE VI. time, however, this right came to be regarded as an estate by the Courts of Chancery possessing all the incidents of an equitable estate in land. The original expression, however, was retained to denote the interest which remained in the mortgagor, although the nature of that interest had been greatly modified by the action of the English Courts of Equity. The expression "equity of redemption" is, therefore, an expression peculiar to the English law, and although its introduction into India may be regretted, it would be idle to protest against it at this time of day. I do not wish to be hypercritical, and I have made the foregoing observations, simply because I know of instances in which the whole discussion has been materially colored by notions, which would not have suggested themselves if the argument had not been conducted in the technical language of the English law.

The position of the mortgagor in possession has given rise in England to a good deal of, not altogether profitable, discussion, which, however, cannot find any place in our law. The mortgagor does not part with the ownership of the property by pledging it to his creditor by way of conditional sale, and his position before foreclosure does not differ in any material feature from that of the mortgagor by way of simple mortgage. It has been said (S. D., 1859, p. 1273), that the position of the mortgagor in possession is that of a trustee. He is not the absolute owner of the land, but holds it subject to the rights of the mortgagee. This proposition, however, must be received with considerable reserve. It is true that the indefinite power of dealing with a property which we call ownership is in some respects controlled by a mortgage, but I venture to think it is not an accurate use of language to say that the mortgagor becomes a trustee for the mortgagee.

From what I have already said, it must be clear to you that the mortgagor is competent to alienate the property notwithstanding the mortgage, although he cannot pass any greater interest than he himself possesses. The assignee must take subject to the rights of the mortgagee, who, in the event of a foreclosure, acquires the property free of all subsequent incumbrances. The mortgagor may either transfer the property absolutely, or create a second mortgage, subject, however, to the same limitation. It is hardly necessary to add that the interest of the mortgagor may be taken in execution, although the sale must be subject to the charge created in favor of the mortgagee. In short, the mortgagor is competent to deal with the property in any way he likes, so that the rights of the mortgagee are not defeated. I may add, that the mortgagor in possession is never liable to account for the rents and profits received by him. This is the law in England, and it also seems to be the law in this country. The mortgagor,

LECTURE VI. however, while in possession, must not do anything to impair the security of the mortgagee, and, as I have already said, there can be very little doubt that he will be restrained from committing wilful waste. (S. D., 1859, p. 1273.)

We have already seen that, notwithstanding the mutual agreement of the parties, the ownership does not pass from the mortgagor to the mortgagee immediately on default. The mortgagor, notwithstanding the default, continues to be the owner, or, to use the language of the English law, retains an equity of redemption, which may be successfully asserted against the mortgagee. I told you in the last lecture that this right was created for the first time in Bengal by Regulation XVII of 1806. No such provision is to be found in the statute law relating to the other Presidencies, but the doctrine of the English Court of Chancery, that the time stipulated in a mortgage is not of the essence of the contract, has been introduced into those provinces by the Courts of Justice as a rule founded in "equity and good conscience." In the case of *Puttaveramier* v. *Vencatta Row Naiker*, however, the Lords of the Privy Council observed, that, in the absence of any known rule of law, a Court of Justice is not at liberty to qualify the rights and obligations of the parties as defined by their mutual contract. "What is known in the law of England as 'the equity of redemption' depends on the doctrine established by Courts of Equity, that the time stipulated in the mortgage deed is not of the essence of the contract. Such a doctrine was unknown to the ancient law of India; and if it could have been introduced by the decisions of the Courts of the East Indian Company, their Lordships can find no such course of decision." (Per Colvile, Sir James, 13 Moo. Ind. App., 560; S. C., B. L. R., 136; 15 W. R., P. C., 37.) Their Lordships, however, concluded by observing,—" It must not then be supposed that, in allowing this appeal, their Lordships design to disturb any rule of property established by judicial decisions so as to form part of the law of the forum, wherever such may prevail, or to affect any title founded thereon." Since this judgment was delivered by the Privy Council, the question again came before the High Courts of Bombay and Madras, but the learned Judges thought that a rule of property had been established in those provinces by judicial decisions which ought not to be disturbed, and which the Privy Council never designed to disturb. (*Shankarbhai Gulabbhai* v. *Kassibhai Vithalbhai*, 9 Bom., 69; *Lakshmi Chelliah Garee* v. *Krisha Bhupati Devi*, 7 Mad., 6.) LECTURE VI.

We thus find that, in nearly all the provinces of this country, the debtor retains a right to redeem, which is not extinguished by the non-payment of the money on the appointed day. This right is very jealously guarded, and in England a large number of maxims have clustered round it. One of these is the well-known proposition "once a mortgage always a mortgage." This maxim requires some explanation, as the language in which it is expressed is likely to mislead the student. It means that no agreement of the parties should control the right of redemption, but then it has reference only to stipulations entered into *at the time* of the mortgage, and not to agreements entered into subsequently; and, as I shall presently explain, there is good reason for this distinction. Any agreement, therefore, at the time of the mortgage, by which the right of redemption is limited, either as to the persons entitled to redeem, or the period within which the right must be exercised, is wholly inoperative. Thus, for instance, if the mortgagor should agree that the right to redeem shall be confined to his life, his heirs after his death will be permitted to redeem. In fact, no limitation can be successfully imposed on the mortgagor's equity of redemption, a right which the law will not suffer to be clogged or fettered even with the assent of the mortgagor.

The maxim "once a mortgage always a mortgage" is a logical corollary to the doctrine which is the very foundation of the law of mortgages, that time is not of the essence of the contract in such transactions. The protection which the law throws round the mortgagor would be wholly illusory if the mortgagee were permitted to restrict the right of redemption within such limits as he might choose to impose on the mortgagor. The debtor, who agrees to forfeit his property if the money is not paid on the appointed day, might be easily induced by the creditor to waive the benefit which the law has secured to him, and this accounts for the jealousy with which the right of redemption is guarded in every system of jurisprudence. There is a curious case which you will find in the English books, in which the mortgagor was permitted to redeem, although he had solemnly sworn never to exercise the right. To the general rule that a mortgagee shall not derive any collateral advantage from his mortgage, English lawyers recognise one exception. An agreement securing to the creditor a right of pre-emption of the equity of redemption is regarded as valid by the English Court of Chancery. I am not, however, aware of any case in which the doctrine has been followed in India.

I have already said, that the rule directed against any attempt to fetter the equity of redemption applies only to agreements made at the time of the mortgage, as the law presumes that the debtor is then completely at the mercy of the creditor, who, unless restrained by the law, might impose his own terms, however exorbitant. The parties are at liberty to contract with one another, in any manner they please, after the execution of the mortgage, although

LECTURE VI. such transactions are not, on other grounds, viewed with favor by a Court of Justice. The distinction, however, between transactions at the time of the mortgage, and those subsequent to the mortgage, is extremely important, and must be carefully borne in mind. I have heard it seriously argued that a mortgagee may not buy in the equity of redemption, and that, except by the process of foreclosure, he cannot become the absolute owner of the pledge. This would, however, be an unjustifiable extension of the maxim, suggested probably by the language in which it is frequently expressed. There is another familiar maxim in connection with the subject—"he who seeks equity must do equity;" but I reserve the discussion of this maxim for another lecture.

I propose to discuss in the next place the persons who are entitled to redeem. Now it may be laid down generally that not only the mortgagor himself, but also any person having an interest in, or lien on, the property, is entitled to redeem. As a judgment debt in this country does not create in itself a charge on land, it is doubtful if a judgment-creditor, merely as such, has a right of redemption. He has, however, only to attach the property, and as an attachment operates as a statutory hypothecation, the attaching creditor acquires the right to redeem the mortgage. The point was substantially decided in the case of Mohun Lall Sukul, to which I have already had occasion to refer.

I need hardly add that the right of redemption may be claimed by the heir or devisee of the mortgagor, and, generally speaking, by any person who, either by voluntary or involuntary assignment, succeeds to the whole or a portion of the rights of the mortgagor in the whole or a portion of the mortgaged property.

This is the present state of the law in Bengal, which has been gradually built up on the provisions of the 17th Regulation of 1806, which impose upon the mortgagee the necessity of serving the foreclosure proceedings upon the "mortgagor or his legal representative," an expression which, as we have already seen, has been held by judicial interpretation to embrace every person who claims an interest in the mortgaged property.

There is no statutory enactment in the other provinces, but the law, as it is administered at the present day by the Courts of Justice, is, in this respect, substantially the same as in Bengal.

The question has been raised in the Calcutta High Court, but, so far as I am aware, not yet decided, whether a lessee, claiming under a beneficial lease created after the mortgage, is entitled to redeem. The English law permits the lessee to redeem (*Keech* v. *Hall*, 1 Smith, L. C., 523), and there is little doubt that this ruling will be followed in India. The expression "legal representative," if wide enough to include an attaching creditor, is

25

LECTURE VI. surely large enough to embrace a tenant claiming under a beneficial lease.

It is necessary to observe that a mortgage security is indivisible, and that no one is entitled to redeem a part of the estate in mortgage on payment of a proportionate amount of the debt secured by the mortgage; you must either redeem the whole, or not at all. Thus, if four brothers, each of whom is entitled to a fourth share of an estate, mortgage it to a creditor as security for a debt contracted by them, one of the brothers cannot redeem his share on payment of a fourth part of the debt secured by the mortgage. He would, no doubt, have a right to redeem the whole, but he cannot redeem a part, although there may be no question as to the extent of his share. If, however, any one or more of several joint mortgagors redeem the whole estate, he will be entitled to possession and receipt of the whole of the rents subject to account with his co-mortgagors. (Macpherson, p. 112; Fisher's Mort., § 304.)

You will, no doubt, find in the books several cases in which a mortgagor has been permitted to bring a suit for redemption of a portion of the mortgaged property, on the allegation that the whole of the debt secured by the mortgage has been satisfied. These cases, however, are no exception to the rule that a mortgage debt is indivisible, for, in the cases to which I refer, there is no longer any debt due to the mortgagee. (*Hurdeo* v. *Ganeshee Lall*, 1 Agra, 3; see also 1 Agra, 36; 4 Agra, 33.) It would not, however, be always safe to bring such an action, and the co-mortgagors should, if possible, be placed on the record as defendants if they refuse to join in the action; and, although the plaintiff might sue for his own share, the suit ought to be brought in the Court which would have jurisdiction over the whole of the subject-matter. (*Unnoda Persaud Roy* v. *Erskine & Co.*, 21 W. R., 68.) If a different rule were laid down, the mortgagee might be harassed by twenty different suits, and although the language used by the Court in some reported cases is not free from ambiguity, I venture to think that it was never intended to lay down the broad proposition that one of several mortgagors could sue without making his co-mortgagors party defendants.

Cases in which the interests of the mortgagors appear to be distinct and separate on the face of instrument are sometimes supposed to form an exception to the rule that a mortgage security is indivisible. There is, however, no foundation for the notion except some carelessly reported dicta in *Mulik Basab* v. *Dhana Bebee* (5 N. W. P., 220). It is true an instrument may be so worded that each of the mortgagors may redeem his share on payment of a rateable portion of the mortgage debt, but such a clause is seldom, if ever, found in a

LECTURE VI. mortgage deed, and cannot safely be inferred merely from a recital of the different shares of the mortgagors in the document.

To the general rule, however, that a mortgage must be redeemed entirely or not at all, there is one exception, and that is where the equity of redemption in a portion of the mortgaged property becomes vested in the mortgagee himself. In such cases the mortgage security is broken up, and the mortgagor or his representatives become entitled to redeem on payment of a proportionate part of the debt charged on the property. Thus, where two villages were mortgaged by the same instrument as security for one sum, and they were both subsequently sold under an execution against the mortgagor, and one of them was purchased by the mortgagee himself, and the other by a third person, the execution-purchaser was allowed to redeem on paying a proportionate part of the mortgage debt. As pointed out by Morgan, C.J., in giving the judgment of the Court in *Mahtab Singh* v. *Misree Lall*, — "A mortgagee is entitled to say to each of several persons who may have succeeded to the mortgagor's interest, that he shall not be entitled to redeem a part of the property on payment of part of the debt, because the whole and every part of the land mortgaged is liable for the whole debt. But it does not follow from this, that a mortgagee, who has acquired by purchase a part of the mortgagor's rights and interests, is entitled to throw the whole burden of the mortgage debt on the remaining portion of the equity of redemption in the hands of one who has purchased it at a sale in execution of a decree against the mortgagor. Each has bought subject to a proportionate share of the burden, and must discharge it." (2 Agra, 88; see also *Nathu Sahu* v. *Lalla Ameer Chund*, 24 W. R., 24.)

These cases, however, must be carefully distinguished from another class of cases with which they may be easily confounded. The principle laid down in *Mahtab Singh* v. *Misree Lall* (2 Agra, 88) will not apply to a case in which the equity of redemption of a portion of the mortgaged property becomes vested in one or more of several mortgagees, and the reason of this distinction is obvious. Where the whole estate as to one portion of the pledged property becomes vested in the mortgagee, or in all the mortgagees, if there are more than one, the mortgagor, if compelled to redeem on condition of paying the whole debt, would have an action for contribution for the excess payment, and thus two suits would be necessary in the place of one for the purpose of attaining the same end. This reason, however, which is founded only upon convenience, does not hold good where the purchaser happens to be one of several mortgagees. In such a case the other mortgagees

LECTURE VI. could not be sued for contribution, and they might very reasonably complain if by the acts of one of them the indivisible nature of the security was altered. Where, therefore, one of several mortgagees purchases a part of the property mortgaged, the case is governed by the general rule, and the purchaser of another part has no right to redeem except on payment of the whole of the mortgage debt. (*Sobha Sah* v. *Inderjeet*, 5 All., 149.)

We have seen that when the mortgagee, or if there are more than one, all of them jointly purchase the equity of redemption of a part of the mortgaged property, they cannot insist upon the payment of the whole of the debt secured by the mortgage as a condition of the redemption of the rest of the mortgaged property. Questions, however, of considerable difficulty sometimes arise when the equity of redemption of a portion becoming vested in the mortgagee, that of the rest passes to two or more different persons. In the case of *Nowab Ahmed Ali Khan* v. *Jowhir Sing*, the estate having been sold subject to mortgage to different persons, one of them being the mortgagee himself, a purchaser of a portion of the mortgaged property sought to redeem his share on payment of a rateable part of the mortgage debt. The purchasers of the other portions were not parties to the suit, and the mortgagee insisting that the plaintiff could not succeed without an offer to redeem the portion which had passed to the other purchasers, the Court refused to make any decree for redemption, being of opinion that the mortgagee had a right to insist upon the redemption of the whole of the property, with the exception of that purchased by himself, on payment of a proportionate part of the mortgage debt. (N. W. P., 1864, 425.)

You will observe that all that the Court ruled in the above case was, that the plaintiff was *bound to offer* to redeem the whole of the estate with the exception of that purchased by the defendant, and not that he was *entitled* to do so if the mortgagee should refuse to part with the shares of the other persons. The distinction is important, and is well illustrated by the judgment of the Privy Council in the subsequent suit for redemption between the same parties, in which the plaintiff claimed to redeem the whole of the mortgaged property with the exception of that which had passed to the mortgagee. The defendant, while conceding to the plaintiff the right to redeem the portion which had been purchased by him, resisted his right to redeem the rest. The Court below being of opinion that the mortgagee could not be permitted to turn round after having "forced the plaintiff to bring the second suit," made a decree for redemption in the terms of the prayer in the plaint. (*Nawab Ahmed Ali Khan* v. *Jowhir Sing*, 1 Agra, 3.) From this decree there was an appeal to the Privy Council

LECTURE VI. when the mortgagee again insisted upon his right to retain possession of that portion of the estate which had not been purchased by the plaintiff. Their Lordships observed:—"The remaining question is what, upon the facts found by the Courts below, ought to have been their decree. The appellant now complains that the plaintiffs have been allowed to redeem as against him the villages other than their own village of Hosseinpore, *i.e.*, to put themselves in his shoes as mortgagee in respect of these villages; and further, that the decrees were wrong in refusing to treat him as the owner under a subsequent purchase of three-fourths of Rookumpore.

" The first objection does not come with a good grace from the appellant, who defeated the plaintiffs' former suit, on the ground that they had not offered to redeem the villages in question, and who, in this very suit, has included in his calculation of the amount, which, as he alleges, ought to have been brought into Court, the shares of the mortgage debt which he said were chargeable on those villages. The Courts below, however, seem to their Lordships to have mistaken the effect of the former decision of the Sudder Court. It merely ruled that the plaintiffs were bound to offer to redeem the villages in question; it did not rule that they were entitled to do so, or to acquire the interest of the mortgagee in them against his will. It is unnecessary to determine in this suit whether, in the peculiar circumstances of this case, the former proposition is correct. Their Lordships are of opinion that the latter cannot be supported. They think that the appellant, if desirous of retaining possession of these villages as mortgagee, is entitled to do so against the plaintiffs, whose right in that case is limited to the redemption and recovery of their village of Hosseinpore upon payment of so much of the sum deposited in Court as represents the portion of the mortgage debt chargeable on that village." (13 Moo. Ind. App., 404; S. C., 14 W. R., P. C., 20.)

You will observe that the Judicial Committee refused to express any opinion as to the correctness or otherwise of the proposition laid down by the Sudder Dewany Adalut in the previous suit. The latter ruling, however, has since been followed by our Courts, and it certainly does not seem to be open to any serious objection. (4 All., 92.) A mortgagee, by purchasing a portion of the mortgaged property, does no doubt destroy the indivisible character of his security to a certain extent; but it would be going too far to hold that the indivisibility of the debt was absolutely destroyed, so that any one of the other persons interested in the equity of redemption might be let in to redeem on payment of the proportion of the debt attributable to the portion in which he might be interested. To take a simple case, suppose two brothers execute a mortgage of their property. If one of the brothers

LECTURE VI. should die leaving three sons, and the other brother should sell his share in the mortgaged property to the mortgagee, I do not think any one of these sons could redeem his share without offering to redeem the shares of the other representatives of the deceased mortgagor.

The foregoing observations are applicable to all kinds of securities. In cases of conditional sales governed by the Bengal Regulations, it may, however, be doubted how far these general principles can be given effect to, the language of the Regulations being curt and applicable only to the more common cases. In the absence of any direct authority, I do not wish to hazard any opinion on the point.

I shall now proceed to consider the method by which redemption may be accomplished, and I propose, in the first instance, to state the law as it is administered in this Presidency. Now the mortgagor may either assert his right of redemption actively, or he may be proceeded against by the mortgagee seeking to foreclose, when the mortgagor may prevent a foreclosure by the repayment of the debt within a limited time. For reasons which are obvious, except when the mortgagee is in possession, a mortgagor seldom, if ever, takes any steps to redeem the mortgage till the mortgagee applies for foreclosure. Section 7 of Regulation XVII of 1806, however, applies as well to cases in which the mortgagee is in possession as to those in which the mortgagor has never parted with the possession of the pledge. That section provides, that "when the mortgagee may have obtained possession of the land on execution of the mortgage deed, or at any time before a final foreclosure of the mortgage, the payment or established tender of the sum lent under any such deed of mortgage and conditional sale, or of the balance due, if any part of the principal amount shall have been discharged,—or, when the mortgagee may not have been put in possession of the mortgaged property, the payment or established tender of the principal sum lent with any interest due thereupon, shall entitle the mortgagor and owner of such property or his legal representative of the redemption of his property." Instead, however, of paying or tendering the money to the mortgagee, the debtor may deposit the money in the Dewany Adalut of the zillah in which the property is situated.

In the last lecture I had occasion to refer in some detail to the provisions of the 8th section of Regulation XVII of 1806, which relates to foreclosure. That very section points out the method by which a foreclosure may be prevented, and the redemption of the mortgage accomplished, by the mortgagor. When an application for foreclosure is made, the mortgagor is bound to pay to the mortgagee, or to deposit in the Dewany Adawlut the principal, or the balance, if any part of the principal shall have been paid, together with interest, if possession has not been taken by the mortgagor. Now the tender or deposit, in order to be good, must be unconditional. It must not be made in such a way as that its acceptance will impose a condition upon the creditor, or supply evidence of an admission that no more is due than the amount tendered or deposited; and I need hardly add, that, as it is the very essence of a tender that the person to whom it is made should be at liberty to take the money at once, a deposit under the Regulation, which takes the place of a tender, must necessarily be bad if accompanied by a protest that the money should not be paid away to the mortgagee immediately. (*Goluckmonee Debea* v. *Nobongomonjoree Debea*, Suth. F. B., 14. See also S. D. A., 1847, p. 462; S. D. A., 1848, p. 897; S. D. A., 1859, p. 352.)

A somewhat different question arises when the deposit, instead of being clogged with any condition, is merely accompanied by a protest that the money is not due, and that the mortgage deed is invalid. The question actually arose in the case of *Prannath Chowdhry* v. *Rookea Begum*, which was heard in the last resort by the Privy Council, when their Lordships held that such a deposit is bad. In delivering the judgment of the Board, Lord Kingsdown said :—
"The remaining objection relates to the payment into Court, in the nature of a tender, which was made by the defendant Ramruttun Roy. Ramruttun Roy

directed the money to be paid out to the appellant, but at the same time, in his petition to the Court, he disputed the validity of the appellant's title to foreclosure, and expressed an intention, amounting to a notice, to sue the appellant to recover back the very money which he was tendering.

"The meaning of the direction that the money may be paid into Court clearly is, that the mortgagor may have adequate and lasting evidence of that which is put in place of a tender, and the mortgagee the security and advantage of a deposit in acknowledgment of the title. The mortgagee would have little inducement to take the money, waiving his lien by its acceptance, if litigation on the very same subject were to recommence upon the acceptance of the money; and though mere words, in the form of a protest, which may accompany a tender, will not defeat, where they can reasonably be regarded as idle words, their Lordships think that the proceedings of Ramruttun Roy with respect to the mortgagee's title to foreclosure forbid such an interpretation of his language and his act." (7 Moo. Ind. App., 323. See also *Abdar Ruhman* v. *Kisto Lall Ghose*, 6 W. R., 225.)

I may mention that this decision has been criticised a good deal. But although at first sight it may seem to treat a tender with a threat that the money is not due as a conditional tender, the judgment really proceeds upon the ground that the

LECTURE VI.

Indian Regulations contemplate cases in which the relation of mortgagor and mortgagee is undisputed, and that section 7 of Regulation XVII of 1806 was not intended to apply to a case in which an alleged mortgagor makes, under protest, a tender of money upon a mortgage, the validity of which he refuses to acknowledge.

We now come to the time within which the money must be tendered or deposited. Now, the Regulation, as you will observe, allows one year from the date of the 'notification.' It is now, however, settled, so far at least as the Calcutta High Court is concerned, that the statutory period runs only from the date of the service, and not of the mere issue of the notice. This was decided in the case of *Mohesh Chunder Sein* v. *Mussamut Tarinee* (10 W. R., 27, F. B.) The Court, however, refused to say from what point of time the period should run when the mortgagor cannot be served. There can, however, be little doubt, that where substituted service is permitted, the period would run from the date of such substituted service. I may mention that, in calculating the year of grace, the date on which the service is effected is excluded. (*Mohesh Chunder Sein* v. *Tarinee*, 10 W. R., F. B., 27; S. C., 1 B. L. R., F. B., 14.) It would appear that, in the Allahabad Court, the year is still reckoned from the date of the *issue* of the notice. (*Gazeeudeen* v. *Bhookhun Dhobee*, 3 All., 301.)

We have seen that the mortgagor is at liberty either to tender the money to the borrower, or to deposit it in Court within the statutory period of one year. If, however, the Court be closed on the day on which the year of grace expires, a deposit cannot be properly made on the first day on which the Court reopens. In order to save the equity of redemption it must be made strictly within the year allowed by the Regulation, and the rule would seem to be the same as well when the Court is closed accidentally and unexpectedly, as when it is closed during an authorized vacation. In the case of mortgages the law allows the mortgagor an alternative, and if he prefer, for his own security, to deposit the money in the Zillah Court, he must avail himself of the privilege at a time when it is within his reach. As observed by the Court in a recent case:—"If we were to hold otherwise, we should be allowing the mortgagor to extend the year of grace at pleasure. He might say, 'If I pay the money to the mortgagor, I must do it within one year; but if I pay it into Court, I shall have thirteen or fourteen months.'" (*Komala Kant Mytee* v. *Narainee Dossee*, 9 W. R., 583.)

The class of cases of which the above is an illustration must be carefully distinguished from those in which, by an agreement between the mortgagor and mortgagee, the time for payment is extended beyond the statutory period, and owing

LECTURE VI. to the unexpected closing of the Court, the deposit cannot be made within the time fixed by the parties. This was decided in the case of *Davi Rawoot* v. *Heeramon Mahatoon*, in which the mortgagee having extended the time for repayment to the 25th of November 1863, on which day the Court was unexpectedly closed, the mortgagor deposited the money on the first day on which the Court reopened, and the question arose whether the deposit was made in time to save the equity of redemption. The Court held that the deposit was good, but in giving judgment the Chief Justice, Sir Barnes Peacock, made certain observations which were certainly not necessary to the decision of the case, and are perhaps open to criticism. The learned Chief Justice is reported to have said:—"The day fixed for payment to prevent a foreclosure of the estate was not a day peremptorily fixed by the law, but a day fixed by the mortgagee himself. Now Courts of Equity, as a general rule, will relieve from forfeiture caused by not doing an act on a day fixed by the parties; and I think they ought also to relieve when the day is fixed by law, and the act is prevented by some accident which the person to be affected by the forfeiture could not prevent, and which was not caused by any default or misconduct on his part. Courts of Equity will not allow a lessor to forfeit a lease, because the rent is not paid on a particular day." Now, although Courts of Equity are always willing to relieve against forfeitures caused by the non-performance of an act on the day fixed by the parties, I do not believe that there is any instance of the exercise of such power when the time is appointed by statute. Indeed, it is difficult to see how such a power could be exercised without trenching on the province of the Legislature, and any argument from analogy would be simply misleading. Take the Statute of Limitations for instance: I do not think it could be contended for a moment that if the plaintiff was prevented by some unforeseen accident, without any default on his part, from suing in time, that a Court of Justice would be justified in receiving his plaint. I should, therefore, venture to think that where the period for doing the act is fixed by law, the person who would be affected by the non-performance must perform it within the statutory period at his peril.

There is another observation of Sir Barnes Peacock which would also seem to be open to question. The learned Judge says,—"I should hold that the plaintiff has the option, either of depositing the money in the Judge's Court, or of tendering it; and that if there is a sufficient excuse for not depositing it in the Judge's Court, he is not bound to tender the money and prove that tender." (8 W. R., 223.) Now, although the mortgagor may not be bound to tender the money to the mortgagee, he should certainly deposit it in Court at a time when

LECTURE VI. it is within his reach to do so. The case may be a very hard one when the Court is closed unexpectedly, but the mortgagor who defers paying till the last moment, perhaps does not deserve much pity.

It very frequently happens that the mortgagee, during the currency of the year of grace, allows an extended period to the mortgagor to repay the debt. In such cases the mortgagor must take care to tender or deposit the money within the limited period, otherwise the mortgage would be foreclosed at the expiration of the time. (*Goonomonee Dassee* v. *Parbutty Dassee*, 10 W. R., 326.)

I have said that the mortgagor may, without waiting till the mortgagee attempts to foreclose, take steps for the purpose of redeeming the mortgage, a right which may be exercised even before the stipulated period. Under the Regulations the mortgagor may, on deposit of the principal in cases in which the mortgagee has been in possession, call upon the Court to restore the possession of the property to him, subject, however, to an adjustment of accounts between the parties. (Section 2, Regulation I of 1798.) If, however, a less sum is deposited, the mortgagor cannot get back into possession except under a decree in a regular suit, in which any question of right between the parties may be regularly brought before, and determined by, the Courts of Civil Justice.

In provinces to which the Bengal Regulations do

not apply, the mortgagor may, at any time before foreclosure and after default, bring a suit for redemption against the mortgagee, when the Court takes an account of the amount due on the mortgage security, and allows the mortgagor a certain period, usually six months, to pay the money. If, however, the mortgagor fail to pay the money within the appointed time, the equity of redemption is foreclosed precisely in the same manner as if the mortgagee had got a decree for foreclosure. This is the practice in the English Court of Chancery, and is followed in Bombay and Madras. In Bengal and the North-West the law on this point cannot be said to be quite settled. I shall, however, discuss the point at some length in the next lecture, in which I propose to treat of usufructuary mortgages.

I now come to the time within which, under the Statute of Limitations, the right of redemption must be asserted. The provisions of the present law are substantially the same as those of Act XIV of 1859, and I shall, therefore, confine myself to the later statute. Now Article 148, Schedule 2, Act IX of 1871, provides a period of sixty years, commencing from the date of the mortgage, unless where an acknowledgment of the title of the mortgagor or of his right of redemption has, before the expiration of the prescribed period, been made in writing signed by the mortgagee or some person claiming under him, and in such case from the date of the acknowledgment.

LECTURE VI.

In the case, however, of a purchase for value and in good faith from the mortgagee, the suit must be brought within twelve years from the date of the purchase. (As to the meaning of the words "purchaser for value and in good faith," see the case of *Radhanath Dass* v. *Gisborne and Co.*, 14 Moo. In. App., 1; S. C., 15 W. R., P. C., 24.) It is true there is no provision in Act IX of 1871 similar to the proviso contained in section 5 of the previous Act, by which the mortgagor was bound to sue the purchaser within the time limited to a suit for redemption, but there can be no doubt that the mortgagor will not, under the new Act, have an extended period against the purchaser from the mortgagee. The proviso in section 5 was probably inserted out of excessive caution.

It is necessary to observe that the period of sixty years allowed to the mortgagor is wholly irrespective of the nature of the title which the mortgagee in possession may assert. The enactment itself is a departure from the rule that derivative possession is inoperative for purposes of prescription; and I know of no principle on which, the law being silent, we should be justified in holding that a derivative possessor could, by his own act, change the character of his possession so as to shorten the period of limitation. But even if there was any doubt upon the language of the Act, the fact that the period may be extended by an acknowledgment shows, that the assertion by the mortgagee in possession of a hostile title would not have the effect of abridging the time fixed by the statute. As pointed out by Mr. Justice Holloway in *Tauji* v. *Nagamma* (3 Mad., 137), the period may be extended by an acknowledgment, but by no process can it be curtailed. I must, however, confess that this view is perhaps not quite consistent with certain reported decisions of the Calcutta High Court. I shall only notice one of these cases, not only because it was decided by a very eminent Judge, but also because it seems to have been the first case in which it was laid down that the period of sixty years may, under certain conditions, be curtailed. In *Loft Hussen* v. *Abdul Ali* (8 W. R., 476), Mr. Justice Dwarkanath Mitter is reported to have held that where more than twelve years had expired from the date of the expiration of the year of grace, the mortgagor lost his right of redemption. It was found in the case as a fact that the foreclosure proceedings were regular, and the Court seems to have thought that the mortgagor was bound to assert his right of redemption within twelve years of the expiration of the statutory year of grace. I must, however, confess that I do not understand the reasoning by which the proposition is maintained. A plea founded upon the statute always assumes that the plaintiff has the right which he claims, but that he cannot be permitted to assert the right successfully in a Court of Justice by reason of lapse of time. This being so, I do not see how any proceedings taken by the mortgagee for the purpose of foreclosure could have any other effect given to them than as evidence of a determination by the mortgagee to hold possession, not derivatively as pledgee, but absolutely as owner. But, as I have already endeavoured to explain, the assertion of a hostile title by the mortgagee cannot curtail the period of sixty years which the statute allows to the mortgagor to redeem his property.

It may be suggested that the clause which allows a period of sixty years from the date of the mortgage applies only to cases in which no particular period is fixed for the redemption of the property; and the fact that the period on any other construction would begin to run even before the accrual of the right to redeem, as also when the possession of the mortgagee was perfectly consistent with the intentions of the parties, might perhaps lend some support to the suggestion. But there is no authority for such a limited construction, and the Privy Council, in *Luchmi Bux Roy* v. *Runjit Ram Panday* (20 W. R., 375), held, that the section applies to all descriptions of mortgages.

I shall now proceed to discuss the nature of the acknowledgment required to extend the period. Now, in the first place, it must be in writing and signed by the mortgagee or some person claiming under him. An acknowledgment, therefore, which is only sealed or signed, not by the mortgagee, but by an agent, would be insufficient. It is, however, not necessary that the acknowledgment should be made to the mortgagor or his representative, and on this point our law differs from the English law on the subject.

You will observe that, by the clause in question, there may be an acknowledgment of the title of the mortgagor or of a right to redeem. An acknowledgment that a certain person is the owner of an estate, is an acknowledgment of the title of that person; while an acknowledgment that the mortgage is subsisting, would be an acknowledgment of a right to redeem which might be availed of by the person entitled to the property. It is not, therefore, necessary that the person entitled to the equity of redemption should be mentioned in the acknowledgment. This was decided in the recent case of *Daia Chand* v. *Sarfraz* (Indian Law Reports, Allahabad Series, 117) by a Full Bench of the Allahabad High Court, who were of opinion that a statement in a record of rights made by a Settlement Officer, that the persons in possession were mortgagees, and signed by the alleged mortgagees, was sufficient to take the case out of the statute. The English law also does not require an express acknowledgment; and any expression referring to the estate as mortgaged will be sufficient.

LECTURE VI.

I have not been able to find any other Indian case in which the nature of the acknowledgment required for the purpose of enlarging the period of limitation has been discussed; and it may, therefore, I think, be useful to refer to certain English cases in which the question was raised. In one case it appears that the solicitor of the mortgagor wrote to the mortgagee requesting to know when he could see the mortgagee upon the subject of the mortgage, and the mortgagee in reply wrote to say,—"I do not see the use of a meeting unless some one is ready to pay me off." It was held by the Court that this was a sufficient acknowledgment in writing to exclude the statute. (3 DeG., Mac. & G., 620.)

An offer by the mortgagee to purchase the equity of redemption has also been held to be a sufficient acknowledgment of the right to redeem; while in an old case, which, however, has never been questioned, it was held, that where the mortgagee described an estate in his will as his "mortgaged estate," there was an acknowledgment sufficient to take the case out of the statute. (See the cases cited in White and Tudor's notes to *Howard* v. *Harris*, pp. 886-891.) I might mention other cases in which the English Courts have permitted the mortgagor to redeem after the expiration of the statutory period on the basis of an acknowledgment; but the above, I think, will show how the Court will seize even the slightest act or expression of the mortgagee as an acknowledgment of the right to redeem. LECTURE VI.

I would conclude by calling your attention to a somewhat remarkable difference between our law and the English statute on which our own is certainly modelled. Our Act speaks of an acknowledgment by the mortgagee; but suppose there are two or more mortgagees, and one of them only makes the acknowledgment, would such an acknowledgment be sufficient to take a case out of the statute against both or either of them ? The English Act expressly provides that such an acknowledgment will hold good but only against the mortgagee by whom an acknowledgment may have been made. Our Act is wholly silent, although section 20 provides that an acknowledgment by one of several debtors shall not have the effect of enlarging the period against his co-debtors. Having regard to the way in which our Acts are frequently drawn, it would not be safe to raise any inference upon the omission of any such clause in the article under consideration. The case may be merely one of omission. There is, however, no reported case on the point, and I do not think it necessary to offer any opinion on it one way or the other.

LECTURE VII.

Usufructuary mortgage—What constitutes usufructuary mortgages—Personal liability of mortgagor—Zuripeshgee leases—Difference between Zuripeshgee and ordinary leases—Hanuman Persad Pandey's case—Origin of Zuripeshgee leases—Rights and liabilities of usufructuary mortgagee before and after repeal of Usury Laws—Liability to account—Right of redemption of mortgagor—Simple usufructuary mortgagee not entitled to decree for sale—Limitation.

A USUFRUCTUARY mortgage is a very common form of security in this country. The creditor is put into possession of the mortgaged property, the rents and profits being applied either to the discharge of the interest alone, or to the gradual reduction of both principal and interest according to the agreement of the parties. No formal words are necessary to constitute a usufructuary mortgage, although in this, as in other cases, inartificially drawn instruments not seldom give rise to much useless litigation. In one case, in which a sum of money being advanced, the person making the advance was put into the receipt of the rents and profits of certain land belonging to the debtor, it was contended that the transaction was not a mortgage, but a mere license to the creditor to receive the rents which might be revoked at any time by the debtor. The Court, however, held otherwise, and directed the creditor to render an account of his receipts as mortgagee in possession. (*Khusul Rai* v. *Jankee Dass*, 2 Alla., 9.) LECTURE VII.

A very familiar kind of usufructuary mortgage is one in which the profits are enjoyed by the creditor in lieu of interest, the debtor being entitled at any time to redeem the property on payment of the principal. It closely resembles a Welch mortgage in its incidents. Another form of usufructuary mortgage is that in which the creditor is let into possession on the understanding that he is to enjoy the usufruct till the whole debt is gradually liquidated. This kind of security resembles the *vivum vadium* of the English law, a form of mortgage which, although once common, has now fallen into disuse in England. The mortgagor, however, instead of mortgaging his whole estate, may mortgage it for a term of years, and there is one kind of usufructuary mortgage by means of a lease, known as a zuripeshgee, which forms a class by itself, and deserves careful consideration. I shall explain hereafter the origin and nature of this remarkable class of usufructuary mortgages which possesses a history of its own very interesting to the student of law. But before I do so, I wish to point out that it is not always easy to say whether a transaction is to be viewed as a mortgage, or simply as a lease. I can only ask you to consult the cases on the point, and the only rule

Lecture VII. — that can be safely extracted from them is, that the intention of the parties must be looked into, and that when "once you get a debt with the security of land for its repayment, then the arrangement is a mortgage by whatever name it is called." In the case of *Masuk Amin Suzzada* against *Marem Reddy* (8 Mad., 34), where, by the terms of the arrangement, a pending suit was compromised, and the payment of a balance ascertained to be due was secured by the creditor being allowed to occupy the land for fifty-five years at a fixed rent, of which, after deduction of a certain sum for the maintenance of the debtor, the rest was to be applied to the gradual reduction of the debt, which it was calculated would be satisfied in full in 55 years, the Court held that the transaction was a mortgage, and that the parties in providing for the gradual liquidation of the debt, did not intend to put an end to the relation of debtor and creditor, and that, upon a true construction of the document, it created only a mortgage security. Now, compare the above case with the case of *Baboo Kowar Sing* v. *Dullun Amrit Koer* (S. D., 1857, p. 1232), in which there was a lease for twelve years, the lessee advancing a certain sum of money to the lessor, and it being provided that the lessor should be entitled to re-enter on the expiration of the term, the lessee taking his chance of good and bad seasons. It was argued that the transaction was in substance a mortgage, and that the lessee was bound to account as mortgagee in possession. The contention, however, was overruled. The Court, in giving judgment, observed :—"The point to consider is, whether there was a fair and reasonable prospect of risk to the debt itself in what the banker (mortgagee) undertook; and, if so, no question of usury can arise out of it, and for the same reason the possession of the lessee cannot be regarded as that of a mortgagee." . . . . . "We think that the deed of Bhurun ijara before us is, in fact, an absolute sale of a lease for a fixed period to which the rules common to mortgage transactions cannot be applied, as the extinction of the original debt is not solely dependent on the receipt of adequate profits, but on profits, whatever they may be, during the continuance of the lease. Should they fail, the debt is neither realizable from, nor secured by, any other resources. This is no device but a substantial risk, entitling the lender to any benefit from the bargain." LECTURE VII.

It is sometimes said that where the principal is risked, the transaction cannot be regarded as other than a lease. This, however, is by no means generally true, and there may be usufructuary mortgages for terms of years, although the parties may expressly covenant that the creditor shall have no claim against the debtor, either for principal or for interest, after the expiration of the prescribed period. It would be impossible to say that the

LECTURE VII. principal was not risked in such cases, but there are several instances in our books, in which such transactions have been regarded as mortgages redeemable on the usual terms.

It would seem that in a pure usufructuary mortgage, where the mortgagee takes possession of the estate, on the understanding that he shall repay himself out of the rents and profits, the mortgagor undertakes no personal liability, and the mortgagee must, therefore, look exclusively to the land for the repayment of the debt. In the case of *Thaku Beebee* (S. D. A., 1850, p. 44), which has since been followed, the Sudder Dewany of Calcutta held that, in the absence of any covenant, the mortgagor cannot be sued personally. A doubt, however, has been thrown upon this doctrine by the observations of the Privy Council in the case of *Jugjewan Dass* v. *Ramdass Brijbhukun Dass* (2 Moo. Ind. App., 487; S. C., 6 W. R., p. 610.) In that case the mortgage deed contained a clause that the mortgagee should continue to enjoy and appropriate the annual produce till the whole debt was liquidated. Their Lordships observed that the mortgagee would have a full right to recover this debt by reason of the mortgage, and that the clause in question was merely a power for the mortgagee to satisfy himself just as an English mortgagee may by taking possession of the rents and profits. The case, however, can hardly be regarded as an authority for the proposition, that in every pure usufructuary mortgage, the mortgagor incurs a personal obligation to repay the debt. There is a distinction between an English mortgage, with a power reserved to the mortgagee to enter upon possession and satisfy himself out of the rents and profits, and a usufructuary mortgage in this country where there is no covenant by the mortgagor for the repayment of the loan. I have already had occasion to point out that in India there is no implied personal obligation in a mortgage by conditional sale, and the same distinction would also seem to hold good in the case of usufructuary mortgages. I need, however, hardly point out that the mortgagor may expressly agree to be personally responsible, and it would no doubt be extremely convenient to the mortgagee to insist upon such a covenant by the mortgagor.

The mortgagor, however, is bound to deliver over possession of the property to the mortgagee and to secure his quiet possession. If, therefore, the mortgagor should refuse, or be unable, to put the mortgagee in possession of the mortgaged property, the mortgagee may sue him at once for the recovery of his money. (*Rajah Odit Perkash Sing* v. *Martindell*, 4 Moo. Ind. App., 444; see also S. D., 1859, p. 118.) Again, if the mortgagee should, before the debt has been liquidated, be disturbed in his possession by the mortgagor, or persons claiming under him, the mortgagee is not bound to bring a suit for

LECTURE VII. possession, but may sue for the balance due to him, and the mortgagor will be personally directed to pay it. (N. W. P., Vol. XI, 115 ; S. D. A., 1856, p. 846 ; N. W. P., Vol. VIII, 286.)

In connection with this topic I may mention that the right created by a usufructuary mortgage is a real right, and that, although the mortgage deed may contain a covenant for the repayment of the money by the mortgagor in the event of the eviction of the mortgagee, the mortgagee is not bound to sue for the money, but may maintain ejectment, his right to possession as mortgagee not being inconsistent with his right to bring an action against the mortgagor.

I will now proceed to treat of zuripeshgee leases. A zuripeshgee lease, or a lease for a consideration, is in form a lease by the debtor to his creditor on a fixed rent reserved by the lease, which is generally a little over the amount of interest payable by the debtor. The excess is paid to the debtor, and is called huq haziree, the rest being retained by the creditor in discharge of the interest. The lease is generally for the term during which the loan is to remain out at interest, although there is usually a provision to the effect that, if the loan is not repaid on the appointed day, the lease is to continue for such further period as the debt may remain unpaid on the same conditions. Thus, suppose Rs. 10,000 are lent at 6 per cent. repayable in five years, the interest on the whole sum would be Rs. 600

per annum; the debtor gives a lease of his property for five years at a rent, say of Rs. 650 per annum, the Rs. 50 representing the huq haziree, and the Rs. 600 the interest, which the creditor retains under the terms of the agreement between the parties. The excess, however, instead of being paid to the mortgagor is not unfrequently applied to the gradual reduction of the principal. LECTURE VII.

I have already said that zuripeshgee leases have a history of their own. They were originally invented to evade the laws against usury, which continued in the Indian Statute Book from 1793 down to a very recent period, when they were repealed by Act XXVIII of 1855. It is not necessary to dwell at any length on the usury laws, but as they moulded the law of securities on the principles introduced by the Regulations, and as cases sometimes still occur, in which the old law has to be applied, I think it necessary to draw your attention to some of the leading provisions on the subject. Regulation XV of 1793, by which the maximum rate of interest was limited to 12 per cent., after enacting in the 10th section, that all mortgages are to be considered as virtually and in effect cancelled and redeemed, whenever the principal sum, with the simple interest due upon it, not exceeding 12 per cent., shall have been realized from the usufruct of the mortgaged property, provides in the next section for the adjustment of the accounts in the cases of

LECTURE VII. mortgages specified in section 10. "Where the mortgagee shall have had the usufruct of the mortgaged property, the mortgagee is to be required to deliver in the accounts of his gross receipts from the property mortgaged, and also of his expenditure for the management or preservation of it. The mortgagee is to swear, or (if he be of the description of persons whom the Courts are empowered to exempt from taking oaths) to subscribe a solemn declaration, that the accounts which he may deliver in are true and authentic. The mortgagor is to be permitted to examine the accounts, and after hearing any objections he may have to offer, or any evidence that either party may have to adduce respecting them, the Court is to adjust the account."

You will observe that these enactments rendered it extremely difficult for the mortgagee to realize more than 12 per cent. on the principal money. If he entered upon possession, he was liable to account for the rents and profits, and anything received in excess of the rate of interest sanctioned by the law was applied to the reduction of the principal. Mortgagees thereupon hit upon the expedient of entering upon possession, not as mortgagees, but as lessees at a fixed rent. The lease was sometimes taken in the name of a third person, but the object in either case was the same, to evade the liability, which the Regulations imposed upon the mortgagee in possession. Such a transparent device was, however, not sanctioned by our Courts of Justice, and zuripeshgee leases were regarded as mortgages, and the mortgagee was not permitted to use them as a shield against the claim of the mortgagor for an account. The rule was not relaxed even when the rent reserved by the lease was shown to be a fair rent. In the case of Hanuman Persad Pandey, in which the mortgagee insisted that he was in possession only as lessee, and was not liable to account for the gross proceeds, the rent reserved on the lease not being shown to be unfair, and it not being suggested that there was any attempt to evade the usury laws, Lord Justice Knight Bruce, in giving the judgment of the Privy Council, observed:—"One point remains to be considered, namely, whether, in taking the account between these parties, the defendant is to be charged as mortgagee in possession, with the actual rents and profits, or only with the rent fixed by the pottah. It is said for the appellant that the Sudder Dewany Adawlut did not set aside the pottah. In terms they certainly did not. But their Lordships think that it was part of one mortgage security, consisting of several instruments of equal date with the mortgage bond; and that it was intended to create, not a distinct estate, but only a security for the mortgage money. Mr. Palmer contended that a stipulation, such as this pottah evidences, may stand in India between mortgagor and mortgagee, and that the Regulations as to interest do

LECTURE VII. not touch such a case. The Regulations provide for the case of an evasion of the law as to interest by invalidating the mortgage security, and forfeiting the claim of the mortgagee to the principal and interest; but Mr. Palmer contends that, where there is no such evasion, and a *bonâ fide* and fair rent is fixed upon as representing *communibus annis*, the rents and profits of the estate, the Court ought to stand on that agreement of the parties, and not to direct the taking of the accounts between mortgagor and mortgagee on any other basis. It is certainly possible that, by reason of the provision that the rent shall be a fixed one, notwithstanding losses and casualties, the mortgagee might be a loser, in his character of lessee, on an account calculated on this basis; but, notwithstanding that contingency, their Lordships think that, as it was not meant that the principal should be risked, it was virtually a provision to exclude an account of the rents and profits, and that the decree of the Sudder Dewany Adawlut, directing an account of the actual rents and profits, therefore proceeds on the right principle, and it is in accordance with the true nature of the security and the spirit of the Regulations.

"In the case of *Roy Juswant Lall* v. *Sree Kishen Lall* (14 S. D. A., 1852, p. 577) the Court seems to have thought that, where a mortgage lease was granted, and whilst the term was running, the mortgage account could not be taken; but it appears from that case that, in former decisions of the Court, not reported, where the lease had expired, the Court directed the account to be taken on the ordinary footing of the receipts of rents and profits of the mortgaged estate. Their Lordships think that, under the Regulations, unless the principal is meant to be risked, and is put in risk, the estate created as part of the mortgage security, whatever be its form or duration, can be viewed only as a security for a mortgage debt, and must be restored when the debt, interest, and costs are satisfied by the receipts."

It followed, therefore, that not only could the mortgage be redeemed before the end of the term, but that the rent reserved on the lease could not be taken as settling beforehand the annual amount with which the mortgagee was to be chargeable in account. The arrangement might be in every respect a fair one, but our Courts, in their anxiety to protect the debtor from usurious contracts, refused to give effect to such an agreement.

The position, however, of the usufructuary mortgagee has been greatly modified by the repeal of the usury laws, and I shall therefore ask you carefully to contrast the rights and liabilities of the usufructuary mortgagee as they stood before the repeal of the usury laws, and as they stand at the present day.

LECTURE VII.

I have already stated that down to the year 1855, a usufructuary mortgage, whatever might be the terms of the contract between the parties, came to an end by virtue of the enactment contained in Section 9 of Regulation XV of 1793, as soon as the principal, together with interest at 12 per cent, if no lower rate should have been agreed upon between the parties, was realized from the usufruct of the mortgaged property, or otherwise liquidated by the mortgagor. The mortgagor, therefore, might redeem the property at any time, and, as in the case of conditional sales, the Court was bound to allow him to do so without any regard to the period mentioned in the mortgage. There might, perhaps, be good reasons for enacting that the mortgage should be cancelled as soon as the money was realized from the usufruct, but it is difficult to see why the mortgagee should be compelled to be paid off by the mortgagor before the appointed time. There is, perhaps, no system of law which guards the rights of the mortgagor with greater jealousy than the English, and yet the Court of Chancery, in the absence of any fraud or improper dealing, will not set aside an agreement, postponing the equity of redemption to a long deferred day, and in one case, the Court refused to relieve the mortgagor, even though he offered to pay the whole of the interest receivable by the mortgagee in advance.

The mortgagor, therefore, under the Regulations, had the right to redeem at any time on payment of the money due, either on account of principal, or interest, or both, and it was no answer to such a suit that the term for which the mortgage had been granted had not expired, or that the money had not been realized from the usufruct.

The position of the zuripeshgeedar, perhaps, deserves a closer examination. I have already called your attention to the light in which zuripeshgee leases were always regarded by our Courts. They were not regarded as mere leases, and could not therefore be set up as a defence in an action by the mortgagor for possession instituted before the expiration of the term. It is true that the decisions of the Sudder Dewany Adawlut of Calcutta at one time showed a considerable fluctuation of opinion, but all the more recent authorities are in favor of the view that a zuripeshgee, before the repeal of the usury laws, might be redeemed, even before the expiration of the term. (*Pungun Sing* v. *Amina Khatun*, 6 W. R., 6; S. D. A., 1860, p. 174; S. D. A., 1852, pp. 280, 304.)

I will now discuss the nature of usufructuary mortgages created after the repeal of the usury laws. The utmost latitude is now given to the parties to contract in any manner they choose, and the restrictions, which the Regulations imposed on the creditor, have been wholly withdrawn. While the usury laws were in force, the mortgagee was bound to account for the gross profits, allowance

LECTURE VII. being only made for necessary outlay and expenses of collection, and the mortgagor could not deprive himself of this right even by contract. Since the repeal, however, of those laws, the mortgagor and mortgagee may make any contract they please, and the mortgagor may by contract deprive himself of the right to call for an account of every farthing received by the mortgagee out of the estate. In the case of *Munnoo Lall* v. *Reet Bhoobun Singh* (6 W. R., 284), the Court observed :—"With regard to the first part of the contention that a mortgagee in possession is bound in every case to account for the profits, and that a mortgagor cannot by contract deprive himself of his right, it is no doubt true that, while the usury laws were in force, a restriction in this respect did certainly exist. But this prohibition on the free power of the parties to contract as they please was solely a consequence of the usury laws then in force ; and on the abolition of those laws, the restriction in question fell with them. By Section 4 of Act XXVIII of 1855, it is expressly enacted that an agreement that the use of usufruct of any property shall be allowed in lieu of interest, shall be binding upon the parties. We are of opinion that a mortgagor and mortgagee are now at liberty to make what contract they please with reference to the profits of the mortgaged estate." This case is, therefore, an authority that the mortgagor is at liberty to contract in any manner he pleases, and will not be relieved from any covenant binding him not to ask for an account of the actual profits. A zuripeshgeedar, therefore, is, as the law now stands, bound to account, not for the profits actually received by him out of the estate, but only for the rent reserved on the lease.

The question has arisen whether a zuripeshgee, created since the repeal of the usury laws, may be redeemed before the expiration of the term specified in the deed; and the reported cases on the point show the inclination of our Courts to treat zuripeshgees as ordinary leases, which cannot be put an end to before the expiration of the term for which they have been created. Zuripeshgee leases, however, are seldom intended to create a distinct estate, but are only effected as security for the mortgage money. In this view, it would perhaps be difficult to treat them as ordinary leases. Be that, however, as it may, there is little doubt that a zuripeshgee, created since the repeal of the usury laws, cannot be redeemed before the term for which it has been executed has expired. (*Khajeh Lootf Ali* v. *Goozraz Thakoor*, 11 W. R., 428; *Soorjun Chowdry* v. *Imam Bandee Begum*, 12 W. R., 527.) It is perfectly valid as an agreement settling beforehand the annual amounts with which the mortgagee would be chargeable in account, and as the equity of redemption may be postponed to any day that the parties may agree upon, I do

LECTURE VII. — not think that the Court will permit the mortgagor to pay off the mortgage money and re-enter upon the estate before the expiration of the term for which the zuripeshgee has been created, that being the period fixed for the redemption of the mortgage. It may, no doubt, be suggested that, in the absence of any express stipulation, postponing the right of redemption, the mortgagor ought to be permitted to redeem, but except in very badly-drawn instruments, there is sufficient indication of the intention of the parties, that the money shall be repaid on the determination of the term for which the zuripeshgee is effected, and as in the case of an ordinary creditor, the mortgagee has the right to refuse payment at an earlier date. It may, perhaps, strike some of you, that it is of no consequence whether you treat the zuripeshgee as a lease on a reserved rent, or as an agreement settling the basis on which the accounts between the parties are to be taken. This, however, is by no means so, and the distinction is an important one, as I shall endeavour to show in the next lecture. In either view, however, a zuripeshgee is valid since the repeal of Regulation XV of 1793 as an engagement excluding an account of the actual profits realized by the mortgagee in possession.

It is necessary to observe that, in the absence of any express contract, a zuripeshgeedar has no right either to foreclose or to sell the property comprised in the zuripeshgee. In a recent case, the Court observed:—"Although it is true that these leases are treated by the Courts as usufructuary mortgages, and that parties to them have to some extent the rights of mortgagor and mortgagee, it does not follow that in a case of this kind the lessee is entitled to have the property sold. To do that would be to give him a greater security than he has stipulated for. All that has been held by the Courts in regard to transactions of this kind, as I understand it, is, that the parties ought to be considered, not simply as lessor and lessee, but as mortgagor and mortgagee, the lease being granted as a security for repayment of the money. This would put the lessor in the position of a mortgagor and give him the rights of a mortgagor, and, to the extent of the security given, would put the lessee in the position of mortgagee with the rights and liabilities attached to that character. What is now asked for is beyond that. We think that the decision of the lower Appellate Court is right, and that the plaintiff is not entitled to the decree which he sought in this suit." (*Kewal Sahu* v. *Rashnarain Sing*, 13 W. R., 446.) A zuripeshgeedar, to whom the property itself is not pledged, has therefore a very imperfect security.

A usufructuary mortgage may be redeemed within the same period as any other mortgage. Before the passing of Act XIV of 1859, however, a usufructuary mortgage might be redeemed at any time, but, as the law stands at present, the mortgagor must exercise the right of redemption within sixty years from the date of the mortgage, or of a written acknowledgment.

There are many other points connected with usufructuary mortgages, which, however, I propose to discuss in the next lecture when I come to treat of accounting.

LECTURE VIII.

Liability of mortgagee in possession to account—Regulation XV of 1793—Meaning of "gross receipts"—Mortgagee not competent to create middlemen—Allowance for expenses of collection—Practice of our Courts—Nature of accounts which mortgagee is bound to produce—Verification of accounts—Right of mortgagee to interest not exceeding 12 per cent.—*Shah Makhun Loll* v. *Sreekissen Sing*—Liability of mortgagee since Act XXVIII of 1855—Zuripeshgee leases—Allowance for necessary repairs—Improvements how far allowed—Payment of Government revenue—Mode of taking accounts—Liability of mortgagee after notice of subsequent encumbrance—Mortgagor not liable to account—Mortgagee not a trustee for mortgagor—Wassilat distinct from usufruct—Mortgagee chargeable with occupation rent—Suit for redemption—Practice of the Courts in Bengal—Procedure in such cases elsewhere.

I STATED in the last lecture that the position of the mortgagee in possession has been considerably modified by the passing of Act XXVIII of 1855. It will, therefore, be convenient to deal in the first place with mortgages governed by Regulation XV of 1793, and then to deal with those which are governed by Act XXVIII of 1855.

In mortgages created before the repeal of the usury laws, the mortgagee, if in possession, is bound to account for the gross proceeds, allowance however being made for the "costs of collection and preservation of the estate in mortgage," and any contract excluding an account of the actual rents

LECTURE VIII. and profits, is, as I said in the last lecture, wholly inoperative. The duty of the mortgagee is defined in Section 11 of Regulation XV of 1793, which says:—"For the adjustment of the accounts, in the cases of mortgages specified in Section 10 where the mortgagee shall have had the usufruct of the mortgaged property, the mortgagee is to be required to deliver in the accounts of his gross receipts from the property mortgaged, and also of his expenditure for the management or preservation of it. The mortgagee is to swear, or (if he be of the description of persons whom the Courts are empowered to exempt from taking oaths) to subscribe a solemn declaration, that the accounts which he may deliver in are true and authentic."

Now, although the section speaks of the gross receipts, they must be such as the mortgagor himself could have realized before the mortgage, and if he could not by reason of an intervening lease call for the account of the collections, neither can the mortgagee. The terms of the law are not inflexible, and must receive a construction such as may suffice to accommodate its provisions to the variable and different natures of estates and possession. (*Shah Makhun Loll* v. *Sreekissen Sing*, 12 Moo. Ind. App., 157; S. C., 11 W. R., P. C., 19.) The mortgagee, however, must not create a middleman between himself and the tenants, and if he does so, he is not relieved from the responsibility of accounting for the gross rents payable by the tenants. (S. D. A., 1852, p. 1137; S. D. A., 1857, p. 1513.)

The mortgagee, however, is not an assurer of the continuation of the same rate of profit as the mortgagor was able to raise, although he is liable for the non-receipt of profits which he might have received with common care and attention. In taking the accounts, our Courts usually hold the mortgagee answerable for the rents exhibited in the rent-roll of the estate in the absence of any satisfactory explanation as to the reasons for the non-realization of any portion of the rents. The rule may, in certain cases, operate with hardship upon the mortgagee, but it is well calculated to prevent fraudulent practices.

You will observe that the mortgagee is entitled to the expenses of collection, and a fixed percentage on the gross collections is generally allowed to him varying from 5 to 10 per cent. In one case, however, the Court observed:—"No item should be allowed to the mortgagee which is not either admitted by the mortgagor, or supported by evidence of some sort. For instance, neither 10 per cent. nor 5 per cent. should be allowed for collection charges, but only so much as the expenses of collection actually amounted to, and if proper vouchers for this are not forthcoming, at least some

LECTURE VIII. evidence should be adduced sufficient to lead to a reasonable estimate of what the expenses under this head probably were." (*Mukund Loll Sukul* v. *Goluk Chunder Dutt*, 9 W. R., 575.)

I need hardly observe that the accounts which the mortgagee is bound to deliver must be full and complete. They must exhibit detailed items of all actual receipts and disbursements, and must be accompanied by all vouchers. In one case in which the mortgagee put in certain jumma-wasil-bakee papers, the Court observed:—"Jumma-wasil bakee papers, although they may, and perhaps may very strongly and directly, support a mortgagee's account put in under the law (section 3, Regulation I of 1798), are not and cannot be that account itself. That account which the mortgagee by law has to put into Court, is not that of his agent or tehsildar, given by the latter for his master's (the mortgagee's) information as to such agent's collections. The jumma-wasil-bakee paper, however, is this latter only. The account to be put in under the law is one to be made, verified, and proved by the mortgagee himself in the way before indicated. His jumma-wasil-bakee papers duly attested by those who prepared them, or who collected according to them, and supported by the receipts of the talookdars or ryots, who also may be called to depose to those receipts and to what was the real demand, collection, and balance of each of their respective tenures, may well be adduced to support the mortgagee's own account when made and put into Court under the law cited. LECTURE VIII.

"In fact, the account required from the mortgagee is one setting forth what he has realized, from what portions of the mortgaged property, in what terms or periods, with what loss and gain on the several assets, with what necessary reductions, and what remains then as the net profits which can be taken as actual realizations towards liquidating the sum due under the mortgaged transaction." (*Mohun Loll Sukul* v. *Goluk Chunder Dutt*, 5 W. R., 276).

It used to be thought at one time that the accounts must, in every case, be verified by the mortgagee himself, and that the terms of the law were inflexible. The Privy Council, however, observed in a recent case:—"Their Lordships think that the language which, like other provisions of the earlier Regulations, is curt and applied to the more common cases, must, to preserve even the spirit of the enactment itself, be construed reasonably, as admitting in case of necessity, of some delegation, also in the person deputed to perform the duty of attesting the accounts. If the general manager who did all, and knows all; with whom the mortgagors, with that knowledge, contracted; whose name is used; whose accounts in one sense they are; and who far more than mere representatives knowing

LECTURE VIII. nothing of their own knowledge of the transactions, satisfies the spirit of the law, swears to the truth of them, it is such a reasonable compliance with the spirit of the law, at least that its performance, in a case circumstanced like the present, by a substitute, furnishes no ground whatever, for suspecting malpractice or designed evasion of the law ; and with that alone, their Lordships are concerned in this case, since the mere mode of the verification has no other importance in this case than as it raises a case of suspicion against the accounts themselves." (*Shah Makhun Loll* v. *Sreekishen Sing* 12 Moo. Ind. App., 157; S. C., 11 W. R., P. C., 25.)

The necessity for an account, however, does not arise in every case. In the case of a usufructuary conditional sale for instance, the mortgagee is bound to account only when the mortgagor has deposited the principal, leaving the question of interest to be afterwards settled, or has deposited all that he alleges to be due, or asserts that the whole of the debt has been liquidated by the usufruct. (*Forbes* v. *Ameerunissa*, 10 Moo. Ind. App., 340.) If the mortgagee refuse or neglect to deliver in the accounts, the Court must take the best evidence available and decide upon it. The general presumption will, no doubt, be against the mortgagee; but this would not justify the Court in accepting without examination any evidence which may be offered by the mortgagor. Presumptions in *odium spolitoris* have known limits, although it may fairly be doubted if those limits have not been overstepped in some of the cases in the books.

I have already said that in a mortgage, created before the repeal of the usury laws, the mortgagee cannot take any higher interest than 12 per cent. on his money. He may, no doubt, agree to take less, and such agreement will be binding upon him. But he cannot in any case exceed the limit fixed by the Regulation. Cases, however, may occur in which the interest reserved by the mortgage will not be the true measure of the annual stipulated return for the loan. A very interesting question on this point arose in the case of *Shah Makhun Loll* v. *Sreekissen Sing*. The interest reserved by the instrument of mortgage was 9 per cent., but the mortgagor, as part of the transaction, executed a lease in favor of the mortgagee, which would leave to the mortgagee an annual profit of something more than 3 per cent. on the principal money. The mortgagee thus secured to himself a return of something more than 12 per cent. on his money. The mortgagor brought a suit, not for avoiding the transaction altogether as a device to evade the laws against usury, but for redemption, and contended that, under the Regulation, the mortgagee, while he could not demand more than the rate of interest specified in the deed of mortgage, was bound to account for the actual collections, and that such

LECTURE VIII. account could not be excluded by the lease which was only part of the mortgage security. The Privy Council, while holding that the mortgagor had a right to insist on the mortgagee's accounting for the actual collections, were of opinion that the latter was entitled to have the bargain performed, so far as the law allowed, and that the rate of interest reserved by the mortgage was only a part of the annual stipulated return for the loan which would not have been granted at 9 per cent. only, the rate mentioned in the deed of mortgage. In giving judgment their Lordships observed :—"It is clear that if the mortgagees had been suing the mortgagor on the mortgage deed for the debt, they could have recovered no higher rate of interest than 9 per cent., the contract being in writing and incapable of being varied by parol evidence ; but this is by no means decisive of the question, for, supposing that the extra profits on the several engagements forming one mortgage security had amounted only in the whole to 3 per cent., making a 12 per cent. only in all, precisely the same consequence would have ensued ; the reserved interest would have been correctly viewed as constituting part only of the profit, and as such would have been all that the parties stipulated for as to that part of the transaction ; but it would not have measured the stipulated return for the loan annually. The rules of evidence and the law of estoppel forbid any addition to, or variation from, deeds or written contracts. The law, however, furnishes exceptions to its own salutary protections ; one of which is, when one party for the advancement of justice is permitted to remove the blind which hides the real transaction, as for instance in cases of fraud, illegality, and redemption, in such cases the maxim applies that a man cannot both affirm and disaffirm the same transaction to show its true nature for his own relief, and insist on its apparent character to prejudice his adversary. This principle, so just and reasonable in itself, and often expressed in the terms that you cannot both approbate and reprobate the same transaction, has been applied by their Lordships in this Committee to the consideration of Indian appeals as one applicable also in the Courts of that country which are to administer justice according to equity and good conscience. The maxim is founded not so much on any positive law, as on the broad and universally applicable principles of justice. The case of *Forbes* v. *Amerunissa Begum* (10 Moo. Ind. App., p. 356) furnishes one instance of this doctrine having been so applied, where it is said in the judgment of their Lordships:—'The respondent cannot both repudiate the obligations of the lease and claim the benefit of it.' Unless, therefore, some positive law has said that, in cases similar to the present, the written engagement, though not extending to

LECTURE VIII. — the whole profit stipulated, must be adhered to against the defendant, though the plaintiff may go beyond it to show the full extent of the profit, and so to be relieved from the consequences of his actual contract, their Lordships must hold that the bargain disclosed should be performed so far as the law allows; in other words that 12 per cent. was in this instance the interest to be computed." (*Shah Makhun Loll* v. *Sreekishen Sing*, 12 Moo. Ind. App., 157; S. C., 11 W. R., P. C., 21.)

We saw in the last lecture that, since the repeal of the laws against usury, a mortgagee may always relieve himself from the liability of accounting for the actual profits by an agreement with the debtor. The prohibition on the free power of the parties to contract in any manner they please has been withdrawn. The profits may be either taken in lieu of interest (Section 5), or the parties may agree upon a certain sum beforehand, as the basis on which the account between them is to be taken, and this brings me back to the question of zuripesghee leases. You will remember that our Courts refused to acknowledge zuripeshgees as leases on a reserved rent, because they might be made the means of obtaining usurious interest. That argument cannot any longer hold good, now that the laws against usury have been repealed, and a mortgagee, entering into possession as a zuripeshgeedar, will probably be now regarded, not as mortgagee in possession, but as lessee at a fixed rent. (Lec. VII.) In any point of view, however, the relation is so peculiar that we must be cautious in extending to it all the incidents of an ordinary tenancy. The English Court of Chancery, however, looks upon such transactions with extreme jealousy ; a jealousy which has not been relaxed by the repeal of the usury laws. "One effect," says Vice-Chancellor Stuart, "of the repeal of the usury laws was to bring into operation, to a greater extent than formerly, another branch of the jurisdiction of the English Equity Courts, namely, the principle which prevented any oppressive bargain, or any advantage exacted from a man under grievous necessity, from prevailing against him." "In order," adds the learned Judge, "to render a contract or an agreement of any kind binding, there must be the assent of both parties to the agreement, under such circumstances as to show there was no pressure, no influence existing of a kind to make the assent an imperfect assent, or an assent which, under other circumstances, would have been refused. If the assent to the agreement is not an assent given under such circumstances as that both parties are on an equal footing, and the agreement one perfectly free from any influence or pressure in the eye of this Court, it is not an assent sufficient to constitute an agreement." (*Barret* v. *Hartly*, 2 L. R , Eq., 795.)

LECTURE VIII. It may, however, be suggested that such a doctrine, unless fenced in by limitations, which would narrow its application only to very exceptional cases, is likely to introduce the very same evils which the Legislature intended to remove when it applied the sweeping brush to the usury laws in our statute book. Indeed the doctrine itself in its relation to debtors and creditors is a "survival." It is another illustration of the "half-conscious repulsions" which we feel to doctrines which we cannot deny. In speaking of them Sir Henry Maine says :—"It seems to me that the half-conscious repulsions which men feel to doctrines which they do not deny, might often be examined with more profit than is usually supposed. They will sometimes be found to be the reflection of an older order of ideas. Much of moral opinion is no doubt in advance of law, for it is the fruit of religious or philosophical theories having a different origin from law, and not yet incorporated with it. But a good deal of it seems to me to preserve rules of conduct which, though expelled from law, linger in sentiment or practice. The repeal of the usury laws has made it lawful to take any rate of interest, yet the taking of usurious interest is not thought to be respectable, and our Courts of Equity have evidently great difficulty in bringing themselves to a complete recognition of the new principle." (Maine's Village Communities, p. 195.)

I have dwelt at some length on the point, as there are indications at the present moment of a desire on the part of our Courts to introduce into this country some of the doctrines of the English Court of Chancery, which rest, not upon the basis of economical science, but upon certain vague moral sentiments, which lie outside the pale of positive law. LECTURE VIII.

We saw that since the repeal of the usury laws, a mortgagee may not only receive the rents and profits in lieu of interest, but he may also protect himself from accounting for the actual receipts by an agreement with the mortgagor. In the absence, however, of any such agreement, the mortgagee is still bound to account for every farthing received by him out of the estate, and he will not only have to account for the rents actually realized, but also for such as he might have received but for his wilful default.

A mortgagee, however, is entitled in account to any outlay made by him in the preservation of the property, as for necessary repairs, and interest is generally allowed on the amount of the outlay at the rate reserved by the mortgage. In the case of *Jogendranath Mullick* v. *Rajnarain Palooye*, Mr. Justice Kemp observed:—"Under the law as administered in this country, a mortgagee in possession is in the position of a trustee. The mortgagee must use the mortgaged premises as liable to become the property

LECTURE VIII. of the mortgagor, and must not do anything to diminish the security upon which the money was lent. In this case, the mortgaged property was a thatched house. To allow it to fall out of repair and to become uninhabitable, would have been diminishing the value of the security on which the money was advanced, and preventing the mortgagor from paying off the debt from the usufruct. It is the bounden duty of the mortgagee in possession to keep the premises in necessary repair, and he will be allowed to charge for the same with interest." (9 W. R., p. 488; See also 5 Bom., 114; 5 Bom., 116.)

You will observe that in the judgment of the Court in *Jogendranath Mullick* v. *Rajnarain Palooye*, it is said that it is the duty of the mortgagee to keep the mortgaged premises in repair. This is no doubt true in a certain sense, but the proposition requires one qualification. A mortgagee is not bound to make any outlay, even in necessary repairs, except where there is a surplus left after the deduction of the interest from the rents. Any other rule would be excessively harsh to the mortgagee.

To sum up what I have said, the right of the mortgagee to be reimbursed for necessary repairs is not co-extensive with his liability to answer for non-repair by which the mortgaged premises may be diminished in value or wholly destroyed. The mortgagee in possession is not bound to rebuild a ruinous house, or increase his debt by laying out anything beyond the rent. The property may deteriorate by lapse of time, or even owing to want of repair, but the mortgagee will not be held answerable in the absence of gross or wilful negligence. The extent to which the mortgagee may safely go in repairing the mortgaged estate, is thus laid down by Fisher in his work on mortgages, and the rule has been followed in this country as founded in equity and good conscience. "The mortgagee will be allowed for proper and necessary repairs to the estate, and if buildings are incomplete or become ruinous so as to be unfit for use, he may complete or pull them down and rebuild for the preservation of his security. And the rebuilding or repairing may be done in an improved manner and more substantially than before, so that the work be done providently, and that no new or expensive buildings be erected for purposes different from those for which the former buildings were used, for the property when restored ought to be of the same nature as when the mortgagee received it; and if it be thus wholly, or in part, converted from its original purposes, the money expended will not be allowed to be charged upon it." (Fisher on Mortgage, p. 887.) LECTURE VIII.

The question of improvements presents much greater difficulty. It would, however, seem that as a rule, allowance will not be made to the mortgagee

LECTURE VIII.

for improvements, even of a lasting kind, unless they are made with the sanction of the mortgagor, or are absolutely necessary for the preservation of the estate. The mortgagor must not be improved out of the estate. (*Sandon* v. *Hooper*, 12 L. J. Ch., 309.)

In the absence of any express contract to the contrary, it is the duty of the mortgagee in possession to pay the Government revenue, and if the mortgagee wilfully default to pay the revenue and purchase the property himself, the Court will fasten a trust upon the purchase in favor of the mortgagor. The mortgagee, who properly or improperly allows an estate to fall into arrear, cannot purchase it, so as to acquire an irredeemable interest. (*Nawab Sidhi Nazzir Ally Khan* v. *Adjudharam Khan*, 10 Moo. Ind. App., 540; 5 W. R., P. C., 83; See also *Raja Adjudharam Khan* v. *Ashootosh Dey*, Supreme Court, 6th July, 1855, and *Kelsall* v. *Freeman*, Englishman, 4th September 1854.) Any payment, however, made by the mortgagee, either to prevent a forfeiture, or a sale for non-payment of revenue or rent, will be credited to him in account. In *Nurjoon Sahoo* v. *Shah Moozeerooddeen* (3 W. R., 26), which was a suit to redeem a usufructuary mortgage on payment of the principal only, there being no stipulation for interest, the mortgagee in his defence insisted upon his righ to retain possession so long as the sums which he had been obliged to pay as revenue, the estate having been assessed with revenue subsequently to the mortgage, were not repaid by the mortgagor or realized from the rents and profits, the Court observed:—"Ordinarily the law gives to a person interested in land a lien against the defaulting owner for sums of money paid by the former in discharge of the public revenue. The payments made by the defendant appear to us to entitle him to a lien within this principle. His equitable claim to such protection is certainly not diminished in this case by the fact that the plaintiff has pledged to him, as lakheraj, land which was not valid lakheraj, and has now been actually assessed with revenue; nor can the plaintiff contend that the annual receipts from the land, which, when it passed into the defendant's hands, were clearly to be appropriated solely to the defendant's use (subject to the mortgagor's right to an account), became subsequently bound for the mortgagor's benefit, although in violation of his express agreement to discharge his estate from the lien of the person who actually paid the revenue. This right is, we think, sufficient to qualify the otherwise undoubted right of the mortgagor to redeem his land on payment of the principal alone. If we gave effect to the latter right in the present suit, we should, in the probable event of the mortgagor requiring no accounts of the mortgagee's receipts while in possession, leave only to the mortgagee a

LECTURE VIII. doubtful remedy by suit for the money which he has paid, a great portion of which would be met by setting up the law of limitation as a defence."

I shall now discuss the mode of taking accounts against the mortgagee in possession. The gross collections are ascertained at the end of each year, and after deducting the necessary outlay on account of revenue, expenses of collection, and preservation of the estate, the balance goes to reduce either in whole or in part the interest, and if there is a surplus over, it goes to the reduction of the principal; the account being closed at the end of each year. In England it is not of course to direct annual rests against the mortgagee in possession, but a different rule obtains in this country. If, however, the mortgage debt is paid off by means of the rents and profits during the possession of the mortgagee, he will ordinarily be liable to pay interest on all subsequent receipts.

The question of the liability of the mortgagee in possession after assignment, when it is not made with the assent of the mortgagor, for the rents and profits received by the assignee, does not seem to have been ever raised in this country. In England, the mortgagee continues to be liable on the principle that the mortgagee must be responsible for the person to whom he assigns the mortgagor's estate. It may, however, be doubted whether the doctrine will be recognized in our Courts.

The jealousy with which the Court of Chancery guards the interest of the mortgagor, is well illustrated by the rule invariably acted upon, that no personal allowance is to be allowed to the mortgagee himself, although the salary of an agent may be allowed when the collections cannot conveniently be made otherwise. Any agreement to make an allowance to the mortgagee is absolutely void, and the repeal of the usury laws has made no change in this respect in the practice of the English Court of Chancery. LECTURE VIII.

I shall now treat of the rights and liabilities of the mortgagee when he allows the profits to be received by the mortgagor instead of entering upon possession himself. The rule of English law on the subject is thus stated by Fisher as the result of the authorities: "After receiving notice of a puisne mortgage, the mortgagee in possession becomes liable to account to the puisne incumbrancer for so much of the surplus rent as he has paid to the mortgagor or his representatives; but so long as the mortgagee in possession is without notice, the puisne mortgagee cannot call upon him or the mortgagor for an account of the by-gone rents." (Fisher on Mortgage, p. 875.) This rule was applied to an Indian mortgage in this country by the Privy Council in *Jugjeewan Dass* v. *Ram Dass*. In that case, the mortgage deed, after stating that the village of Mujeegum

LECTURE VIII. and the house at Sural should be mortgaged for a certain sum, went on to say :—"The profit of this money is settled for 12 annas, on these conditions, that the holders of the mortgage are to receive in redemption the whole of the produce of the said village, about 3,000 or 3,200 rupees, and after allowing for interest, the remainder will go for the purpose of liquidating the principal, and they shall continue so to receive and appropriate the annual produce until the whole of their demand be liquidated. The risk of collecting the income, and of any deficiency in the revenue, is upon our heads, that is the mortgagor's; and we do further declare that the holders of the said mortgage shall station a mehta or clerk of their own in the said village, for the purpose of making the collections; and we, the mortgagors, so long as this property remains in mortgage, do agree to give him a monthly salary of 5 rupees and his daily food so long as we can afford to do so." It seems that the mortgagee continued in possession under this deed for a short time, but afterwards allowed the mortgagors to receive the rents and profits. In execution of a decree obtained by the plaintiff against the mortgagors, the property was placed under attachment when the mortgagee for the first time had notice of the plaintiff's claim. In determining the respective rights of the parties the Privy Council said:—"Now the question will be, in what way the mortgagee's rights are affected by this conduct; and that will depend, first, upon the construction of the instrument itself. If this is a binding contract,—binding between him and the mortgagors,—binding him to apply the rents and profits to the payment of the debt, he might be considered as having forfeited his right to payment in consequence of having allowed the mortgagors themselves to take possession of the rents and profits during some of the years during which his mehta was in possession. But their Lordships are of opinion that that is not the true construction of the deed, but that it is merely a power to satisfy himself, just as an English mortgagee may, by taking possession of the rents and profits of the estate; and if an English mortgagee chooses to forego the benefit of receiving the rents and profits, and permits the mortgagor to take them, it would have no effect as between him and the mortgagor; he would have a full right to recover his debt by reason of the mortgage. The only effect would be, when some subsequent incumbrancer came in, and he had notice of that claim. In that case the rule and law in England would be that if, after notice, he permits the mortgagor to receive the rents and profits, he exposes himself to the claim of the second incumbrancer; and that is the principle which their Lordships think ought to be applied to the present case." (*Jugjewan Dass* against *Ram*

LECTURE VIII. *Dass Brijbhukun*, 2 Moo. Ind. App., 487 ; S. C., 6 W R., p. 11, P. C.)

By the decree which was ultimately made, the mortgagees were postponed to the attaching creditor in respect of the rents which might have been received by them, but for their allowing the mortgagors to continue in possession. The rights of the mortgagee against the mortgagors personally were left untouched, and they were only permitted to continue in possession till the balance settled on the above principle was realized.

While on the subject of accounting, I may mention that the mortgagor in possession is not bound to account, although the security may be insufficient. This is the rule of English law, and is also the law in this country. A mortgagor, however, will be liable to an action for mesne profits, if he withhold possession from the mortgagee in violation of the terms of his contract. It is scarcely necessary to repeat that the mortgagor is also liable for mesne profits from the date of the final foreclosure (*i.e.*, from the expiration of the year of grace). There are expressions in some of the reported decisions of the Sudder Dewany Adawlut which might, at first sight, seem to countenance the notion that it was only from the date of the decree for foreclosure that the mortgagor was liable for mesne profits. I need, however, hardly point out to you that the rights of the parties, after a decree for foreclosure, are precisely those which they possessed at the date of the expiration of the year of grace. The decree only declares those rights, and it must therefore follow, that, if there is any liability in the mortgagor for mesne profits, that liability must exist before the decree for foreclosure, and consequently at the expiration of the year of grace, which is the dividing point of time. LECTURE VIII.

The question has arisen as to the precise position of a mortgagee after the mortgage debt has been liquidated by the usufruct. It seems to have been held in some cases that his position was that of a trustee, and that therefore no limitation was applicable to a suit brought by the mortgagor for surplus profits. These decisions were, however, overruled by a Full Bench of the Calcutta High Court, and the period of limitation was held to be six years. (*Baboo Lall Doss* v. *Jamal Ali*, 9 W. R., 187.) This was under the old law. Under the new, a suit for surplus profits must be brought within three years of the date on which the mortgage comes to an end. The interpretation clause also tells us that a mortgagee is not a trustee within the meaning of the Act.

A question of some nicety arose a few years ago in the High Court of Calcutta, which was ultimately heard by a Full Bench. In that case which was a suit for redemption, the principal having been deposited, the mortgagee was called upon to account

LECTURE VIII. for moneys which he had realised by means of a decree for mesne profits against the mortgagor, who had evicted him from the mortgaged premises. The question arose under Regulation XV of 1793, and it was contended for the mortgagor that the mortgagee was bound to account to him for the moneys which he had succeeded in realizing from the mortgagor in excess of the legal interest of 12 per cent. per annum. It was, however, held by the Full Bench that the mortgagee was not liable to account for the mesne profits. In giving judgment, Peacock, C. J., said:—"There is a wide distinction between usufruct collected by a mortgagee in possession, and damages which are awarded to a mortgagee in a suit brought by him against the mortgagor for evicting him. We think that the defendants were not bound under the words or the spirit of Regulation XV of 1793, or Regulation I of 1798, to account for the wasilat or damages which they have received under the decree in the suit brought by them against the mortgagor for possession. If a mortgagor wrongfully turns a mortgagee out of possession, it is his own fault, and the mortgagee is entitled to retain any wasilat which he may recover against the mortgagor, and is not bound to account for it. To prevent an evasion of the usury laws, the Regulation compelled the mortgagee to account for the usufruct; if that exceeded interest at 12 per cent., the balance was to be accounted for. We think that a Regulation of this kind must be construed strictly, and that we ought not so to construe it as to substitute wasilat recovered by a decree of Court for usufruct enjoyed by a mortgagee. The case of *Chutterdharee Kowar* v. *Ramdoolun Kowar*, (Sudder Decisions of 1859, p. 1181), is a case very much in point, though the question arose in a different form." (*Joymungul Sing* v. *Sardeen*, 6 W. R., 240).

In the case of *Nilkant Sen and another*, the facts of which were somewhat peculiar, the mortgagee had wrongfully dispossessed the mortgagor, the mortgage being one by conditional sale, and not giving the mortgagee power to receive the rents and profits. The mortgagor brought a suit for possession and mesne profits. He got a decree for possession, but the prayer for mesne profits was rejected, apparently because there was some technical informality in the prayer in the plaint. The mortgagee subsequently proceeded to foreclose, and when he brought a regular suit for possession as absolute owner, the Court held that he was bound to account for the profits during the time he was in possession, just in the same manner as if he had been let into possession by the mortgagor. It would seem, although the fact is not clear from the report, that a suit for mesne profits would have been barred. (*Nilkant Sen* v. *Joynedin*, 7 W. R., 30).

A mortgagee in possession, who instead of letting

LECTURE VIII. the land to tenants and realizing the rent in the ordinary way, cultivates it himself, is not liable to account for the whole of the profits arising to him from farming the land, but only for such profits as he would have received, if he had let the land to a tenant, and so in the case of any other profits, the mortgagee, if in possession, is chargeable only with an occupation rent. (*Rughunath Roy* v. *Gridhari Sing*, 7 W. R., 244.)

In concluding this lecture, I wish to say a few words on the manner in which suits for redemption are treated by the Courts in Bengal and the North-Western Provinces. The practice has been to treat a suit for redemption as a suit for ejectment, and to refuse any relief to the plaintiff, except upon proof that every condition necessary to the right to immediate possession, has been fulfilled. You will find it laid down in several cases, that, in a suit for redemption, the mortgagor must fail if any thing is due to the mortgagee on the security, and the plaintiff cannot show that he had deposited or tendered the amount. In some instances, however, conditional decrees have been made, and in recent cases the Court has shown some disinclination to adhere to the old practice; a practice, which I venture to think, is attended with inconvenience as well to the mortgagor as to the mortgagee. It is true that plaints are not very artificially framed in the Mofussil Courts, and they are very frequently brought for recovery of possession on the allegation that the mortgage debt has been satisfied. Such suits, however, are substantially brought for the purpose of ascertaining as between the parties what is the state of the account, a right which is expressly given by statute to the mortgagor. We saw that, according to the practice of the English Court of Chancery (and which is followed in the other provinces of this country), the Court, in a suit for redemption, invariably takes an account of the monies due to the mortgagee on his security, and if anything is due to the mortgagee, the mortgagor is directed to pay it by the time appointed by the Court, and on his failure to do so, the bill for redemption is dismissed; such dismissal having the same effect, and carrying with it the same consequences, as a decree for foreclosure. It would be difficult to suggest any reason why the same practice should not be followed in Bengal. According to the present practice of our Courts, the Court is bound to take an account in a suit for redemption, but, even if a single shilling be found due to the mortgagee, the suit is dismissed, and, however carefully the account may have been taken, the finding of the Court will not be binding upon either party in any subsequent suit. This naturally leads to a perfect waste of litigation which might be easily prevented by the exercise of the power, which our Courts undoubtedly possess, of moulding their decrees in such a way as

LECTURE VIII. to meet the exigencies of each case. (See the observations of Phear, J., in *Mukund Loll Sukul* v. *Goluk Chunder Dutt*, 9 W. R., 572. Compare 4 N. W. P., 37; 5 N. W. P., 104; 6 N. W. P., 221; 10 N. W. P., 543; S. D. A., 1849, p. 392.) The following recent cases may be usefully consulted by the student:—*Shah Lutafut Hossein* v. *Chowdry Mahomed Moneim*, 22 W. R., 269; *Rajah Saheb Perladh* v. *Broughton*, 24 W. R., 275. See also 18 W. R., 65; 22 W. R., 172. Compare 8 W. R., 369; Suth. F. B., 33.

LECTURE IX.

Liens—Legal and Judicial — Distinction between — Statutory liens — Regulation VIII of 1819 and Act VIII of 1869 (B.C.)—Act XI of 1859—Salvor's lien—Lien of co-sharer for revenue paid by him—Unpaid vendor's lien— *Mackreth* v. *Symmons* —What constitutes waiver of lien—Objections to legal liens—Registration—Purchasers without notice—Practice of English Court of Chancery—Purchaser's lien—Lien of partners and agents—Tenants in common—No lien for dower in Mahomedan law—None in favor of creditors on assets of deceased debtor in Hindu or Mahomedan law—Judicial lien—Attachment before and after judgment—Operation of—Section 240 of Act VIII of 1859—Alienation by debtor not absolutely void—*Anund Mohun Dass* against *Radha Mohun Shah*—Striking off attachment—Effect of—*Puddomoney* against *Roy Mothuranath Chowdhry*.

In the present lecture I propose to treat of liens or securities created by the operation of law. In the introductory lecture I pointed out to you the difference between these charges and charges created by the express or implied consent of the parties. I also stated that liens may be divided into two groups, legal and judicial; the one constituting a part of substantive law, and the other, a part of the law of procedure. I propose to discuss the law relating to legal liens in the first place, and then to treat of judicial liens.

I have already said that there are some cases in which a lien is expressly conferred by statute, while

LECTURE IX. there are others in which the right has been recognised by our Courts of Justice as resting on those principles of equity which the Indian Courts are bound to administer. But though they are the growth of 'judicial legislation,' I need hardly point out they do not differ in any essential feature from the class of liens which I shall call statutory liens. The earliest instance of the latter is furnished by the enactment contained in the 13th section of Regulation VIII of 1819. That section says:—"If the person or persons making such a deposit in order to stay the sale of the superior tenure, shall have already paid the whole of the rent due from himself or themselves, so that the amount lodged is an advance from private funds, and not a disbursement on account of the said rent, such deposit shall not be carried to credit in, or set against, future demands for rent, but shall be considered as a loan made to the proprietor of the tenure preserved from sale by such means, and the taluk so preserved shall be the security to the person or persons making the advance, who shall be considered to have a lien thereupon in the same manner as if the loan had been made upon mortgage; and he or they shall be entitled, on applying for the same, to obtain immediate possession of the tenure of the defaulter in order to recover the amount so advanced from any profits belonging thereto. If the defaulter shall desire to recover his tenure from the hands of the person or persons who by making the advance may have acquired such an interest therein and entered in possession in consequence, he shall not be entitled to do so except upon repayment of the entire sum advanced with interest at the rate of twelve per cent. per annum up to the date of possession having been given as above, or upon exhibiting proof in a regular suit to be instituted for the purpose that the full amount so advanced, with interest, has been realized from the usufruct of the tenure."

This, I need hardly point out, is a very beneficent provision. It has since been extended to all classes of tenants by whom the superior tenure may be preserved from sale. (See section 62, Act VIII of 1869, B.C.)

Another provision of a similar character, but less ample, is to be found in section 9 of Act XI of 1859. That section, after enacting that the revenue in arrear may be tendered in certain cases by a person who is not the proprietor of the estate, goes on to say:—"And if the person so depositing, whose money shall have been credited as aforesaid, shall prove before a competent Civil Court that the deposit was made in order to protect an interest of the said person, which would have been endangered or damaged by the sale, he shall be entitled to recover the amount of the deposit, with or without interest as the Court may determine, from

LECTURE IX. — the defaulting proprietor. And if the party so depositing, whose money shall have been credited as aforesaid, shall prove before such a Court that the deposit was necessary in order to protect any lien he had on the estate or share, or part thereof, the amount so credited shall be added to the amount of the original lien."

It is somewhat remarkable that the section does not, in so many words, confer a lien on every person by whom the estate may be saved, and apparently limits it only to a mortgagee making the deposit in order to protect his security. Advances in the nature of salvage, however, are recognised in every system of law as conferring a lien on the estate itself, and such advances may be made not only by a person having an interest in the property, but even by a simple creditor, although his debt is disputed. In the case of *Nogender Chunder Ghose* against *Sreemutty Dasi*, their Lordships of the Privy Council observed:—"Considering that the payment of the revenue by the mortgagee will prevent the taluk from being sold, their Lordships would, if that were the sole question for their consideration, find it difficult to come to any other conclusion than that the person who had such an interest in the taluk as entitled him to pay the revenue due to the Government, and did actually pay it, was thereby entitled to a charge on the taluk, as against all persons interested therein, for the amount of the money so paid." (11 Moo. Ind. App.; S. C., 8 W. R., p. 617.)

This doctrine rests upon the plainest principles of equity, and the Calcutta High Court held in a recent case that a co-sharer who is compelled to pay the revenue due from his shareholder is entitled to a lien on the share of the latter. (*Syud Enayet Hossein* v. *Madon Mohun Shahun*, 22 W. R., 411; See also *Manik Mulla Chowdhry* v. *Parbutty Churn*, S. D., 1859, p. 515.)

The language of the ninth section of the Act may, perhaps, suggest a doubt as to whether or not the Legislature intended to confer a lien in any other case except where the payment is made by a mortgagee; but we must remember what one of the sages of the English law says about law-making, and should not be too ready to infer that the express mention of one excludes all other cases.

The lien of the co-sharer is an instance of the recognition by our Courts of Justice of a right not expressly given by any statute. This, however, is by no means an isolated case. In the absence of any specific rule, the Indian Courts are bound to administer the principles of equity and good conscience, and thus a good deal of English law has not unnaturally worked its way into our jurisprudence.

I, therefore, propose to give a short outline of the liens recognised by the English Court of Chancery, pointing out those that have been adopted in this country. Foremost among them is the lien of the unpaid vendor for the purchase money. It is thus defined by Lord Eldon in *Mackreth* v. *Symmons*:—"Where the vendor conveys, without more, though the consideration is upon the face of the instrument expressed to be paid, and by a receipt endorsed upon the back, if it is the simple case of a conveyance, the money or part of it not being paid as between the vendor and vendee, and persons claiming as volunteers, upon the doctrine of this Court, which, when it is settled, has the effect of contract, though perhaps no actual contract has taken place, a lien shall prevail—in the one case, for the whole consideration; in the other, for that part of the money which was not paid." (1 White and Tudor, L. C., p. 269.) If it were not now too late to do so, I should venture to protest against the introduction of this doctrine into our system, if on no other account, at least on account of the number of refined distinctions which have clustered round it in the English law, and which must inevitably be introduced with it. In order to explain myself I ought to state that, in the English law, a vendor may waive his lien either expressly or by implication, and the circumstances which will be sufficient to raise an inference of waiver have given rise to a cloud of distinctions which are extremely refined, and which have produced a degree of uncertainty such as led Lord Eldon to say,—"that it would have been better at once to have held, that the lien should exist in no case, and the vendor should suffer the consequences of his want of caution; or to have laid down the rule the other way so distinctly, that a purchaser might be able to know, without the judgment of a Court, in what cases it would not exist." It has been held in England that the lien exists even when the money is secured to be paid at a future day (*Winter* v. *Lord Anson*, 3 Russ., 488), while the mere taking of a security does not amount to an abandonment of the lien. If, however, the vendor take a totally distinct and independent security, it will then become a case of substitution for the lien. The question, however, in all these cases is simply whether or not the circumstances show a clear and unequivocal intention to give up the lien—a question on which there must necessarily be a great conflict of opinion. It is, therefore, to be regretted that the doctrine should have worked its way into our law. It rests upon grounds altogether different from those on which the lien of the salvor has been recognised. In the case of the vendor of land it is always open to him to protect himself against the consequences of the fraud or insolvency of the purchaser, and if he does not choose to take the most ordinary precautions he hardly deserves much sympathy. I need scarcely point out that the case of a person who is obliged to make a payment for the protection of his own interests, is essentially different. But there is another and a still more serious objection, which applies to all legal liens alike. They are neither agreements, nor declarations, and are therefore wholly untouched by the Registration Acts. They, however, confer real rights, and a *bonâ fide* purchaser for value may be easily misled. This is a serious evil. We know how it is guarded against in England. The right being merely "equitable," the English Court of Chancery, acting upon a well-known doctrine, will not suffer it to be enforced against a *bonâ fide* purchaser for value without notice of the lien. The doctrine itself is a curious illustration of the way in which the rights and obligations of parties have been gradually moulded by equity. We saw that in archaic law it was not easy to make a secret transfer of land. The transaction must be attended with a number of solemnities which served to give it publicity, and the omission of any one of them was fatal to the validity of the transfer. It is hardly necessary to observe that a rigid adherence to the doctrine was likely to lead to considerable hardship, and the Court of Chancery, therefore, allowed in certain cases the same relief as if the plaintiff had acquired a real right, notwithstanding his inability to make out a complete legal title. But, in order to prevent injustice to third persons, equity allowed a peculiar defence to a purchaser for value who may have been misled by the presumable want of publicity. As a fact, in modern times, a conveyance does not necessarily carry with it greater publicity than a contract, but the old doctrine still remains as a "survival." LECTURE IX.

In countries in which this peculiar defence is not admitted, the same object is accomplished by the hypothec books in which all transfers of real rights are carefully entered. In the French Code, for instance, the registration of legal mortgages is as compulsory as the registration of conventional securities. But the Indian statute does not permit the registration of such transactions. This fact of itself ought to induce our Courts to be cautious in the admission of legal liens. If, however, we adopt the law as administered by the English Court of Chancery on this subject, the equitable defence open to a purchaser for value should also be admitted. So long as the registration of legal mortgages is not rendered compulsory, any other course must necessarily lead to very great hardship. It may, no doubt, be said that it would be inconsistent with the logic of the law to hold that a real right may not be enforced against a subsequent purchaser; but, as observed by an eminent jurist, logical antinomy is more easily to be borne than a rule which fails to do justice between man and man.

I shall now treat of some other liens recognised by the English law. A lien arises in favor of a purchaser for purchase money prematurely paid by him. There is also a lien in favor of partners on the partnership estate, on dissolution, in satisfaction of any demands arising out of the partnership business. An agent also is, in certain cases, protected by a lien on property on which he has made advances on account of his principal. As a general rule, however, a person is not entitled to a charge simply because he has laid out money on the property of another. I am not sure whether, according to English law, one of the tenants-in-common of a house is entitled to a lien for money laid out in necessary repairs. The question does not seem to have been ever raised in this country, but I venture to think that the person who lays out money in repairing a house to which he is entitled in common with others, has a much stronger equity in his favor than the unpaid vendor. In this country properties are frequently held in coparcenary, and although the remedy may, in one sense, be said to be in their own hands, we all know, a partition cannot be made without great delay and expense to the parties.

The principles of justice, equity, and good conscience, however, so long as they do not harden into system, are often extremely vague. They should, therefore, be applied with very great caution. Various liens, for instance, are recognised by the Civil law and the Continental Codes, which find no place in the English system. The lien of the lender who advances money for the purchase of land, or for repairing a building, or of the architect or laborer employed in the construction of any works, is not recognised by the English Court of Chancery; and yet it would be difficult to deny that the creditor in the one case, and the architect in the other, have at least as strong an "equity" in their favor as the unpaid vendor. The truth is, the principles of justice, equity, and good conscience are at best but an uncertain guide, and not unfrequently wear an appearance of vagueness, which, it must be confessed, is rather bewildering to the student of Indian law. Indeed, it may fairly be doubted whether our Courts ought not to confine the right to a legal mortgage only to those cases in which, as in the case of the salvor, the person claiming the right could not have protected himself by an express agreement. In every other case the parties may be safely left to take the consequences of their own want of caution.

I shall now treat of one or two cases in which it is sometimes thought that a lien exists. It is sometimes said that a Mahomedan widow has a lien on the estate of her husband for dower due to her. The question was very fully discussed in the case of *Mir Meher Ali* v. *Mussamut Amanee*, and the Court, after a review of all the authorities, came to the conclusion that the widow has no special charge on the property, but ranks *pari passu* with other ordinary

LECTURE IX.

creditors. (11 W. R., p 212, see also *Shah Enayet Hossain* v. *Syud Romzan*, 10 W. R., 216.) But dower, like every other debt, must be paid before the heirs are entitled to take anything, and the authorities show that a Mahomedan widow in possession of her husband's estate upon a claim of dower, has a lien upon it as against those entitled as heirs, and is entitled to the rents and profits till the claim of dower is satisfied. (See Macnaughten's Precedents, case 24, p. 275, *Womatul Fatima* v. *Mirunnissa*, 9 W. R., p. 318, reported also in 8 W. R., 51.)

A similar right is sometimes put forward on behalf of the creditor of a deceased Hindu, but it is now conclusively settled that a creditor has no lien on the assets in the hands of the heir, and cannot, therefore, reach any property which may have been transferred by the heir in good faith to a third party. Sir Thomas Strange, indeed, in his book on Hindu law, says, that "debts are a charge on the inheritance, and that they follow the assets into whatsoever hands it comes." (Strange's Hindu Law, Vol. I, p. 166.) And the learned author cites the very high authority of Colebrooke in support of his opinion. (Strange's Hindu Law, App., p. 282.) There is also the text of Katyayana:—"If any debts exist against the father, his son shall not take possession of his effects. They must be given to his creditors." (Stokes's Vabahara Mayukha, p. 122.) Our Courts, however, have laid down a different doctrine, although it may fairly be doubted if this is not one of the many instances in which English lawyers have unconsciously introduced the doctrines of their own law, moulded by the commercial necessities of of the country, into a system comparatively archaic, and not shaped by such economic considerations. The Sudder Dewany Adawlut, presided over by Judges not so familiar with English law, adhered to the doctrine laid down by Strange and Colebrooke. But the law has been differently interpreted in recent decisions. In the case of *Zuburdust Khan* v. *Inderman* (Agra, F. B., 71), the Court, in giving judgment, observed:—"In our judgment the real test to be applied in deciding the issue of law raised is to be found in the answer to the question—to whom does the property pass on the death of the deceased? Does it pass immediately and entirely to his heirs, or is the normal devolution interrupted, so that the whole or a portion of the estate sufficient to discharge his debts, vests, as if by hypothecation, in the creditors, and does only the residue pass to the heir?

"We can find no authority for the latter proposition; nor has any other text been cited in support of it than that from Katyayana referred to by the Division Bench. Although Sir T. Strange enumerates debts among the charges on the inheritance, he nowhere expresses himself to the effect, that any

LECTURE IX. interest in the inheritance vests in the creditor; on the contrary, the language used by him rather shows that the whole estate of the deceased's ancestor passes to his heirs, affecting them with a liability for the debts of the ancestor to the extent of the assets received by them. The heirs may, if they please, avoid this liability by disclaiming the estate, but into the hands of whatever volunteer it comes, the liability attaches on him; and so long as the estate remains in the hands of the heirs or any other volunteers, so long does it constitute a fund, to which the creditor is entitled to have resort for satisfaction of his claim. This is, in our opinion, the correct interpretation of the dictum that 'debts follow the assets into whatsoever hands they come.' We have examined the authorities referred to by Sir T. Strange on this point, and can find nothing in them which warrants any stronger position in favor of creditors than that which we have expressed above. The text of Katyayana may, at first sight, seem to justify the contention that the whole estate of a deceased ancestor does not pass directly to the heirs; but that there rests in them only the residue after satisfaction of the debts. But this text must be read in connection with other texts of writers of high authority on Hindu law; and so reading it, we are of opinion, that the proper construction of it is to hold, that it declares that the resulting benefit to the heirs from the succession cannot be greater than the surplus of assets over liabilities; not that the estate does not altogether and absolutely vest in the heirs. Numerous texts may be referred to which indicate a power in the heirs to deal with the whole estate before satisfaction of the debts. The very fact that they may sell it to satisfy debts shows an ability to make a good title to the whole of it. LECTURE IX.

"The construction of the text of Katyayana in the sense contended for on behalf of the appellant is therefore untenable." (See also *Annopurna Dassee* v. *Gunganarain Pal*, 2 W R., p. 296 ; compare N. W. P, 1859, p. 23 ; Mad., S. D. A., Vol. I, p. 166.)

It would seem that although a Hindu widow has, in a certain sense, a lien on the estate of her deceased husband for maintenance, the charge cannot be enforced against a purchaser for value without notice of the lien. At any rate the widow cannot seek to charge the estate in the hands of a purchaser without showing that there is no property of her deceased husband in the hands of his heirs. (*Adhiranee Narain Kumaree* v. *Shona Malee*, 1 I. L. R. Calc., 365; see also 8 B. L. R., 225; 9 B. L. R., 11 ; compare 2 Agra, 42; 4 Moo. Ind. App., 246; 1 All., 191.)

I now come to judicial liens or attachments. Now an attachment under the Procedure Code may be either before or after judgment; the process being intended in both cases to guard against the

LECTURE IX. alienation of the property by the defendant. It would be beyond the range of the present lectures to discuss all the various points in connection with attachments. I shall confine myself only to the operation of an attachment under the Code. An attachment operates from the moment that the process is executed as a charge on the property, the judgment itself not having the effect of creating in this country a lien on the property of the judgment-debtor. But, in order to have the benefit of an attachment, the provisions of the Procedure Code must be carefully followed. In one case in which the notice of attachment was not fixed up in the Court-house, or in the office of the Collector, the Court thought that an alienation made by the debtor could not be avoided by the creditor. Mr. Justice Macpherson in giving judgment observed :—

"The objection is by no means a technical objection. The affixing the notice in the Court-house and in the office of the Collector is a far more certain means of giving information to the parties immediately interested, than in the process of reading the notice aloud on the land or on some place adjacent to it. A man can always arrange so as to keep himself acquainted with all notices fixed up in the Court of the Judge or the Collector of a district. But there can be no certainty that he will happen to hear, or to be made acquainted with, orders which are merely read aloud on his land or on some place adjacent to it. In the case before us, it is not proved that the judgment-debtor was in personal possession of the lands which were the subject of attachment, and there is nothing whatever to show or to lead to the presumption that he was acquainted with the fact of the order of attachment having been read aloud by the peon who was sent to attach the property. The probability of the judgment-debtors having known that the attachment had been issued, would have been far stronger if the order had been fixed up in the Court-house or in the office of the Collector.

"Section 240 says that alienations after attachment are to be void, if the attachment or the written order 'shall have been duly intimated and made known in manner aforesaid.' The words 'manner aforesaid' relate to the provisions of Section 239, and when two out of the three methods prescribed by that Section for intimating and making known attachments have been wholly omitted, it cannot possibly be said that the order of attachment was duly intimated and made known within the meaning of Section 240." (*Inderchund Baboo* v. *The Agra Bank*, 10 W. R., 264.)

An attachment before judgment is not, according to the view taken by a Full Bench of the Calcutta High Court, an attachment which would entitle the creditor to preference in an order for distribution. The scope and object of an attachment before judg-

LECTURE IX. ment are merely to guard against the debtors making away with the property pending the suit. It does not secure to the creditor priority, if any question should arise as between rival decree-holders as to the distribution of the sale proceeds of the attached property. (*Sreeram Manik* v. *Tincowree Roy*, 13 W R., F.B., p. 9.) An attachment before judgment, therefore, confers only a somewhat precarious right. An attachment after judgment and in execution is, however, a perfect real security. The judgment-debtor may not alienate the property, the purchaser under the execution following upon such attachment not being bound by a transfer made by the debtor subsequently to the attachment. What passes to the purchaser is, therefore, not the rights and interests of the debtor as they stand at the time of the sale, but the rights and interests of the debtor as they stood at the time of the attachment. Section 240 of the Procedure Code has, however, received a somewhat limited construction, the Privy Council, in the case of *Anund Mohun Dass* against *Jullodhur Shah*, having held that a private alienation is void only as respects the attaching creditor and those who claim under or through the attachment. (14 Moo. Ind. Ap., 543; S. C., 17 W. R., 313.) The construction suggested by one of the learned Judges in the Court below would have given the creditors of the debtor an ampler remedy, but the point has been settled otherwise by the highest

Court of Appeal. It must, however, be borne in mind that an attachment does, to a certain extent, enure to the benefit of all the judgment-creditors. Thus, suppose A attaches property belonging to his judgment-debtor worth 5,000 rupees, and that the debt due to A is only 1,000 rupees. Now, if the debtor should sell the property to a third person before it has been attached by any other creditor, and the property should eventually be sold under an execution, the balance of the purchase money will not be paid over to the purchaser, but will be distributed among such of the other creditors as may have taken out execution prior to the order for distribution. (Sections 270 and 271, Act VIII of 1859.)

In conclusion, it is necessary to observe that if an attachment has been permanently struck off, and a new attachment has become necessary, a conveyance which is executed between the two attachments will be valid. (*Govindo Sing* v. *Mir Mushun Ali*, S. D. A., 1855, page 244.) A question of much greater difficulty arises when the conveyance has been executed while the first attachment was subsisting. Does such a conveyance become valid by relation, or is it void against the execution-creditor and those claiming under him. In the case of *Puddomoney* against *Roy Muthooranath Chowdry*, the Privy Council observed:—"It seems to their Lordships that generally where the party prosecuting the decree is compelled to take out another execution, his title should be presumed to date from the second attachment. Their Lordships do not mean to lay down broadly that, in all cases in which an execution is struck off the file, such consequences must follow. The reported cases sufficiently show that in India the striking an execution proceeding off the file is an act which may admit of different interpretations according to the circumstances under which it is done, and accordingly their Lordships do not desire to lay down any general rule which would govern all cases of that kind; but they are of opinion that when, as in this case, a very long time has elapsed between the original execution and the date at which it was struck off, it should be presumed that the execution was abandoned and ceased to be operative, unless the circumstances are otherwise explained." (20 W. R., 133.)

LECTURE X.

Subrogation—Application of rule—Rights of puisne incumbrancers—Rights of surety—Entitled to benefit of securities held by creditor—How far discharged by relinquishment of security—Security not relinquished by payment—Rule of English law—Followed in India—Co-debtors—How far entitled to benefit of securities—Purchasers of mortgagor's rights redeeming a mortgage, how far entitled to benefit of subrogation—Other cases illustrative of the rule—Contribution—Principle on which founded—Doctrine followed in India—Marshalling of securities—Rule of English law—Adopted by our Courts—Distinction between purchasers and incumbrancers—Notice immaterial in the case of a mortgage.

In the last lecture I treated of the various circumstances under which a lien is created by the operation of law, independently of the assent of the parties between whom the relation is created. In the present lecture I propose to discuss a class of securities which, although distinguishable from the class considered in the last lecture, have yet some features in common with them. I refer to cases in which a person, by whom an incumbrance is discharged, is sometimes allowed to stand in the place of the mortgagee, and to avail himself of the security in precisely the same way as if the mortgagee had assigned it to him.

The doctrine of subrogation, as it is called, rests upon the plainest principles of justice and equity,

LECTURE X. and is recognized in almost every system of law. You must not, however, suppose that every person who discharges the mortgage debt is entitled to the benefit of the security held by the mortgagee. As a rule, in the absence of an assignment of the security, the person by whom the debt is discharged has no right to avail himself of it. The discharge of the debt extinguishes the security, and the doctrine of subrogation or involuntary assignment is an exception to this rule.

We have seen that every person who is entitled to redeem acquires, on redemption, the right to stand in the place of the mortgagee, and that it is not necessary that he should obtain an actual assignment of the mortgage in order that he may avail himself of the security. (*Bhekun Sing* v. *Din Doyal*, 24 W. R., 47.) But there are other cases also in which the discharge of a debt secured by a mortgage is followed by the same result. A surety who pays the debt due from his principal is entitled to enforce any security against the debtor possessed by the creditor. "A surety," to use the language of Sir S. Romilly, in his argument in *Craythorne* v. *Swinburne*, "will be entitled to every remedy which the creditor has against the principal debtor; to enforce every security and all means of payment; to stand in the place of the creditor, not only through the medium of contract, but even by means of securities entered into without the knowledge of the surety; having a right to have those securities transferred to him, though there was no stipulation for that; and to avail himself of all those securities against the debtor." In a recent case in the Calcutta High Court, the question arose whether or not a surety, by whom the debt had been paid, could proceed against the original debtor upon the instrument itself by which the debt had been created. The facts were shortly these: The plaintiff brought a suit in the nature of an action of ejectment upon a mortgage, which had been regularly foreclosed. The defence was that, prior to the mortgage under which the plaintiff made title to the property, the debtor had borrowed money from a third person on the security of that very property, and that the defendant was his surety on that occasion. The money not having been repaid by the principal debtor, the defendant paid the debt, and the creditor, at his instance, brought an action against the debtor on the mortgage bond; and in execution of the decree obtained by him, the property in dispute was sold and purchased by the defendant. In this state of facts it was contended for the plaintiff that the payment by the surety discharged the debt, and consequently extinguished the security; and that the defendant under his purchase acquired only the rights and interests of the debtor as in an ordinary execution, and that,

LECTURE X. as the plaintiff's mortgage was prior in date to the defendant's purchase, the facts stated in the defence were no answer to the plaintiff's suit. This contention was, however, overruled by the Court, and Mr. Justice Markby, in giving the judgment of the Court, said:—"We must decide the question by analogy of the law of other countries ; and it appears to us clear, that, by the law of England and the law of Scotland, and, as far as we are aware, by the general law of Europe, when a surety has paid off the debt of his principal, not only all the collateral securities are transferred to the surety, but, by what is called subrogation, the right is also transferred to him to stand in the place of the original creditor, and to use against the principal debtor every remedy which the principal creditor himself could have used. It seems to us, therefore, that the law of this country may be reasonably taken to be that which has been considered equitable in other countries, namely, that the surety is not debarred from proceeding against the original debtor upon the instrument itself which created the debt, by reason of the debt having been paid by himself." (*Heera Lall Samunt* v. *Syud Oozeer Ali,* 21 W. R., 347.)

The English law on the subject is contained in the Mercantile Law Amendment Act, 1856 (19 & 20 Vict., c. 97), which provides, that "every person who being surety for the debt or duty of another, or being liable with another for any debt or duty, shall pay such debt or perform such duty, shall be entitled to have assigned to him, or to a trustee for him, every judgment, specialty, or other security which shall be held by the creditor in respect of such debt or duty, whether such judgment, specialty, or other security shall or shall not be deemed at law to have been satisfied by the payment of the debt or performance of the duty; and such person shall be entitled to stand in the place of the creditor, and to use all the remedies, and, if need be, and upon a proper indemnity, to use the name of the creditor, in any action or other proceeding at law or equity, in order to obtain from the principal debtor, or any co-security, co-contractor, or co-debtor, as the case may be, indemnification for the advances made and loss sustained by the person, who shall have so paid such debt or performed such duty; and such payment or performance so made by such surety shall not be pleadable in bar of any such action or other proceeding by him."

The surety being entitled to use against the principal debtor every remedy which the creditor himself could have used, it follows that, if the principal creditor improperly deals with the securities or relinquishes them, the surety will be discharged. This is the law in England, and has been followed in this country. (*Narain Govind*

LECTURE X. v. *Gunesh Attaram*, 7 Bom., 118.) Whether the surety will be absolutely discharged or exonerated only to the extent of the value of the securities relinquished by the creditor, is a question which admits of some doubt, and cannot perhaps be said to be yet settled.

You will observe that the English Statute, following in this respect the law of other countries, allows to the surety, not only the benefit of any security possessed by the creditor, but also the benefit of any judgment which may be held by the creditor. The same right is extended to one of several debtors who may have been obliged to pay the whole of the debt due to the creditor. The co-debtor has the same equity as the surety, and ought in justice to have the same facilities for reimbursement. It is true that the question has not been directly raised in any case in this country, except where one of several mortgagors redeems a usufructuary mortgage, when it has been held that he is entitled to retain possession of the whole estate till the mortgage debt is discharged by the rents and profits. It would be, however, difficult to suggest any reason why the same principle should not be extended to other cases, in which one of several joint debtors pays the whole debt, such debt being secured by a mortgage. It is true, if the mortgage is one by way of conditional sale, difficulties may arise in the way of the enforcement of it as against the other debtors; but there is no reason why the payment should not be regarded as a charge on the property in the nature of a simple mortgage. There are some expressions in the judgment of the Court in *Degumburee Dabee* v. *Eshan Chunder Sen* (9 W. R., 230), which would at first sight seem to show that a co-debtor cannot have the benefit of any securities held by the creditor; but the point really decided in the case was, that a co-debtor purchasing a judgment against himself and the other debtors, had no right to issue execution on the judgment for the purpose of recovering the whole amount from the other debtors. It is, however, unfortunate that the Court should have rested their judgment in great measure upon the English case of *Dowbiggin* v. *Bourne* (2 Young and Collyer, 462), which followed *Copis* v. *Middleton* (Turner and Russell, 231), in which a somewhat refined distinction was taken between securities that were merged by the judgment, and those that were available to the surety notwithstanding the judgment. The rule, however, laid down in those cases was considered to be unsatisfactory; and, as we have already seen, the English Legislature has since passed an Act for the purpose of giving increased facilities to sureties and co-debtors for reimbursement.

I have already said that, as the law stands at present, one of several joint debtors cannot have the benefit of any judgment held by the creditor. The procedure of our Courts in matters of execution is ill adapted to the determination of the various questions which must necessarily arise in such cases; but, as I have already pointed out, it does not, by any means, follow that the debtor will not be permitted to avail himself of any securities held by the creditor, and which the creditor might have enforced against the debtor.

There are several other cases in which the law allows a person who discharges an incumbrance to stand in the place of the mortgagee. A purchaser of the debtor's equity of redemption, who pays off incumbrances on the purchased property in order to acquire a safe title, may, under certain circumstances, use such incumbrances as a shield against the claims of a subsequent incumbrancer who may not have been paid off. (*Syud Ajid Hossein* v. *Hafiz Amed Reza*, 17 W. R., 480.) The question, however, is not entirely free from difficulty, and I reserve a fuller discussion of it for the next lecture. Many other instances of subrogation will also be found in the books. Thus, in the case of *Syud Mohamed Shamsal Hasla* v. *Shewak Ram*, which was a suit by a reversioner to avoid a conveyance by a Hindu widow, it appearing that there was a valid mortgage upon the property for a certain sum which had been redeemed by money paid into Court by the defendant, the Court refused to make a decree for the plaintiff, except on the condition that the plaintiff should pay to the defendant the amount of the mortgage which had been redeemed by him. (14 W. R., 315; S. C. on appeal, 22 W. R., 409.) An analogus rule is followed when a conveyance is set aside, the Court frequently directing that the conveyance should stand as a security for the amount actually advanced to the plaintiff, or applied to his benefit.

I now come to the subject of contribution. This involves the determination of the proportions in which two or more owners of an estate, subject to a common charge, ought to contribute to its redemption, or what is the same question under another aspect, the extent of the right which one of such persons, who has been compelled to discharge the common debt, has to be reimbursed by the others. This is only a branch of the general law of contribution, and rests on the plainest principles of justice and equity. Any other rule would leave it open to the creditor to select his own victim, and from caprice or favoritism, what ought to be a "common burden," might be turned into "a gross personal oppression." We have already seen that a mortgage debt is one and indivisible, and if several distinct parcels of land are hypothecated to the creditor, and subsequently pass to different purchasers, the creditor may proceed against any one of those parcels; and the only way to prevent a sale of it would be

LECTURE X. to tender to him the whole of the mortgage debt. It is but reasonable that, in such a case, the person who is compelled to discharge a common burden, should be permitted to seek indemnification from the other purchasers, and no fairer rule can be suggested than that each of the purchasers should contribute according to the value of the property purchased by him. This was laid down by the Calcutta High Court in the case of *Bhoyrub Chunder Moduk* v. *Nudear Chand Pal* (12 W. R., 291). It would be manifestly unjust to allow a mere accident to cast upon a particular portion of the land, and, therefore, upon the owner of that portion, a burden which was originally imposed, and which ought in fairness, notwithstanding the proceedings of the creditor, to be laid equally on the whole, and, therefore, on all the purchasers; and, as I have already said, no proportion can be suggested which is so equitable as that of the respective values at the date of the severance.

It would seem, although the point was not directly before the Court, that no personal liability is incurred by the defendant, the plaintiff being only entitled to a charge on the portion purchased by the person from whom he seeks to be reimbursed. You will find the law similarly laid down by Story in his Equity Jurisprudence:—"Cases may be easily stated where apportionment of a common charge, or, more properly speaking, where contribution towards a common charge, seems indispensable for the purposes of justice, and accordingly has been declared by the common law in the nature of an apportionment towards the discharge of a common burden. Thus, if a man owning several acres of land is bound in a judgment or statute, or recognizance, operating as a lien on the land, and afterwards he alienes one acre to A, another to B, and another to C, &c.; there, if one alienee is compelled, in order to save his land, to pay the judgment, statute, or recognizance, he will be entitled to contribution from the other alienees. The same principle will apply in the like case, where land descends to parceners who make partition, and then one is compelled to pay the whole charge; contribution will lie against the other parceners. The same doctrine will apply to co-feoffees of the land, or of different parts of the land." (§ 477.) And again in § 484 the learned author says:— "Let us suppose a case where different parcels of land are included in the same mortgage, and these different parcels are afterwards sold to different purchasers, each holding in fee and severalty the parcel sold to himself. In such case, each purchaser is bound to contribute to the discharge of the common burden or charge, in proportion to the value which his parcel bears to the whole included in the mortgage." (Story's Equity Jurisprudence.) A somewhat curious case on the point is to be

LECTURE X. found in the books: *Jeetram Dutt* v. *Durga Dass Chatterjee* (22 W. R., 430.) It appears that the creditor, who had a charge in the nature of a simple mortgage on two properties belonging to two different persons, levied the whole of the debt from one of the debtors. The person who was obliged to repay the whole of the debt brought a suit for contribution against his co-debtors, and, in execution of the decree obtained by him, seized the property which had belonged to his co-debtor, and which formed a portion of the land on which the debt due to the principal creditor was secured. The creditor, who had in the meantime purchased the property, asked that the attachment might be withdrawn, and on the dismissal of the application deposited in Court under protest the money due to the judgment-creditor, which was subsequently paid away to him. He then brought a suit for the money which he had been obliged to pay under protest, but the Court was of opinion that he was not entitled to recover back the money, apparently because the judgment-creditor had a lien on the land which formed a portion of the property on which the debt was originally secured; and that he was entitled, "in respect of the security given for the original debt, to stand in the same position as the creditor whose claim on that security had been satisfied."

I now come to the doctrine of marshalling of securities, which is intimately connected with the right of subrogation, which I have already considered. Whenever a person has a lien on two properties, and another a charge only on one of such properties, the Court will compel the mortgagee whose debt is secured on two properties, to take his satisfaction in the first instance out of the estate not in mortgage to the other, provided that his rights are not in any way prejudiced, or his remedies improperly controlled. The very same result is accomplished in some systems, by allowing the mortgagee who has a mortgage only upon one estate to stand in the place of the other mortgagee, if the latter shall have taken his satisfaction out of that estate. LECTURE X.

The doctrine of marshalling rests upon the principle, that a person having two funds to resort to should not be permitted from wantonness or caprice to disappoint another who has only one fund to go upon. If, therefore, the person with a claim upon two funds elects to proceed against that to which alone the right of the other is limited, the latter will be allowed to stand in the place of the former, and to satisfy his demand out of the other fund.

The result of the English and American authorities on the subject is thus stated by Story in his Equity Jurisprudence:—

"The general principle is that where one party has a lien on or interest in two funds for a debt, and another party has a lien or an interest in one only of the funds for another debt, the latter has a right in equity to compel the former to resort to the other fund in the first instance for satisfaction, if that course is necessary for the satisfaction of the claims of both parties, whenever it does not trench upon the rights or operate to the prejudice of the party entitled to the double fund."

"If A has a mortgage upon two different estates for the same debt, and B has a mortgage upon only one of the estates for another debt, B has a right to throw A in the first instance for satisfaction upon the security which he, B, cannot touch, at least where it will not prejudice A's rights or improperly control his remedies." (§§ 633, 642, 643.)

I need hardly point out that, ordinarily, a subsequent purchaser of one of the estates has just as strong a claim as a mortgagee. There is, however, this difference between the position of a purchaser and that of an incumbrancer. In the case of a purchaser, if the purchase was made with knowledge of the mortgage, there is no reason why, as between the purchaser and the mortgagor, the burden should be thrown in the first instance on the mortgagor; although, as I have already endeavoured to explain, the person who is compelled to pay the whole would be entitled to bring an action for contribution. A mortgagee, however, stands upon a different footing. He has a right to enforce the payment of his debt, and whether the mortgage to him was or was not with notice of the prior incumbrance, the mortgagor cannot complain with reason of any facility which may be offered to the second mortgagee by compelling the prior mortgagee to resort, in the first instance, to the estate which is not the subject of mortgage to the puisne incumbrancer. The case, in fact, is analogous to the familiar case of a mortgagor redeeming the first mortgagee. Such redemption enures to the benefit of the puisne mortgagee, and the mortgagor will not be permitted to say to him "you shall satisfy yourself only out of the equity of redemption on which alone the debt was secured." The point is a very important one, and must be carefully borne in mind. In some of the earlier English cases, you will find it laid down that marshalling could not be insisted upon by an incumbrancer with notice of the prior mortgage. (*Lanoy* v. *Duke of Athol*, 2 Atk., 4446.) The rule, however, was considered too narrow, and the distinction has since been abolished. (*Gibson* v. *Seagrim*, 20 Beav., 614; *Tidd* v. *Lister*, 10 Hare, 157.) LECTURE X.

The doctrine of marshalling has been adopted by our own Courts as a rule founded in equity and good conscience, although it may perhaps be doubted if the reservations by which the doctrine is qualified have been sufficiently attended to in some of the reported cases on the subject.

In the case of *Mussamut Nowa Koer* v. *Sheikh*

Abdul Rohim (Sutherland, 1864, p. 374) one of the estates in mortgage having been sold under an execution levied by an ordinary creditor, the purchaser under the execution resisted the attempt of the mortgagee to enforce his security against the property which had been purchased by him, without in the first instance proceeding against the properties which still belonged to the mortgagor. The defence was allowed, and the Court, in giving judgment, observed:—"The sale (*i.e.*, the execution sale) does not release that estate from the mortgage, but it forces the plaintiff to take measures in the first place to recover the amount due to him from the remaining estates included in his mortgage deed. If any balance remains after he has realized all which he can realize from these two remaining estates, he can then return to the third estate to recover the balance. No injustice is done to the plaintiff by requiring him to take satisfaction out of funds which are within his power for this purpose, and so placed by the deed; while, on the other hand, very great injustice might be done to other parties by allowing plaintiff to proceed against the estate which has been already sold."

It is probable, although the fact does not appear from the report, that the purchaser bought without notice of the mortgage, and paid, not for the equity of redemption, but for an absolute interest in the property. Even in that case, however, it is extremely doubtful, as I have already explained, if the purchaser under the execution could set up the defence of a *bonâ fide* purchase for value and without notice of the incumbrance. LECTURE X.

There are other cases also in the books in which securities have been marshalled, and which you may usefully consult. (*Tulsi Ram* v. *Munu Lall*, 1 W. R., 353; consider *Bissonath Mookerjee* v. *Kisto Mohun Mookerjee*, 7 W. R., 483; *Khetoosee Churria* v. *Bany Madhub Dass*, 12 W. R., 114.)

LECTURE XI.

Pledge of moveables—Paucity of authority—Contract Act—Definition of pledge—Validity of hypothecation of moveables—Danger of fraud—Distinction between a pledge and a mortgage of chattels—Power of sale—Pawnee's lien extends to interest and necessary expenses—Extraordinary expenses—Right of pawnee to tack subsequent advances—Rule of English law—Right of pawnee to make use of pledge—Degree of diligence imposed on pawnee—Differences between Indian law and English and Roman law on the point—Pawnor's right to accessions—Right of redemption—Passes to the legal representative—Possessory heirs—General and special—Unpaid seller's lien—May be varied—Right of resales—Differences between Indian and English law—Lien of artificers—Banker's and attorney's lien for general balance of account.

I NOW propose to treat of pledges of moveable property. This class of securities is, by no means, unimportant, although, in a country like India, the wealth of which mainly consists in agriculture, they are not so common as in commercial countries. It is for this reason that there are so few cases on the subject in the books. Pledges, however, occupy a distinct chapter in the Contract Act; and, although it cannot be said that the Legislature has dealt with every point in connection with the subject, it has certainly removed a good deal of that obscurity which must necessarily cluster round such a topic in the absence of well-defined rules.

A pledge is defined in the Act to be the "bailment of goods for the payment of a debt, or performance of a promise." But, although the bailment itself is called a pledge, the bailor and bailee are severally called pawnor and pawnee,—a change of phraseology for which it is somewhat difficult to account. LECTURE XI.

You will have observed from the definition of a pledge, that it must be accompanied by a delivery of possession. The Act is silent on the subject of the hypothecation of moveables. I told you in the introductory lecture that, in most modern systems of law, the hypothecation of moveables is, either not permitted at all, or is fenced in by a multitude of rules which are absolutely necessary for the prevention of fraud. We do not purchase land without examining the title-deeds, but moveables are daily transferred from one person to another, simply on the faith of the vendor's possession; and one of the most difficult problems which modern legislation has to solve is the reconciliation of the interests of commerce with the prevention of fraudulent transfers of moveables by persons in possession of them. It is, therefore, to be regretted, that the Contract Act is silent on the subject of hypothecation of moveables. We must not, however, infer from the silence of the Legislature that such transactions are invalid in this country, or that they may not be enforced against *bonâ fide* purchasers

LECTURE XI. without notice. In the case of *Deans* v. *Richardson* (3 All., 54), the Allahabad High Court affirmed the validity of a mortgage of moveable property, although unaccompanied by delivery of possession. In giving judgment, the Court observed,—"Now, without going at length into the numerous English authorities cited by the learned counsel in the course of their arguments, we may lay it down as the result of the latest rulings, that, by the common law of England, where goods are mortgaged and left in the possession of the original owner, the circumstance that they are so left is not to be held as a fraud '*per se*' rendering the mortgage liable to be defeated as between the mortgagee and third parties, such as *bonâ fide* purchasers or judgment-creditors ; but when possession is left with the mortgagor, this is a circumstance which warrants the Court in leaving it to the jury to determine whether or not the mortgage was fraudulent and colourable, or otherwise. We are not aware that any difference prevails between the law on this point, which has heretofore been accepted in this country, and the English common law. When recently the proposed Code of Contract Law was discussed in this country, the provision which the Indian Law Commissioners proposed for the security of *bonâ fide* purchasers of chattels from persons in possession was not only denounced as at variance with the received practice of the Courts, but as undesirable in this country. We do not feel at liberty to hold that the rule which has heretofore been accepted is so inequitable that we are at liberty to disregard it in our judgment. The circumstances of each case should be closely scanned; and, where it is shown that the original dealing is *bonâ fide*, it should be supported, notwithstanding there has been no delivery. In the present case no fraud other than alleged legal fraud and laches is imputed to the Bank. It is not denied that the advance was made and the security bargained for, it is only urged that the Bank should have taken possession at least when failure occurred in payment of the loan. The Bank was not, in our judgment, bound to take possession immediately after default was made. The machines were the means whereby the debtor earned moneys ; and it may, therefore, have been imagined that, in course of time, the debtor would be in a position to discharge his debts if indulgence were shown him. The Court, after considering the arguments urged, finds that the property in suit passed to the auction-purchaser, subject to the lien created in favour of the Bank ; and a decree will issue accordingly in favour of the Bank."

This doctrine was adhered to in the subsequent case of *Shyam Surder* v *Cheytaloll*, and the pledgee was allowed to enforce his security against a purchaser without notice. (3 All., 71.)

LECTURE XI. — It may here be necessary to notice the distinction between a mortgage and a pledge of chattels. A mortgage, although it is subject to a condition, passes the whole title to the creditor, but a pledge passes only what English lawyers call a special property. "A mortgage is a pledge and more; for it is an absolute pledge to become an absolute interest, if not redeemed at a certain time. A pledge is a deposit of personal effects, not to be taken back but on payment of a certain sum, by express stipulation or the course of trade to be a lien upon them." (*Jones* v. *Smith*, 2 Ves. Jun., 378.) The mortgagor of chattels may, therefore, be allowed to retain possession till default, but such a proceeding is open to the same objections as a hypothecation.

To return. If the pawnor make default, the pawnee may sell the pledge of his own authority and without judicial process. But he is bound to give previous notice of the sale to the pawnor. The pawnee may also, at his option, bring an action against the pawnor, and retain the goods pledged to him as collateral security. The lien of the pawnee extends not only to the principal debt, but also to the interest and any necessary outlay in the preservation or custody of the pledge. The language of the law, however, leaves us in some uncertainty whether the right of the pawnee to interest and necessary expenses is confined to a bare right of detention, or whether he is entitled to retain the amount out of the proceeds of the pledge. The Legislature could hardly have intended to confer the somewhat precarious right of a bare lien in such cases. But it is unfortunate that it has expressed itself in language which is certainly open to misconstruction.

It is hardly necessary to observe that the pawnee may obtain a sale of the pledge through judicial process, and having regard to the jealousy with which a private sale is regarded, and the possibility of further litigation, a sale through the intervention of a Court of Justice would certainly seem to be desirable in ordinary cases. In commercial transactions, however, this is not always either practicable or convenient; but the pawnee, as a fiduciary vendor, is bound to attend to the interests of the pawnor, and an improper sale will certainly be set aside as an abuse of the duty cast upon him. Again, you must remember that there is not the same danger of fraud in the sale of chattels as there is in the sale of land. Moveables may be appraised with sufficient accuracy for all practical purposes, but the case is very different with landed property. Besides, the exigencies of commerce may absolutely require, in many cases, a prompt sale of goods; but I need hardly point out that the analogy cannot be safely extended to land. I have, however, dwelt at length on the subject in a preceding lecture, and if I recur to it, it is only to point out that a power

LECTURE XI. of sale, which may be safely given to a pawnee, may yet be denied to a mortgagee of immoveable property.

I omitted to mention that extraordinary expenses for the preservation of the pledge, expenses which could not have been foreseen, may be recovered by the pawnee from the pawnor. There is, however, this distinction between expenses of this class and necessary expenses. In the case of necessary expenses, the law authorizes the pawnee to retain the pledge till he is reimbursed; while in the case of extraordinary charges, the pawnee has a right of action against the pawnor for the outlay, and it is extremely doubtful if he can add it to the amount of his lien. One learned commentator, indeed, says, that the pawnee has only a lien for necessary expenses, and that the law does not confer on him any right to be reimbursed by the pawnor over and above the right of lien. Such a right, however, I venture to think, may fairly be presumed. (See the observations of Peacock, C.J., in *Ambica Devi* v. *Pranhuri Dass*, 12 W. R., F. B., 1; S. C., 4 B. L. R., F. B., 77.) In the absence of any contract to that effect, the pawnee may not detain the pledge for any other debt than that for which the goods were pawned to him. The right of tacking, however, is recognized to a limited extent, the Court being bound to presume, in the absence of any evidence to the contrary, that subsequent advances made to the pawnor were made on the security of the pledge, and the pawnor is not entitled to redeem, except on condition of repaying the original debt, together with the subsequent advances. It would seem that this qualified right of tacking may be enforced, not only against the pawnor, but also against creditors and purchasers. The rule of the English and American law on the point is thus stated by Mr. Justice Story in his Equity Jurisprudence, § 1034:—" A subsequent advance made by a mortgagee or a pledgee of chattels would attach by tacking to the property in favour of such mortgagee, when a like tacking might not be allowed in cases of real estate. Thus, for instance, in the case of a mortgage of real estate, the mortgagee cannot, as we have seen, compel the mortgagor, upon an application to redeem, to pay any debts subsequently contracted by him with, or advances made to him by, the mortgagee, unless such new debts or advances are distinctly agreed to be made upon the security of the mortgaged property. But in the case of a mortgage or pledge of chattels, the general rule, or at least the general presumption, seems the other way. For it has been held, that, in such a case, without any distinct proof of any contract for that purpose, the pledge may be held until the subsequent debt or advance is paid, as well as the original debt. The ground of this distinction is, that he who seeks equity must do equity; and the plaintiff, seeking the assistance of the Court, ought to pay all the moneys due to the creditor, as it is natural to presume that the pledgee would not have lent the new sum but upon the credit of the pledge which he had in his hands before. The presumption may, indeed, be rebutted by circumstances; but, unless it is rebutted, it will generally, in favour of the lien, stand for verity against the pledgor himself, although not against his creditors or against subsequent purchasers."

A pawnee may not ordinarily use the goods pledged to him without the consent of the pawnor; such consent, however, will be presumed, if the pledge is such that it cannot be duly preserved without being used. A horse, for instance, must be exercised, and the pawnee may ride it for that purpose. If, however, the pledge is of such a nature, that it will be the worse for use, as wearing apparel for instance, the pawnee may not use it himself. If the use is indifferent, a moderate use is not prohibited; but in no case should the pledge be exposed to extraordinary peril.

On this subject the Contract Act says:—"If the bailee makes any use of the goods bailed, which is not according to the conditions of the bailment, he is liable to make compensation to the bailor for any damage arising to the goods from or during such use of them." (Section 154.) But the foregoing rules which have been adopted in other systems of law may be taken to sufficiently illustrate the conditions under which a pledge may or may not be used by the pawnee.

I will next call your attention to the degree of diligence imposed by the law on the pawnee. Section 151 says:—"In all cases of bailment, the bailee is bound to take as much care of the goods bailed to him as a man of ordinary prudence would, under similar circumstances, take of his own goods of the same bulk, quality and value as the goods bailed." This is a very simple rule unincumbered by the somewhat refined, if not fanciful, distinctions which we find in the Roman and English law. (See the case of *Coggs* v. *Bernard*, and the notes to that case in Smith, L. C., p. 177.) It is, however, necessary to observe, that the responsibility of the pawnee is greatly increased when he is in "mora," *i.e.*, when he wrongfully withholds the pledge from the pawnor. He then becomes answerable for any loss, destruction or deterioration from the time of such refusal. (Section 161.)

I told you in a previous lecture that, as a rule, any accession to the pledge, or natural increase, is considered to be itself pledged. A different rule would, however, seem to be laid down in the Contract Act. Section 163 of which says:—"In the absence of any contract to the contrary, the bailee is bound to deliver to the bailor, or according to his directions, any increase or profit which may have accrued from

LECTURE XI. the goods bailed." It is, however, probable that all that the Legislature intended to enact was, that the property, in the accession or increase, should belong to the pawnor and not to the pawnee, although the latter might claim the same qualified right in the increase as in the original pledge. I need hardly say that, in the absence of any authority, I cannot but speak with some reserve.

The pawnor may redeem the pledge at any time before it is actually sold, provided that he asserts his claim within thirty years from the date of the pawn, or of a written acknowledgment by the pawnee. (Act IX of 1871, S. 2, Art. 147.) Any agreement by which the right of redemption was sought to be fettered, would, as in the case of a mortgage of land, be absolutely void; and the pawnor would be let in to redeem, notwithstanding the agreement. If the pawnee should die before redemption, the right may be enforced against his representatives. The right to redeem is, however, not confined to the pawnor during his life, but may be asserted by his legal representatives.

I shall conclude this lecture with a few words on possessory liens—a very imperfect class of securities when confined to a bare right of detention without the means of obtaining material satisfaction. The Contract Act, following the English law on the subject, divides liens into two classes—general and special. A special lien authorizes the holder of the goods to retain them only till the particular debt in respect of the goods is paid. But a general lien extends to any balance which may be due from the owner to the holder of the goods. By section 93 of the Contract Act, the seller has a lien on the goods sold by him for the unpaid price so long as they remain in his possession. As in the case of land, however, the lien may be waived, and the taking of a collateral security will probably raise the inference that the lien was intended to be abandoned. I need hardly point out that, where the goods are sold on credit, the seller has ordinarily no lien; but the insolvency of the buyer before delivery will give the seller the right to retain the goods. The same result follows if the period for which credit is given is allowed to expire, and the goods are suffered to remain in the possession of the seller. (Sections 95—97.) As for the right of stoppage *in transitu*, see sections 99—106.

According to the English law, as I have already explained, a possessory lien is only of value as a means of compelling satisfaction. It does not confer a right of sale. (*Thames Iron Works Co.* v. *Patent Derricks*, 29 L. J., Chan., 714.) Section 107 of the Contract Act, however, contains an important improvement. It says:—"Where the buyer of goods fails to perform his part of the contract, either by not taking the goods sold to him, or by not paying for them, the seller, having a lien on the goods or

LECTURE XI. having stopped them in transit, may, after giving notice to the buyer of his intention to do so, resell them after the lapse of a reasonable time, and the buyer must bear any loss, but is not entitled to any profit, which may occur on such resale."

There are other descriptions of liens, however, which are not accompanied by a power of sale. The lien, for instance, allowed to a person for labor bestowed on goods bailed to him is confined to a bare right of detention. Bankers, factors, and others, who possess a general lien, are also in the same position. (Sections 170 and 171.) They can, no doubt, put a pressure on the will of the debtor, but they may not, in any case, sell the pledge.

LECTURE XII.

Extinction of securities—Consolidation—Merger of debt—Right of prior mortgagee how far extinguished—Rule of Roman law—Doctrine of English Court of Chancery—Conflicting decisions in India—Extinction of security by discharge of obligation—Novation—Substitutionary and cumulative—Extinction of security by destruction or sale of pledge or prescription and renunciation—Priority—Generally determined by order of time—How affected by registration—Notice immaterial—Priority how far affected by possession—Rule of Hindu law—Privileged liens—Salvor's lien—Tacking—Extent to which recognised in Roman law—Doctrine of English law—Origin of doctrine—Not followed in India—Consolidation of securities—Rule of English law—Partial recognition by our Courts—Mortgage to secure future advances—How priority is forfeited—Fraud, actual or constructive, of mortgagee—Laches—Effect of allowing title-deeds to remain in custody of mortgagor—Allowing mortgagor to receive rents after notice of incumbrance—Deeds of further charge—Practice in India—Waiver of security not presumed—*Lis pendens*—Application of doctrine in relation to priority of securities.

I PROPOSE to discuss in the present lecture the various methods by which a security is extinguished. I will also treat of the rules governing the priority of securities, and as intimately connected with the topic, the 'tacking' and 'consolidation' of mortgages. The questions to which I intend to call your attention are extremely important, and deserve very careful attention. I must, however, warn you at the outset that much of this branch of the law of securities is still in a floating condition; and I am, therefore, obliged to speak with some reserve.

LECTURE XII.

A mortgage is, generally speaking, extinguished by consolidation, that is, by the property in the pledge vesting in the mortgagee, or by the acquisition by the mortgagor of the right of the mortgagee. In such case, there is, technically speaking, a complete confusion of the security. The doctrine rests upon the impossibility of a man having a right of pledge over his own property, and is analogous to the extinction of a servitude when the dominant and servient tenement become vested in one and the same person. A very slight examination of the rule will, however, show that the doctrine must be received with some qualification, as cases may be easily put in which the application of the rule would lead to manifest injustice. Thus, supposing the equity of redemption is purchased by the prior mortgagee, if the effect of the purchase were to extinguish the security, the result would be that the subsequent incumbrancers would be entitled to priority, and the prior mortgagee would thus be in a distinctly less favorable position than he occupied before. In such cases, the Roman law admitted an exception and recognised the right of the prior mortgagee to use his mortgage as a shield against the claims of the puisne incumbrancers. It has indeed been suggested by some writers that the exception applied only to those cases in which the pledgee was either ignorant of his own right of pledge or of the subsequent incumbrances; but the better opinion seems to be that the exception was not hedged in by any such limitations. (See the authorities cited in *Ramu Naikun* v. *Subarayu Mudali*, 7 Mad., 229; and the Supplement to Markby's Elements of Law, p. 43.)

A different doctrine, however, prevails in the English law. The purchaser of an equity of redemption, with notice of subsequent incumbrances, stands in the same situation as if he himself had been the mortgagor, and cannot set up against such subsequent incumbrances either a prior mortgage of his own, or a mortgage which he or the mortgagor may have got in. (*Toulmin* v. *Steere*, 3 Mer., 210.) The prior mortgagee, however, may protect himself from the consequences of a merger of the debt by taking distinct steps to keep his security alive. If, however, the mortgage is not kept on foot as a distinct and distinguishable security, there will be complete confusion, and the mortgagee may not use it as a shield to protect himself from the claims of the puisne incumbrancers. (*Watts* v. *Symes*, 21 L. J. Chan., 713; *Heyden* v. *Kirkpatrick*, 34 Beav., 645.)

The rule of the English law on the point may perhaps seem to some persons as extremely artificial, and, on the whole, less equitable than the doctrine of the Roman law. Indeed, English lawyers themselves would seem to share the impression, and the doctrine laid down in *Toulmin* v. *Steere* has been sought to be qualified in more recent cases. (See

LECTURE XII. — the observations of Knight Bruce, L. J., in *Watts* v. *Symes*, 1 DeG., Mac. and G., 240.) It is, therefore, somewhat remarkable that the doctrine should have been adopted without question by some of the superior Courts in India. (*Gournarain Mujumdar* v. *Brojonath Kundu*, 14 W. R., 491; *Itcharam Dyaram* v. *Raiji Joga*, 11 Bom., 41.) I do not wish to say anything which may wear the appearance of presumption or disrespect, but I trust I may be permitted to suggest without offence that the very high estimate which English lawyers almost always set on their own system is scarcely justified by a comparison with other systems of law, and more particularly Roman law.

In the case of *Ramu Naikun* v. *Subarayn Mudali* (7 Mad., 229), the Madras Court, after comparing the doctrine of the Roman law with that of the English law on the point under consideration, refused to follow the English authorities, the learned Judges observing that the "rule of the Civil law is the true rule, and one to which the minds of English Judges are gradually tending." (Compare *Narain Saha* v. *Ochut Saha*, 14 W. R., 233; *Syud Wajed Hossein* v. *Hafez Ahmed Reza*, 17 W. R., 480.) There is thus an unfortunate conflict of opinion on the point among the superior Courts in India. The knot can perhaps be cut only by the Legislature.

I may mention that the foregoing observations apply only to the case of a mortgagee purchasing the equity of redemption, or a purchaser of the mortgaged estate paying off an incumbrance on it. They have no application whatever to the case of a mortgagor himself buying in an incumbrance. If the mortgagor obtains the benefit of a prior mortgage by an assignment of the security, or by purchase from the mortgagee under his power of sale, the charge is absolutely extinguished, and may not be set up against the puisne incumbrancers. (See the English case of *Otter* v. *Lord Vaux*, 2 K. & J., 650.) The distinction rests upon a very intelligible ground, which I had occasion to explain in a previous lecture. (See Lect. X.) A mortgage is only a security for a debt, and the mortgagor cannot be heard to complain of any increased facilities which may be offered to the subsequent incumbrancers for the recovery of their debts by an enlargement of the estate possessed by the mortgagor. A mortgagor cannot protect himself against his own incumbrances.

To return. The second method by which a security comes to an end is by the discharge of the debt for which the security was given. The obligation may be discharged, not only by an actual payment, but also by what is called novation, that is, the substitution of another obligation in place of the first. The substitution, however, may take place without destroying the former obligation when the novation is known as 'cumulative.' The rule of law, however, is, that in the absence of a clear expression of the

LECTURE XII. intention of the parties to the contrary, the former security is not extinguished. The ordinary presumption in all such cases is, that the benefit of a security is not waived by the acceptance of another security in its place. (See Colq. Rom. Law § 1852—1855; Fisher on Mortgage, pp. 811 & 812; and *Gopeebundhee* v. *Kalipodo Banerjee*, 23 W. R., 338.)

The pledgee also loses his right by renunciation, or by destruction of the pledge. The same result follows, if a third person has held the property for a period sufficient to create a prescriptive right. I may mention that a sale for revenue or any other statutory sale, which passes the property to the purchaser free of all incumbrances, does not, in reality, destroy the security of the mortgagee. It only transfers the charge from the land to the purchase money.

In conclusion it is necessary to observe that a sale by the pledgee himself passes the property to the purchaser unincumbered by the security. The result is the same whether the property is sold under a decree for sale or by the mortgagee himself under his power; and, according to a recent decision of the Calcutta High Court, the benefit of the security passes to the purchaser even when the decree is simply for money, and does not expressly authorise a sale of the mortgaged estate. (*Denobundhu Ghose* v. *Haran Bose*, 23 W. R., 186.) A mortgagee may not, in any case, sell the bare equity of redemption. Any other rule would be excessively harsh to the mortgagor; indeed it might be attended by the most disastrous results to him. Take, for instance, the case of a property worth Rs. 4,000, subject to a mortgage for one-half of that sum. If the mortgagee were allowed to sell the equity of redemption, which, by the hypothesis, is worth Rs. 2,000, the price which would be paid by the purchaser would, no doubt, satisfy the mortgage debt, but the property would pass away from the mortgagor for only Rs. 2,000. It is possible that the mortgagor may become entitled by subrogation to the security possessed by the creditor; but, as I pointed in a previous lecture, such a course would certainly lead to a perfect waste of litigation, which may be easily avoided by holding that whenever the mortgagee sells the property on which his debt is secured, what he sells is not an undefined right like the equity of redemption, but the pledge itself unincumbered by his own security. LECTURE XII.

I will now proceed to discuss the rules touching priority, one of the most intricate topics in the law of securities. Now, the general rule is, that priority is determined by the order of time. There are, however, exceptions to this rule either created by statute or recognised by the Court as founded upon those general principles of justice and equity which, in the absence of any express enactment, the Indian Courts are bound to administer.

LECTURE XII. — The first exception is that contained in Section 50 of the Registration Act, which, under certain circumstances, allows a registered mortgage priority over an earlier unregistered security. That Section says:—"Every document of the kinds mentioned in clauses (1) and (2) of Section 18, shall, if duly registered, take effect as regards the property comprised therein, against every unregistered document relating to the same property, and not being a decree or order, whether such unregistered document be of the same nature as the registered document or not." A similar enactment was contained in the earlier Acts.

You will observe one rather remarkable omission in the law. The Act allows preference to a registered instrument over an unregistered writing, where both belong to that group of instruments, the registration of which is optional. If, therefore, the puisne incumbrance is one which the parties are bound to register, it will not be entitled to priority over an earlier unregistered security. (*Hamed Buksh* v. *Bindabun*, 2 All., 37; *Shaik Ryesatulla* v. *Durga Churn Pal*, 24 W. R., 21.) A distinction is also made in favor of parol mortgages when they are accompanied by possession.

It is necessary to observe that, under the Indian Registration Act, notice is immaterial. A registered instrument will be entitled to priority in every case, provided that the transfer is not merely colorable, or as it is usually called a paper, transaction.

It is true the Act is silent as to the effect of notice, but it does not follow that the protection was intended to be confined only to a mortgagee without notice of a prior unregistered security. The construction put by Lord Hardwicke on the English Act has been questioned by several eminent Judges as trenching upon the policy of the registration laws, and it would certainly require strong argument to show that the Indian Legislature intended to introduce into this country a doctrine which would have the effect of frittering away the provisions of a most beneficent enactment. The omission from the recent Acts of the clause in the second Section of Regulation XIX of 1843, by which notice was expressly declared to be immaterial, may perhaps lend some color to the suggestion that the old doctrine embodied in the earliest Regulation on the subject was intended to be revived. It would, however, not be safe to build any argument on such an omission.

It would carry me much beyond the limits which I have proposed to myself in the present lecture, to enter upon a full discussion of the question. I may, however, point out that a comparison of the successive Registration Acts down to the 19th of 1843, shows that it was necessary in the last statute to provide expressly that notice was immaterial in order to guard against the application of the English doctrine which had been embodied in the

LECTURE XII. original Regulation. Besides, it may fairly be asked why has not the Legislature in the later Acts expressly declared its intention to confine the protection afforded by registration only to subsequent alienees taking without notice of a prior alienation. Such an enactment was contained in the original Regulation, and, if the doctrine was intended to be revived after having been advisedly repealed by subsequent legislation, the provision would probably have been repeated in the more recent statutes.

I have been induced to make the foregoing observations, because, in the case of *Jivandass Keshavji* v. *Framji Nanabhai* (7 Bom., 45), the Court seems to have held that the English doctrine of notice was applicable to Act XVI of 1864, the provisions of which on this point are similar to those of the present statute. In that case express notice was alleged; but if you once introduce the doctrine of notice, I do not see how questions of constructive notice can be wholly shut out, and thus the protection afforded by the Registration Act would be, in great measure, if not wholly, illusory. The doctrine, however, laid down by the Court in *Kashavji* v. *Framji* was not actually necessary for the decision of the case, as the mortgage to the registered mortgagee was, on the face of the instrument, subject to the prior unregistered incumbrance. No question of priority, therefore, could possibly arise, as the subsequent mortgage did not purport to be a mortgage of anything more than the bare equity of redemption. (Compare *Kishore Bhat Gullabhai* v. *Jorabhai Daji*, 7 Bom., A. J., 56.)

To return. Another class of exceptions to the general rule, by which priority is determined by the order of time, is to be found in certain decisions of the Bombay High Court, introducing the rule of Hindu law, by which preference is, in some cases, given to a mortgage followed or accompanied by possession. The application of the doctrine is, however, confined only to a few districts in that presidency. As I told you in a preceding lecture, preference is given only to a puisne incumbrancer without notice of the prior security, and, as registration at the present day serves the same purpose of publicity as tradition in ancient law, the delivery of possession affords no protection against an earlier registered security. This is probably the ground on which the application of the rule of Hindu law has been narrowed in recent decisions, for registration, of itself, could not alter a rule of law, except so far as effect may be given to it by statute. (*Itcharam Dyaram* v. *Raiji Joga*, 11 Bom., 4.)

Another important exception to the general rule touching the priority of securities, is recognised in favor of advances in the nature of salvage, that is advances made for the purpose of protecting a property from forfeiture or destruction. The lien of the salvor is known as a privileged lien, and upon

LECTURE XII. the plainest principles of equity, takes rank above every other charge on the property. This rule obtains in almost every system of law, and has been admitted in this country. (See *Sha Enayet Hossein* v. *Madan Mohun Sahun*, 22 W. R., p. 411.) There is another peculiarity about salvage liens which I ought to notice. It is that among themselves they are entitled to priority in the inverse order of their dates. The general order is here reversed, and the charge which is latest in point of time is entitled to preference over others earlier in date. The rule rests upon the obvious ground that, unless the last advance had been made, the property could not have been preserved for the benefit of the previous lenders. It is necessary to observe that, where a payment is made to save an incumbered property from forfeiture, the person making the advance ought to take care that the facts sufficiently appear upon the face of any instrument which may be subsequently executed by the person who is benefited by the payment, as otherwise the creditor might forfeit his priority. In conclusion I must throw out a caution that it does not follow that a person, lending money to another for the purpose of preventing a forfeiture, will be entitled to a privileged lien, even though the fact may appear on the face of the instrument, and the money is actually applied for the purpose. There is no authority on the point, and I do not think it necessary to offer any opinion on it one way or the other.

In some systems of law, however, as I have already pointed out, charges of this nature are entitled to preference over others earlier in date. LECTURE XII.

The principle on which the priority of a mortgage to secure future advances should be determined, is a question of some nicety. The general rule is, that if, by the terms of the instrument, the mortgagee is bound to make the advance, he would be entitled to the same priority as if the money had been advanced at the execution of the mortgage. (§ 1023, Story's Equity Jurisprudence.) If, however, the terms do not bind the mortgagee to make any advances, no present debt is created, and it seems that the mortgagee would be postponed in respect to any advances made by him after notice of a subsequent incumbrance. This is now the law in England (*Shaw* v. *Neale*, 6 Ho. Lo. Cas., 581), and will probably be followed in India. The only doubt that suggests itself to me is, whether in this country the mortgagee will not be postponed even in the absence of any notice in respect to advances made by him after the execution by the debtor of a mortgage on the same property in favor of another person. There is, however, no authoritative decision on the point, and I have drawn your attention to it only for the purpose of pointing out that the English rule must not be accepted without a more careful examination of the principle on which it rests than I am now able to give to the question.

LECTURE XII.

The discussion has conducted us to a topic which is familiarly known to English lawyers as tacking, and on which it is necessary to make a few observations. Now, the right of tacking was, as I told you, recognised to a certain extent in Roman law, which would not suffer the pledgor to redeem the pledge without paying to the pledgee, not only the debt for which the security was given, but also any other claim for money in writing possessed by the creditor against the pledgor. The right, however, could not, in any case, be exercised to the prejudice of a third person. This qualified right, however, is not what English lawyers understand by "tacking." Building upon the maxim "where the equities are equal, the law shall prevail," the English Court of Chancery has introduced a highly artificial rule, by which a mortgagee may, under certain conditions, entitle himself to priority over an incumbrance earlier in point of date. The doctrine may be thus stated: A mortgagee without notice, purchasing the first incumbrance, shall thereby protect his estate against an intermediate incumbrance, although he purchased in the incumbrance after he had notice of the subsequent incumbrance. You will observe that the first mortgagee has what is called the legal estate, and as the mortgagee purchasing in the first incumbrance, advanced the money without notice of the intermediate incumbrance, he has, at least, as strong an equity as the intermediate incumbrancer. Equity will not, therefore, disarm him of the advantage which he has secured for himself, and thus 'the equities being equal, the law shall prevail.' LECTURE XII.

The origin of the doctrine is thus explained by Lord Hardwicke:—"As to the equity of this Court," observes his Lordship, "that a third incumbrancer, having taken his security or mortgage without notice of the second incumbrance, and then being puisne, taking in the first incumbrance, shall squeeze out and have satisfaction before the second, the equity is certainly established in general, and was so in *Marsh* v. *Lee*, by a very solemn determination by Lord Hale, who gave it the term of the 'creditor's *tabula in naufragio*;' that is, the leading case. Perhaps, it might be going a good way at first; but it has been followed ever since, and I believe was rightly settled, only on this foundation, by the particular constitution of the law of this country. It could not happen in any other country but this; because the jurisdiction of law and equity is administered here in different Courts, and creates different kinds of rights in estates; and, therefore, as Courts of Equity break in upon the common law, where necessity and conscience require it, still they allow superior force and strength to a legal title to estates; and, therefore, where there is a legal title and equity on one side, this Court never thought fit that, by reason of a prior equity against a man

LECTURE XII. — who had a legal title, that man should be hurt; and this, by reason of that force, this Court necessarily and rightly allows to the common law and to legal titles. But if this had happened in any other country, it could never have made a question; for, if the law and equity are administered by the same jurisdiction, the rule, *qui prior est tempore potier est jure*, must hold." (*Wortley* v. *Birkhead*, 2 Ves., 571.)

It is hardly necessary to add that our Courts have refused to follow the English doctrine on the subject. (11 W. R., 310.) There is, however, another maxim of the English Court of Chancery less open to objection, which applies not to tacking—properly speaking —but to the right to a consolidation of all the securities possessed by the creditor without any question as to priority. He who seeks equity must do equity, and redemption being an equitable right, the mortgagor may not redeem without on his part doing equity to the mortgagee. Thus, if the owner of two or more different estates mortgage them successively for distinct debts to the same person, the mortgagee has a right to insist that one security shall not be redeemed alone leaving him exposed to the risk of deficiency as to the others, but that the mortgagor must redeem him entirely. The right in fact claimed by the mortgagee in such cases is analogous to the right recognised by the Roman law, and has been admitted by our Courts as resting not upon any technical ground, but upon the plainest principles of justice and equity. (*Vithal Mahadeo* v. *Daud Valad Mahomed Hossein*, 6 Bom., 90.) The doubt, however, which I have expressed in respect to the applicability of these general maxims to mortgages governed by the Bengal Regulations, applies also to the present question. The Courts in the other provinces are not fettered by any positive enactments, and are, therefore, in a position to introduce a larger number of the doctrines of the English Court of Chancery than the Courts of Allahabad or Calcutta.

The rule of English law, however, touching the consolidation of securities, however unexceptionable when confined to the mortgagor or his heir, becomes of questionable propriety when extended to a purchaser, even though he should have purchased without notice of any other mortgage. (*Ireson* v. *Denn*, 2 Cox, 425.) The doctrine has not, however, yet received the same extension in this country, and will probably be recognised only in a qualified form.

It would seem that debts, which are not secured by a mortgage, may not be consolidated. In pledges of moveables, however, the Legislature has recognised a qualified right to tack subsequent advances. There is, however, no authority for extending the right to a mortgage of land. (N. W. P., Vol. IX, p. 465; 1860, p. 122.)

LECTURE XII. I shall next proceed to discuss the various ways in which priority may be forfeited. Now, a mortgagee forfeits his priority if he is guilty of fraud, either actual or constructive. Thus, if he should induce another by concealing his own mortgage to lend money on the security of the property pledged to himself, he will be postponed to the subsequent incumbrancer whom he has misled. There may be no duty upon the prior mortgagee voluntarily, and without being asked, to disclose his security; but any actual misleading, either by acts or declarations, will be followed by a forfeiture of his priority. It would take me much beyond the limits I have proposed to myself in this lecture, to state the various circumstances which would be sufficient to fasten upon the prior mortgagee a charge of actual or constructive fraud. The subject is discussed in Story's Equity Jurisprudence, to which I would refer those who wish to pursue the enquiry. The following cases also may be usefully consulted. (11 W. R., 286; 5 Agra, 402.)

A mortgagee may also forfeit his priority by his own laches. Thus, for instance, if the mortgagee should suffer the title-deeds to remain in the custody of the mortgagor, he will, under certain circumstances, be postponed to a subsequent incumbrancer who may have advanced money on the faith of the title-deeds. The earlier English authorities were very stringent against the mortgagee who put the mortgagor in a position to mislead third persons; but the rule has been considerably relaxed in more recent cases. The mere possession of the title-deeds by the second mortgagee will not give him priority. There must be some act or default on the part of the first mortgagee to have this effect. The non-possession, however, of the title-deeds, is a circumstance which the mortgagee is bound to explain. But if he can satisfy the Court that the absence of the title-deeds was reasonably accounted for by the mortgagor when he obtained his mortgage, or that he was subsequently induced to part with them, under such circumstances as to exonerate him from any serious imputation of negligence, he does not lose his priority. This is how the law stands upon the more recent authorities in England, and it was followed in Madras in *Somasundara Zambiran* v. *Sakkarai Pattan.* (4 Mad., 369.)

I have already explained how the first mortgagee in possession is postponed as regards the rents and profits which he suffers the mortgagor to receive after notice of a puisne incumbrance.

A practice obtains in this country, which is not the less objectionable because it is almost universal. When money is advanced by way of further charge, the original mortgage deed is not unfrequently cancelled, and the property pledged by a second instrument for the consolidated sum. Deeds of further charge are very rarely executed outside the Presi-

LECTURE XII. — dency Towns. Again, it frequently happens that when the mortgagor is unable to repay the loan, an account is taken of the moneys due to the mortgagee on his security, and a fresh bond is executed, by which the property is pledged for the original debt with the accumulated interest. The property, however, may have been intermediately pledged to a third person, and the mortgagee may be thus in danger of losing his priority. The reported cases on the subject, however, show that the Court will not presume, except on very strong grounds, that the original security was intended to be relinquished. (*Gopee Bundhoo Shantra* v. *Kalee Pudo Banerjee*, 23 W. R., p. 338; S. D. A., 1856, p. 942; 1857, p. 1184.) The subject has been already discussed by me when treating of the extinction of securities. It must not, however, be supposed that, as against an intermediate incumbrancer, the security will be entitled to priority, except to the extent of the advances actually made before the execution of the subsequent mortgage, and where the interest is turned into principal, the agreement for compound interest will have no effect as against the intermediate incumbrancer.

In connection with the question of priority there is one topic, on which a few words will not perhaps be thrown away. I allude to the doctrine of *lis pendens*. In consequence of the rule *pendente lite nihil innoveture*, the priority of a security cannot be affected by any incumbrance created by the mortgagor during the pendency of a suit for foreclosure or sale. This maxim is not founded upon any technical ground as to constructive notice, but on the broad principle, that litigation would be interminable if any of the parties to an action could create any right in favor of a third person during the pendency of a suit. As observed by Lord Cranworth in *Bellamy* v. *Sabine* (26 L. J., Ch., 797, N. S.):—"It is scarcely correct to speak of *lis pendens* as affecting a purchaser through the doctrine of notice, though, undoubtedly, the language of the Courts often so describes its operation. It affects him, not because it amounts to notice, but because the law does not allow litigant parties to give to others, pending the litigation, rights to the property in dispute, so as to prejudice the opposite party. Where a litigation is pending between a plaintiff and a defendant as to the right of a particular estate, the necessities of mankind require that the decision of the Court in the suit shall be binding, not only on the litigant parties, but also on those who derive title under them by alienations made pending the suit, whether such alienees had or had not notice of the pending proceedings. If this were not so, there could be no certainty that the litigation would ever come to an end. A mortgage or sale made before final decree to a person who had no notice of the pend-

LECTURE XII. ing proceedings, would always render a new suit necessary, and so interminable litigation might be the consequence." (*Ballajee Gunesh* v. *Khushalji*, 11 Bom., 24; *Gulabchand* v. *Dhondie*, 11 Bom., 64; *Ravji Narain* v. *Krishnajee Lakshman*, 11 Bom., 139; and *Pullukdharee* v. *Mohabir Sing*, 23 W. R., 382.)

It is only necessary to add that, under Regulation XVIII of 1806, the application of the mortgagee for foreclosure would seem to be the commencement of the suit for the purposes of *lis pendens*. I had occasion to consider the question in a previous lecture, and need not, therefore, repeat what I then said (Lect. VI). It would, however, not be safe for the mortgagee to disregard the transfer altogether, and where the alienation takes place after the institution of the foreclosure proceedings, but before the commencement of the regular suit by which they are almost invariably followed in Bengal, the purchaser ought to be made a party defendant, as well as the original mortgagor.

Here I conclude the lectures of the term. I have endeavoured to give you a short account of the law of securities in this country. A mere bead-roll of cases, however useful to the practitioner, would have been of doubtful utility to the student, and I have, therefore, attempted to explain, as fully as I could in the compass of these lectures, the principles on which the law is founded. 'He knoweth not the law who knoweth not the reason of the law' is a saying which the student should always bear in mind, and you will pardon me if I venture to affirm what is now accepted almost as a truism that a careful study of general principles as illustrated in different systems of law, will not be wholly useless to you when you enter upon the practical duties of the profession. It may not be given to every one of us to attain high forensic skill, but depend upon it, the culture gained by the scientific study of law is never wholly thrown away, even though it may not in every case be crowned with professional success. LECTURE XII.

APPENDIX I.

Since these lectures were delivered, my attention has been called to an unreported decision of Bayley and Hobhouse, JJ., in which the Calcutta High Court refused to follow the ruling of the Sudder Dewanny Adalut in Bhowany Churn Mitter's case. The facts sufficiently appear from the judgment.

IN THE HIGH COURT OF JUDICATURE AT FORT WILLIAM IN BENGAL.

The 23rd of September 1869.

PRESENT:

The Honorable Vincent Bayley and the Honorable Sir Charles Parry Hobhouse, two of the Judges of this Court.

CASE No. 135 OF 1869.

Regular Appeal from a decision passed by the Subordinate Judge of Zillah Dacca, dated the 15th of March 1869.

SUNATUN BYSACK, Defendant *(Appellant)*,

versus

KOONJO BIHAREE BYSACK, GOBINDHUN BYSACK, CHYTUNKISTO BYSACK, SADHOO CHURN BYSACK, AND GOBIND CHURN BYSACK, Plaintiffs *(Respondents)*.

Baboo *Romesh Chunder Mitter* for Appellant.

Baboo *Onnoda Persaud Banerjee* for Respondents.

Bayley, J.—THIS was a suit by the plaintiffs to recover from the defendant Rs. 5,600, being the principal of the overdue instalments to be paid under a certain deed of mortgage, together with Rs. 654-4 annas as interest on the said amount, by attachment and sale of the mortgaged properties, mentioned in the schedule of the plaint. The plaint stated that the cause of action, with regard to the first eight instalments, accrued on the 2nd October 1866. In regard to four others on the 9th February 1869, and in regard to four others on the 9th February 1868; that a notice was served on the defendant on the 1st June 1868, requiring him to pay under the deed of mortgage, but that the defendant did not pay the money, and consequently the plaintiff prayed "that the Court may be pleased to award from the defendant and the mortgaged properties the amount claimed, together with costs and interests."

The defendant's answer was to the effect, that as there was a suit already pending in the Original Side of the High Court, in which the mortgage instalment bond in question was filed, until that case is decided, a second suit on the basis of the said instalment bond could not be entertained; that, ere this, the plaintiffs had preferred a similar claim in the Original Side of the High Court for the instalments due on the said bond, but that the suit was dismissed,—hence the present suit was *res adjudicata;* that the terms of the instalment bond were such as enabled the plaintiffs to bring to sale the pledged property by enforcing the said bond without the necessity of having recourse to a suit like the present, especially as the defendant never made any objection to the sum being realized by the sale of the properties mortgaged; that the present suit was brought merely to harass the defendant; and lastly, that the amount of interest was improperly calculated, and that all that was claimed was not in fact due.

The judgment of the Lower Court is not very clear, but it evidently draws a distinction between the Courts where the English law prevails as in Calcutta, in which, under a bond, property can be sold in realization of monies due under it without the intervention of a Court, and the Mofussil Courts, where the Lower Appellate Court remarks, such property cannot be sold without the Court's intervention. It says:—"It is not legal for any mortgagee to sell *of himself* the mortgaged property, situate within the jurisdiction of the Mofussil Courts."

As to interest, the Lower Court considers that the plaintiff's claim was a just one, and the order of the Court is, "that the suit be decreed, and that the amount claimed and interest on the principal amount for the period of pendency of the suit at the rate of Rs. 6 per cent. per annum, and costs in Court, together with interest on the consolidated amount at Rs. 6, be realized from the defendant and the mortgaged properties."

From this decision the defendant appeals to this Court, and the first, second, and sixth grounds of appeal may be well considered together. The first is, that the plaint discloses no cause of action. The second ground is also almost to the same effect, being that, whereas there is nothing in the plaintiffs' statement to show that the defendant was called upon to pay the money due under the mortgaged bond by the sale of any portion of the mortgaged premises and refused to carry out the proposal, the plaintiffs had no right to bring this suit. The sixth ground is, that the contract between the parties was such as that there could be no decree against the person of the defendant as given by the Lower Court. In addition to these, there are other grounds taken in appeal to the effect, that the Lower Court was wrong in holding that, in Mofussil Courts, a claim, such as this, could not be realized without the intervention of a Court of Justice; that the terms of the contract were sufficient to enable the plaintiff to realize what was due from the mortgaged property without bringing an action in Court; and lastly, that the plaintiff was not entitled to the interest he claimed, or to any interest previous to the date of mortgage. It is further urged before us, although the point is not taken in the written grounds of appeal, that, if the plaintiffs are entitled to any decree at all, it must be without any costs.

Now, if we read the grounds of appeal, together with the objections taken in the written statement, there appear in the first place two main objections to the plaintiff's suit. The *first* is, that pending adjudication in the Supreme Court of the suit there, this suit cannot be heard; and the *second* is, that the present suit is of the character of a *res adjudicata*.

With regard to the *first* point I would observe, that the same subject-matter cannot be said to be pending adjudication in the Original Side, for that is a suit on the general question of family right, and that family suit is a 'subject-matter separate and distinct from the matter now in dispute.

In regard to the *second* point, it is stated that a similar suit on the basis of the very instalment bond was brought before the High Court in its Original Side and dismissed, and hence the present suit on the basis of the said bond would be a *res judicata*. But the fact is that that suit only was, and could only be, for property, *within the local jurisdiction of that Court*, whereas the property now in dispute is without the jurisdiction of that Court. The subject-matters therefore of the suit there, and of the suit here, are each entirely different.

Having disposed of these two objections to the suit, the next point to be considered is, whether, by the terms of the contract itself, the plaintiffs could bring this suit. Now, the terms of the contract are these. After reciting that the sums due shall carry interest, (as to which matter I shall have to remark hereafter,) the deed says "the sums shall be recoverable by a separate suit in respect thereof or by sale of a portion of the mortgaged premises sufficient to realize the amount so due." I think that, on the express terms of this contract, it was open to the plaintiffs to sue to have their right declared by a Court of Justice, to realize the money due by sale of the mortgaged property. The word "*or*" clearly indicates that there was the option. It is very strongly pressed on us, that there was no objection made by the defendant, and no consent was withheld as to the property being sold by a private sale or otherwise as the creditor might think best for the realization of his money due, and, therefore, there being no cause of action, the present suit was unnecessary, and to use the terms of the pleader, vexatious. But as I before observed, a clear option was given by the very terms of the contract to the plaintiffs to bring a suit in Court. There may have been good reasons for their instituting the present suit in Court, as the preferential course for a declaration by a Court of their right would probably be less open to future difficulties than might follow a private transfer. It is quite clear, moreover, that it was stipulated in the deed of mortgage, that a notice of a month's date was to be served upon the defendant for the payment of the money. It is also to be remarked that it was quite within the power of the defendant to avoid the necessity of the plaintiff's bringing an action under the specific terms of the contract by at once paying off the money claimed; but he did not do this; so far from paying it when the suit was brought by the plaintiffs in Court, he resisted the claim as it then stood, urging in his written statement that the amount of interest claimed was not really due. Thus, there was a clear dispute raised on the subject of the claim made by the plaintiffs, and accordingly there was thus a cause of action and the necessity of an adjudication by the Court of the point in dispute.

I may, perhaps, properly notice in this place that there is a decision in page 354, S. D. Rep. of 1847, wherein it is held that a party, even under a contract, cannot realize by sale of the mortgaged properties the sums he claims, except with the intervention of a Court of Justice. Now, under the terms of this contract, it was perfectly open to the plaintiffs either to institute the suit, or (to use the terms of the contract) adopt the alternative of proceeding to sell. Of course the decision cited is clear in its terms, but it is one passed about two-and-twenty years ago, and it is not shown to us that it has been followed by a single case after its date. But be that as it may, it seems to me quite clear that, under the general law of contract, when parties agree to alternative remedies to be available to the creditor under their contract, it would be perfectly inequitable in a Court of justice, equity, and good conscience, to refuse to carry out the terms of the contract, unless it is shown that those terms involve direct illegality or immorality. But nothing of this kind is shown or attempted to be shown in this case.

There is then an objection raised to the effect that, under the terms of the contract, the suit would not lie against the person, as also against the properties of the defendant. But in my opinion, the terms are such as quite leave it open to the plaintiffs, either to realize the monies due, from the person of the defendant, or from his properties, or from both. Baboo Onnoda Persaud Banerjee, for the plaintiffs, declares, however, that the main object of his clients is to realize the money from the properties mortgaged.

The only point then that remains to be considered is that of costs. Now, as to costs, the ordinary rule is, that, where the plaintiff gets a decree, he is entitled to his costs; but the question of costs is one, a matter of discretion. In this case, the plaintiffs might, under the alternative terms of the contract, realize the money due to them, by the sale of the properties mortgaged, without having recourse to the Court, and albeit there was an option given to him to come into Court. I am of opinion that, if they have elected the option which has put the other party, who did not oppose the realization of the money due by sale of the mortgaged property, to the trouble and expense of coming into Court, the case is one where, in a proper exercise of our discretion, no costs ought to be awarded to the plaintiffs.

In this view of the case, I would on the main uphold the decree that the Lower Court has passed in the case with this modification, that each party must bear his own costs, both of the Lower Court and of this Court.

Hobhouse, J.—Mr. Justice Bayley has stated so completely the pleadings on either side, that it does not seem to me to be necessary to go over that ground again. I shall, therefore, begin by simply stating what to my mind are the material points of the agreement between the parties, of date the 2nd March 1866, on which the contention before us hinges. I understand that, under that agreement, the defendant held himself bound to pay a certain sum of money to the plaintiffs; that he pledged certain properties as security for the repayment of the money; and that it was then provided that he was to repay the same by certain quarterly instalments. The conditions as to repayment by instalments form an essential part of the contention before us, and I shall, therefore, quote those conditions at length. They are these:—That the defendant was to repay the principal sum of Rs. 29,380 "by quarterly instalments of Rs. 350 on the days and in the manner hereinafter mentioned,—that is to say, the sum of Rs. 3,500, as being the aggregate amount of ten quarterly instalments, to be calculated from the 9th day of February 1864 up to the 8th day of August 1866 (together with such interests as may be due under the covenant hereinafter contained), to be paid and become payable immediately on the execution of these presents, and from thenceforth by quarterly instalments on the 8th day of November next; the second quarterly instalment on the 8th day of February then next following; the third quarterly instalment on the 8th day of May then next following; the fourth quarterly instalment on the 8th day of August then next following; and so on, by quarterly instalments on the like days in every year, until the whole amount, or the full sum of Rs. 29,380-5-3¾, be paid off and liquidated." Then followed certain other conditions which do not seem to be essential to the issue before us, and then we have the following condition in the deed:—"And further, that in case all four of the said quarterly instalments, amounting to Rs. 1,400 in a year, payable by the said Sonatun Bysack to the said Koonjo Biharee Bysack, Gobindhun Bysack, Chytunkisto Bysack, Sadhoo Churn Bysack, and Gobind Churn Bysack and their heirs, representatives and assignees, or any of such instalments or any part of the same shall at the close of every and each year remain in arrears and unpaid, every such year being calculated from the 9th day of February of one year to the 8th day of February of the next year, that then, and in such case, the same or so much thereof as shall remain due at the close of the year, shall carry interest at the rate of 6 per cent. per annum, and shall be recoverable by a separate suit in respect thereof, or by sale of a portion of the mortgaged premises, sufficient to realize the amount so due." These, I think, are all those points of the contract between the parties which it is essential for the purpose of this suit to have clearly before us, and I shall refer to these conditions of the contract as each point arises hereafter. The first contention, as I understand it, made by the appellant before us, is, in reality, that the plaintiff has no cause of action, and he rests his contention, as it seems to me, mainly on these arguments, *viz.*, that the object of the plaintiffs was to obtain the monies in dispute by sale of the properties, and that inasmuch as the plaintiffs had the power to sell those properties by the agreement between the parties, and inasmuch also as the defendant never objected to such sale, therefore there was in reality no cause of action against him. The answer, however, to this contention, seems to me to be this,—*viz.*, that, by the agreement between the parties, the plaintiffs were not bound to realize their monies by the sale of the properties mortgaged, but they had the option, either of so realizing the monies, or else of proceeding against the defendant, by a suit to recover the same, and it seems to me that they had ample cause of action in the notice which was served upon the defendant to pay, and which he disregarded. It is, however, contended, that, so far as that notice is concerned, it was a notice under the terms of the agreement, and that it must, therefore, be considered as a notice of sale, and not a notice giving a cause of action to this suit; but it seems to me that the notiee might be used either way. By the terms of the agreement, there was a sum of Rs. 3,500 principal due to the plaintiffs on the 2nd March 1866, and by the terms of the same agreement there were certain other sums of money, being instalments on the bond, due up to the 8th February 1868. Now, the notice was in the shape of a demand upon the defendant to pay those monies, and when, therefore, the defendant neglected, or refused to pay the same, and it is admitted that he did either the one or the other, then there was clearly a cause of action to the plaintiffs to sue to recover the same. They might, of course, have used the notice simply as preparatory to the sale, but they might equally, as it seems to me, use it, as they did use it, as a cause of action on which to proceed to sue. I think, therefore, that the plaintiffs in this case had a cause of action against the defendant.

The next objection in order of sequence is to the effect that, if it be admitted that the plaintiffs could sue, still they could not sue as well against the defendant personally as also against the properties mortgaged in the bond; and the grounds of this objection are that, when by the agreement between the parties the plaintiff had a specific remedy given to him, by which he could sell the properties without having recourse to the Courts, then he was not entitled unnecessarily to drag the defendant into Court, in order that he might sell that property by resorting to the Court, which he had power to sell without any such resort. I confess that when this argument was first made, I considered that it had very considerable force in it, but on reflection I think, that however much it may affect the case as regards the award of costs, yet it does not affect the case as regards the nature of the suit which it was within the plaintiff's competency to bring.

The words of the contract seem to me, on a careful consideration of them, to be very plain, and go no further than this,—*viz.*, to give an alternative course of procedure to the plaintiffs. They are to the effect, that if the defendant shall fall into arrears of instalments, then the instalments shall be "recoverable by a separate suit in respect thereof or by the sale of a portion of the mortgaged premises sufficient to realize the money due," so that when the defendant fell into arrears, the plaintiffs had clearly a right under the contract, either to sue for those arrears, or else to sell the estates mortgaged, and thereby recover the arrears, and there was no restriction placed upon the kind of suit to be instituted. The contract declared simply, that the plaintiffs were entitled either to sue or to sell, and one of the commonest forms of suit in this country is, as pointed out by Baboo Onnoda Persaud for the respondent, that of a suit on a mortgage bond, praying for the realization of the money due, and also that the amonnt of the said money be declared to be due upon the property mortgaged. When, too, I come to look more carefully at the prayer in the plaint itself, it seems to me that that prayer, in the words of the plaint, is to the effect that "the Court may be pleased to award from the defendant and the mortgaged properties the amount claimed with costs and interests," so that the object was to have it declared, not generally that the plaintiff had a lien on the property for the repayment of the monies advanced, but particularly that the specific sum which the plaintiffs claimed from the defendant was due from the defendant, and that he and the property he had mortgaged were liable for that sum. I think, therefore, that the plaintiffs were not restricted by the terms of the agreement from suing in the form that they adopted, and that the plaint was one which obviously, if there was no special restriction by the agreement, might be brought in a Civil Court.

The only question that remains is as to costs, and, though perhaps on this point I should have been inclined to go even further than my learned colleague, and to have given the defendant, appellant, at least his costs of this Court, yet looking to the fact that there was a contention between the parties as to the interpretation of the bond, I am on the whole content that the judgment as to costs should be as Mr. Justice Bayley has put it. I have said that I think that the plaintiffs were not prevented by the terms of the bond from instituting this suit. But the plaintiffs' pleader informs us that his main object in the suit, and that is also stated in the preamble of the plaint, was to attach and sell the mortgaged properties. The plaintiffs' main object therefore was to sell the properties mortgaged. That was why they sued, but it is manifest that, by the very terms of the agreement, they could have gained that object by selling the mortgaged estates at a private sale, and if they could have done so, then, when it is quite clear, that there was no obstruction or objection to their doing so on the part of the defendant, although we may think that the plaintiffs are entitled to a decree, we should not, I think, be justified in giving them their costs.

I quite agree with Mr. Justice Bayley that the decision of the Sudder Dewany Adawlut of 1847, at p. 354, ought not to bind us. That decision is to the effect that where a mortgagee was entitled under the contract between him and the mortgagor to sell the property mortgaged if the debts were not paid, then when the mortgagee did sell the property, and the vendee claimed possession after the sale, he could not obtain possession because of that policy declared by the laws of this country which made such a sale altogether inoperative. Now, it seems to me that if it were the intention of the Legislature in any instance to prevent contracts between private parties being binding in all their particulars, the Legislature would specially have said so, and would have assigned its reasons ; and in furtherence of this view I find from the very decision relied upon that wherever the Legislature interfered in contracts between parties, it has done so by special legislation, and for special reasons assigned; for instance, Regulation XVII of 1806, which was between the mortgagor and the mortgagee, requires foreclosure proceedings to be carried out through the Court. It seems to me that there is nothing in any proceeding of the Legislature which evinces any desire to interfere in matters of private contracts between parties except in special cases and for special reasons assigned, and I quite agree in the remarks to be found at p. 45 of Macpherson on Mortgageo, Edition of 1868. I am of opinion, therefore, that the plaintiffs could, under the terms of their agreement, have sold the estates mortgaged without resorting to the Court.

In this view of the case, whilst I think that we must uphold the decision of the Lower Court in substance, I also think that both in this Court and in the Court below this is a case in which each party should bear his own costs.

APPENDIX II.

I have not separately discussed the law administered by the High Courts in this country in the exercise of their original jurisdiction. It is, however, in great measure, moulded on the practice of the English Court of Chancery, of which I have endeavoured to give a succinct account in these lectures. The High Court, however, is a Court both of law and equity, and is therefore in a position to deal with any question arising before it according to the true, as opposed to what I may call the artificial, relations between the parties. As to the mode in which mofussil mortgages are dealt with, see Macpherson's Mortgage, Chapter XI. The following cases also, as to the right of the mortgagee to sell the bare equity of redemption under a decree for money on the covenant, may be usefully consulted: *Ramlochun Sircar* v. *Kamini Devya*, 5 B. L. R., 460; S. C. on Appeal, 10 B. L. R., 60; *Brojonath Kundu Chowdhry* v. *Govindmony Dassee*, 4 B. L. R., 83; and *Nerenjun Mookerjee* v. *Opendra Narain Dev*, 10 B. L. R., 57.

INDEX.